The Place of Bows

Cover: **Camp In The Mountains [Bow Valley]** *July 24, 1845 by H. J. Warre*

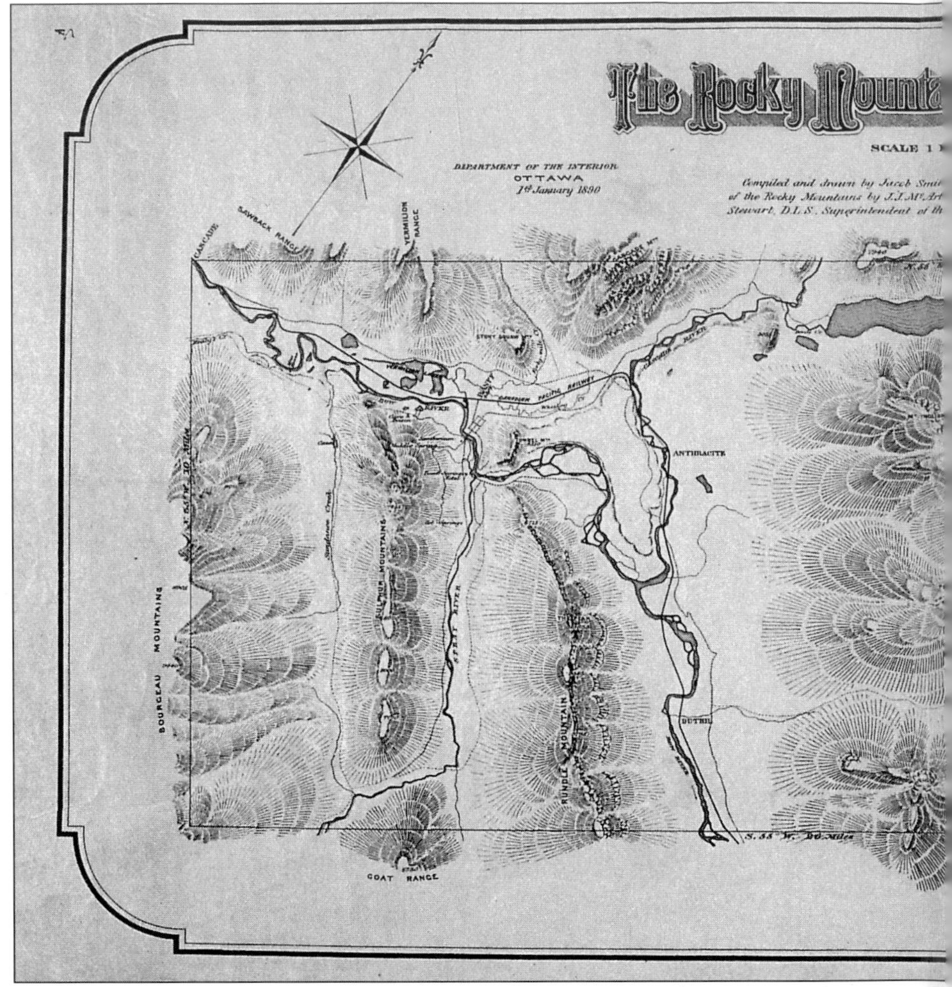

The Place

exploring the heritage of

Part I

E. J.

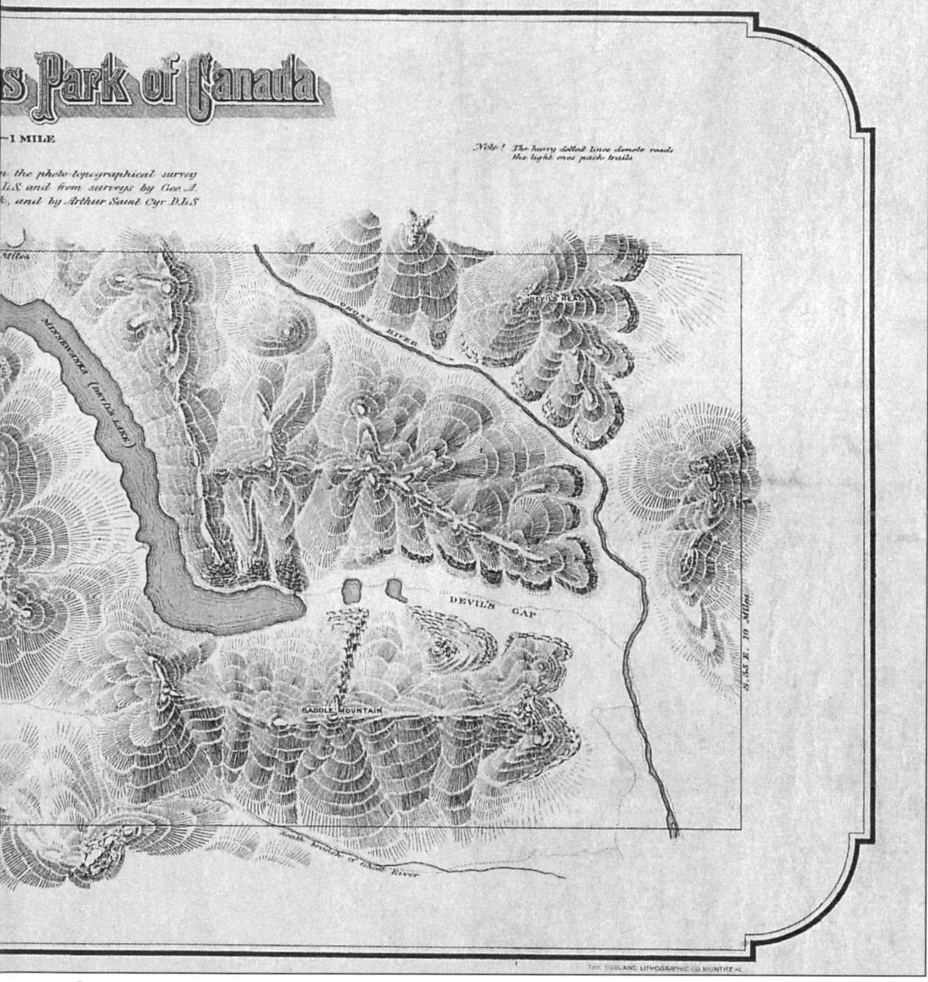

# of Bows

the Banff-Bow Valley
to 1930

Hart

ISBN 0-9699732-5-X

Designed by E. J. Hart

Printed and bound in Canada
by
Friesens
Altona, Manitoba
ROG OBO

First Printing 1999

Distributed by
EJH Literary Enterprises Ltd.
Box 2074
Banff, AB.
TOL OCO
(403) 762-4194

EJH Literary Enterprises Ltd.
Banff

Cover: ***Camp In The Mountains [Mounts Rundle and Cascade] July 24, 1845 by H. J. Warre***

Table of Contents

Three important aspects of the Banff-Bow Valley's heritage are represented in this portrait taken at Lake Louise, ca. 1925 -- l. to r.: Walter Wilcox (tourist explorer and mountaineer); John Hunter (Stoney Indian chief); and Tom Wilson (pioneer outfitter and guide)

Introduction

As one approaches the imposing physical presence of the Rockies following the rushing blue waters of the Bow River from Calgary, they are forced to consider one of the great geographic features of our country. A seemingly impenetrable wall of rock fills the eye, but as they proceed this soon gives way to contemplation of the more individual features that spring to view as the highway makes its way through the Gap. Upthrust peaks, snow, ice, wild tributaries, and remarkably coloured bands of rock speak to the millions of years of sedimentary history of this world on end. The presence of the place soon imposes itself on the viewer — they are transcended into another world, quite unlike the prairie and foothill one they have left behind.

Not as immediately apparent as the physical presence of these mountains is their influence on the mind's eye. This unique world has embodied, over its some 11,000 years of occupation, a human experience that mirrors the rugged individualism of the very peaks themselves. Those who have lived among these high places have been shaped by them, much as the landscape itself has been shaped by ice, wind and water. In this place that so imposes itself on the human psyche, its cultural traditions spring from the human experience of the mountain wilderness and personal reaction to it. It is, as mountain writer Bob Sandford has described it, "a geography of the heart," gradually creating that sense of place which in time defines who we are.

This book, and other volumes to follow, are an effort to identify and understand how the mountain world of the Banff-Bow Valley has shaped those who have come in contact with it. As we enter a new century, I believe that an authentic and identifiable cultural heritage has emerged in the area extending from the Bow River's headwaters at Bow Lake to the point where it debouches from the mountains at its junction with the Kananaskis River at the western edge of the Stoney Reserve. This heritage, while related to that of the remainder of the Rockies, is indeed different, and stands out in even sharper relief from that of the adjacent prairies and foothills and their towns and cities. In the following pages I will attempt to identify those features, activities, movements and individuals that have contributed to the Valley's heritage and have provided this cultural identity. In the process, you shall be introduced to little known and understood first peoples, hardy explorers, intrepid mountain and trail guides, daring mountaineers, pioneer conservationists, accomplished artists and many others who have made these mountains known to the world.

The identity of the area as "the Banff-Bow Valley" springs from the Department of Canadian Heritage's 1995-96 in-depth investigation into the Valley's ecological health, known as the *Banff-Bow Valley Study*. The *Study* correctly looked at the area as a physiographic unit, despite the fact that it is partly within Banff National Park and partly within Alberta provincial lands regulated by a variety of governments and agencies. One of its major recommendations concerned the re-direction of tourism in the Valley, and particularly Banff National Park, towards a more sustainable, heritage-oriented future building on its unique attributes. From that concept arose the creation of a Heritage Tourism Council, whose task it was to design an effective strategy for making heritage an integral part of the area's tourism message and everyday life. Given my quarter-century of involvement in the cultural heritage field in the Canadian Rockies, I was a keen participant in helping to formulate the strategy. However, in trying to explain exactly what the "heritage of the Banff-Bow Valley" was during discussions on the strategy, I had problems articulating the concept. My inability to do so has provided the impetus for this work.

The title of this volume is a translation of the Stoney Indian word *mun-uh-cha-ban*, "the place one takes bows from" or, more literally, "the place of bows," which they applied to the Valley to identify it as a source of one of the key sustaining elements of early native life — the bow — in this case made from the strong branches of the Douglas fir. It implies the Stoney's sense of place of the Valley, and serves as an excellent metaphor in our own search for meaning and sustenance in these glorious mountains.

Chapter One
People of the Shining Mountains

As we contemplate the Banff-Bow Valley today, it is hard to conceive that it has been home to human beings for more than 10,000 years. And, as we watch the crowds of visitors from around the world stroll down Banff Avenue on a summer afternoon, it is equally difficult to imagine that it has always been a meeting place for people from different cultures. Yet, both these things are true. For the more than 400 generations, the Valley has been a beacon and a sanctuary for humanity as disparate as prehistoric hunters clad in rough animal skins seeking bare subsistence and well-heeled international tourists wanting to enjoy the aesthetic pleasures of a world-famous tourist resort.

Few, if any, of the millions of visitors passing each year over the four lanes of pavement on the Trans Canada Highway west of Banff realize they are following the trail of the ages. Skirting the marshy shores of the Vermilion Lakes on the slopes of Mounts Norquay and Cory, they unwittingly pass over the location where peoples little known and understood made seasonal camps for over 100 centuries while pursuing their meagre existence at the margins of retreating glaciers. It is perhaps one of the great ironies of the history of the Banff-Bow Valley that in an area so thoroughly studied and sought to be understood by contemporary observers, virtually nothing is known of the human activity in the Valley which dominated its life for such a great part of its history.

What we do know is that on the south-facing slope of the Bow, prehistoric bands of hunter-gatherers camped on the shore of a glacial lake, much larger than today's Vermilion, and from the rock made fleshers and scrappers that allowed them to butcher the game they killed. They burned fires in hearths, created clothing from the skins of their prey, and left flakes from tool-making activities. Fire-cracked bone fragments from the prehistoric mountain sheep and the Pleistocene bison they hunted litter the site. Generation after generation used the same protected, sunny camp close to wood and water, and it was sometimes covered by mud or rock from a land slippage on the slopes above. Altogether, archaeologists doing investigations preceding the twinning of the highway in 1983-84 found seven separate and distinct living floors exhibiting evidence of human use at what was named site *EhPv-8* during a period of some 11,000 years.

The discovery of *EhPv-8* and the subsequent intensification of archaeological investigation in the four mountain park area has led to somewhat of a reassessment of prehistoric life in the mountains. Discovery of evidence some 2,000 to 3,000 years older than had previously been postulated spurred renewed archaeological activity in valleys tributary to the Bow and even in higher alpine areas. Evidence of smaller seasonal camps in valleys such as the Cascade came to light, as did hitherto undiscovered pit house dwellings at several locales in the Red Deer River Valley, including some at the very foot of the Drummond Glacier. These revelations led to a reconsideration of similar depressions first reported over eighty-five years ago at the margin of the Banff Springs Golf Course and on the lower benches of Tunnel Mountain (on Deer Street) and Mount Norquay (at the Timberline Hotel) in the vicinity of today's Banff townsite. Geological Survey of Canada anthropologist Harlan I. Smith, who had worked on house pits in the Kamloops and Thompson River areas in the interior of British Columbia, was able to convince the government to preserve the golf course find in 1913, making it the first protected archaeological site in Canada. Smith related these pit houses to the Shuswap, a branch of the Interior Salish, an opinion essentially shared by the Parks Canada archaeologists of today. But rather than being winter pit house dwellings, as he supposed, they believe they represent temporary dwellings of Interior Plateau peoples moving through the Bow, Red Deer and North Saskatchewan River valleys on their way to seasonal bison hunts on the plains, timing their passage to engage in the gathering of berries and medicinal plants. The pit houses

Archaeologists working near Vermilion Lakes in 1983-84 found one of the oldest and most important prehistoric sites in Western Canada

appear to have been occupied almost continuously in the period between 2800 and 440 years ago, putting them in the range of use of the Vermilion Lakes and other Banff park sites which exhibit occupation by peoples of a different Plains-Mountain tradition. Senior Parks Canada archaeologist Gwyn Langemann has described, in the evaluation of her research on these sites, what this tells us about the Valley:

But it is becoming clear that there is really no pristine wilderness, that people have been living in the park for a very long time, and have been playing a role in shaping the landscape within the parks for at least 11,000 years. The south-facing fans around the Vermilion wetlands, and along the Bow River just west of Banff townsite, have many extremely early sites, including the Vermilion Lakes site where the lowest component dates to 10,700 BP (Fedje et al. 1995). These sites also have occupations that extend throughout the precontact period right up to historic times. Among these are sites with a housepit component. Banff townsite has been a focus of occupation for a very long time, and a place where people from the west have met people from the plains.

In the late pre-contact period, Banff was already a village. . . .[1]

Overall a picture of consistent and varied use of the mountains and their resources by different peoples is emerging, rather than the view of avoidance and lack of resources that was speculated upon by scientists not many decades ago.

By virtue of there being no way for them to be recorded, we cannot know what the earliest prehistoric peoples who frequented these mountains in their never-ending quest for subsistence thought about them. We can speculate, though, that their forays to the edges of the retreating glaciers of some 11,000 years ago in search of isolated flocks of Pleistocene sheep and other large game, or the roots and berries of gradually emerging plant life, were no worse than their incessant quests for food on the neighbouring plains. Indeed, the fact that the geography and the ice constrained the movements of their prey may have meant that the mountain valleys seemed a desirable location for these migratory peoples, at least in the summer and fall seasons, and that they actually sought them out as preferred hunting grounds. We can also speculate that given the elemental forces of nature that were still very much at work, with huge glaciers alternately retreating and advancing and large glacial rivers and lakes, that the landscape provoked fear and wonder in these simple folk. They likely ascribed religious and symbolic powers to the mountains and thought of them, as would later generations, as sacred places.

Were these prehistoric peoples the forebears of the native peoples of the mountains that European fur-traders first reported near the end of the eighteenth century? While we can speculate that the pit house dwellers were either Interior Salish or closely related to them, it is more difficult to identify other tribes, for there were few peoples anywhere in North America and they dispersed widely as food resources and tribal rivalries waxed and waned. There would have been little incentive for any people to live permanently in the Rockies, although it appears that several groups used them on a seasonal basis. All we do know is that by the 1700s the native bands living near or in the mountains had taken on tribal affiliations and linguistic attributes that allow us to identify them as being different from one another. In the northern Rockies, on the Peace River drainage, lived the Dene-speaking Beaver Indians on the eastern slopes and the Shuswap on the western slopes, although the latter were found on both sides of the divide in the Yellowhead Pass area and as far south as Lake Windermere on the western side. On the headwaters of the North Saskatchewan and Bow Rivers were the Kootenay, a small tribe unrelated to others of the woodlands and plains, who moved seasonally back and forth between the plains for bison hunting and the Columbia-Kootenay area for fishing and agriculture. Further south were more Kootenay in the Oldman River district as well as the Snake, a Shoshone-speaking people, who were found on the headwaters of the Milk and Oldman Rivers.[2]

As far as can be determined the Banff-Bow Valley area was mainly frequented by Kootenay (*Ktunaxa)* prior to the appearance of the fur trade in the west in the second half of the eighteenth century. Even at that, though, its upper reaches in what is currently Banff National Park appear to have been fairly isolated from their main areas of usage. The Kootenay moving back and forth from the interior Columbia Valley to the plains preferred the route over the head of the Kootenay River and down the Beaverfoot to the Kicking Horse, then passing by Emerald Lake over Amiskwi Pass onto the Blaeberry River and thence over Howse Pass to the head of the North Saskatchewan River and the Kootenay Plains, a traditional trading area. Undoubtedly some did use the Vermilion Pass and perhaps, on occasion, Whiteman's Pass when they wished to have direct access to the hunting in the Bow Valley. The Kootenay, unlike the plains tribes, also gained part of their subsistence from fishing, and it was recorded by an early observer that they spoke of an area north of the Bow River, likely Lake Minnewanka, as being particularly favoured.

The appearance of the fur trade was to have far-reaching consequences for the first peoples of the foothills and montane, for it set in train tribal movements and rivalries and created effects in native social and religious life that would fundamentally change the situation in the area within a century. While we will examine the fur trade and its influence on the Valley elsewhere, suffice it to say here that the pressure of the trade, leaving its secure base on the shores of Hudson Bay beginning with Henry Kelsey's journey westward in 1690, forced great changes on all the tribes between the Bay and the mountains. First peoples were forced westward by better armed enemies and some set out on great migrations that would result in their occupying new homelands formerly under the control of others.

When Hudson's Bay Company surveyors Peter Fidler and David Thompson began to explore and map the Front Ranges of the Rocky Mountains in the late 1780s, they noted that the Peigan (*Pikuni*) were the dominant tribe in the area. These people, the largest of the plains Indian groups known as the Blackfoot Nation, were of Algonquin linguistic stock and were among the fiercest of the plains tribes. By this time they had extended their influence all the way from the foot of the mountains at the North Saskatchewan River to what is now Montana. North of the North Saskatchewan the Cree had migrated in from the north to become the dominant tribe of the parkland region and had also begun to frequent the mountain front and valleys. At some time previous to the arrival of the first fur traders, these two tribes, but mainly the Peigan who were particularly aggressive, had uprooted the Kootenay and had forced them permanently across the mountains to the headwaters of the Columbia. Native lore was recorded only in oral traditions but David Thompson made reference to this occurrence in his journal during a winter he spent south of the Bow River in 1787-88 in the lodge of *Saukamappee* (Young Man), a seventy-five-year-old Cree who had come to live among the Peigan to help them in their battles with the Snakes and Assiniboines some forty years earlier. *Saukamappee* stated that "the Peigans were always the frontier tribe" and that the plains where they now held sway "were formerly in full possession of the Kootenays, northward; next the Saleesh and their allies; and the most southern, the Snake Indians and their tribes, now driven across the Mountains."

From *Saukamappee's* account it is apparent that the ascendancy of the Peigan in the Valley was but recently won. He told Thompson of an incident that occurred on a tributary of the Bow in the mountains sometime around 1750 when several Peigan met their fate at the hands of their traditional southern enemies, the Snake:

I think it was about the third falling of the leaves of the trees that five of our tents pitched away to the valleys in the Rocky Mountains, up a branch of this river to hunt the big horn deer as their horns make fine large bowls, and are easily cleaned; they were to return on the first snow. All was quiet and we waited for them until the snow lay on the ground, when we got alarmed for their safety and about thirty warriors set off to seek them. It was only two days' march, and in the evening they came to the camp; it had been destroyed by a large party of Snake Indians, who left their marks of snakes' heads painted black on sticks they had set up. The bodies were all there, with the women and children, but scalped, and partly devoured by the wolves and dogs.[3]

As for the Kootenay, they still wished to trade ochre derived from beds in the Paint Pots area on the Vermilion River with friendly plains tribes, and to continue their tradition of seasonal hunting of the buffalo on the fringes of the plains bordering the mountains. This made the period of first white contact one of jealousy, rivalry and sometimes open hostility at the mountains' foot, particularly after both the Hudson's Bay Company and the rival North West Company opened posts on the upper reaches of the North Saskatchewan River in the 1790s. Peter Fidler, while observing trade between the Kootenay and the Peigan at Livingstone Gap on the Old Man River in 1792, noted how the Peigan had imposed themselves as middle men in the fur trade. In speaking of the matter he noted the Kootenay's difficult situation:

They never was near any of the Trading Settlements, altho they much wish it. But the Muddy river (Peigan), Blood, Black Feet & Southern (Snake) Indians always prevent them, they wishing to monopolize all their Skins to themselves, which they do giving the Poor Indians only a mere trifle for. They scarce given them as much for 10 skins as they can get for one at the Trading Settlement.[4]

David Thompson also provided a reliable witness to these circumstances when in 1800, now as a trader and surveyor with the North West Company, he sought a band of Kootenay rumoured to be coming over Howse Pass at the head of the North Saskatchewan to trade at the company's Rocky Mountain House post. The Peigan in the neighbourhood tried to prevent this taking place. Thompson noted in his journal that "they are so jealous of the Kootanaes coming in to Trade that they do all they can to persuade me to return, assuring me that it is impossible for me to find them, and that in endeavouring to search them out, our Horses will fall by Fatigue and Hunger, and perhaps also ourselves." On October 13, 1800 two Peigan appeared at Thompson's camp and reported that "the Kootanies would be on the Heights of the Mountain the Morrow." This initiated a period of eight days when the Kootenay, composed of twenty-six men and seven women, would come into the post, located some fifty miles from the mountain front, to trade under constant harassment from the Peigan. Thompson observed that they were "but poorly clothed notwithstanding the rigour of the Cold in these Mountains," a comment made about the Kootenay by others as well. The Kootenay were noted for raising fine horses in the warmer climes of the Columbia Valley and during their march from Howse Pass to the fort the Peigan stole five of their eleven mounts and forced them to trade two more for inferior animals. Thompson marvelled at the bravery of this small band in the face of the hostility and superior numbers of their tormentors:

I cannot help admiring the Spirit of these brave, undaunted, but poor Kootanaes; they have all along shown a courage and Fortitude admirable — not the least sign of Weakness or Cowardice, altho' they are in the

The Kootenay, as shown in this view taken in the Columbia Valley, were the foremost users of the mountains in the early historic period

Power of a large Party of Indians, who are at least 20 to one. They are conducted by 4 old Men who seem worthy of being at the Head of such People. This day when the young Pekenow Men seized the Heads of their Horses, they all as if acted by one Soul bent their Bows, got ready their other Weapons, and prepared to make their Oppressors quit their Horses or sell their lives dearly — hardly a single Word was spoken among them.[5]

Thompson had to go ahead to the post to get additional horses to allow the Kootenay to get their furs in, as the Peigan picked off their mounts one by one. He traded with them for their skins, but learned as they were preparing to leave that the Peigan were laying in wait and intended to rob them. He sent them off in a different direction to avoid confrontation, accompanied by two of his own men to learn something of the lay of the land and the Kootenay's situation in their home territory on the Pacific slope.

While it appears from early fur trade accounts that the Peigan held sway at the foot of the Rockies, it is also evident that the Kootenay were the main ones to regularly use the mountain valleys and passes for hunting or travel at the turn of the nineteenth century, with some incursions by the Peigan and Cree as well as the Shuswap and Snake. However, this situation was soon to change as new native elements appeared in the mountain area affecting the ethnography of the region in fundamental ways.

Although not directly associated with the Banff-Bow Valley area, one of the most interesting changes was the introduction of eastern natives directly into the Rockies by the activities of the fur companies. Around the turn-of-the-century the North West Company brought out Iroquois, Nippissing and Saulteaux Indians from the Great Lakes and St. Lawrence River areas to work in the company's interests. In November, 1800 Thompson recorded his discourse with some Peigan on the Highwood River about the matter:

We then spoke to him (the principal chief) about introducing a number of Iroquois & Saulteaux in the Country about the Mountains. We informed them that their country was so very poor as to be utterly incapable of maintaining them — for which reason they had applied to us to bring them up to the Mountains, which request we had not complied with, as we did not know how they would be pleased with it. We also added that those Indians would behave quietly, would reside in the woody Hills at the foot of the Mountains & serve as a Barrier between them & their Enemies — upon which Terms they gave us Permission to bring them up as soon as we pleased.[6]

Because the focus of the trade shifted north to the Athabasca River region after 1811, most of these introduced people were active in that area, frequently travelling over Athabasca and Yellowhead Passes in the interests of the trade. They often intermarried with the Cree and other tribes on the reaches of the Athabasca and became an important element in that area's ethnographic mix.

More specific to the Bow Valley was the appearance of the

Stoney Indians, henceforth the dominant tribe in the area. They were first referred to by Fidler in a later reference to the fate of the two men who Thompson had sent off with the Kootenay in 1800. He recorded that several Kootenay had accompanied these men back to Rocky Mountain House in 1801 but had been killed by a band of "Swampy Ground Stone Indians." These were likely the Stoney (*Nakoda* or *Yanktonnais*), their name deriving from the term *Assinipwat*, or "Stone People," because of their habit of using hot stones in their cooking. They were part of one of three branches of the Sioux Nation, originally splitting off from the main tribe in the area of the Great Lakes about 1600. Although evidence is not entirely clear, it appears they began moving west in three distinct groups and reached the mountains at different times and in different locales. The first to arrive sometime around the mid-eighteenth century were the Chiniki, who frequented the area along the Bow River and were soon crossing the mountains to hunt and steal horses from the Kootenay and other Plateau tribes. A second group, originally known as the Goodstoney, but later as the Wesley, took a migration route that followed a more northerly path along the edge of the parkland, halfway between the bison-rich plains on the south and the lake, forest and river habitat of moose and deer to the north. They mainly inhabited the region on the headwaters of the North Saskatchewan River near the Kootenay Plains, fur trade records first noting their presence about 1800. The third group, the Bearspaw, travelled a more southerly course, one that brought them into contact with the Blackfoot and Peigan, and they occupied the region along the upper headwaters of the Highwood River.

It was not until the late eighteenth century that all three bands were firmly established in their territories.[7] Together they were referred to as "Mountain Stoney" as distinct from other groups of their tribe, often referred to as the "Wood Stoney" or "Thickwood Assiniboine," who settled in areas west of Fort Edmonton near the North Saskatchewan and Athabasca Rivers. It was largely the Chiniki who initially used the Banff-Bow Valley region, although that would change as time went on when the Stoney, like all west-

Early Stoney camp in the Bow Valley

ern tribes, were brought onto reserves. In the Banff region, tradition held that they found Cree inhabiting the area around the hot springs but they forced them out. Their familiarity with the Bow Valley and its montane life-zone supporting an abundance of game also led them to utilize its other resources. Among these were the sturdy branches of the great Douglas fir found at low valley elevations, which they found excellent for making bows. Before long, the Valley was being referred to as *mun-uh-cha-ban*, "the place one takes bows from."[8]

What brought the Stoney to the foot of the mountains at such a relatively late time in the history of western first peoples? The answer lies in the dislocation created by the fur trade, and in this case most likely in the scourge that the trade unleashed on peoples totally incapable of resisting it — smallpox. Over the course of the trade's history more than half of the native population of the west was taken by this whiteman's disease. In the mountains, Peter Fidler related in his journals that around 1781 smallpox had reached the Kootenay and had so decimated the tribe that they had discontinued their use of the trails over the passes to the plains.

The Stoney's oral traditions seem to indicate that an attempt to escape smallpox set off at least part of their migrations. In 1926 a well-known Stoney medicine man, *Tatanga-mani* (George McLean), recounted the story that had been passed down for generations in his family:

Long ago our people who lived in the southeast suffered a great sickness, untsahnihni (sore disease). It was new to them. To-day we call it small-pox. In those days they used to travel in big parties, and any place they saw another party, they would fight a war. When this sickness came upon them, they did not understand how it had happened to them. They lived in tipis, maybe three or four hundred in a party. Sometimes they found in one night a whole lot of tipis with all the occupants dead. Maybe ten or twelve tipis in one night. They did not touch them, just left them, just packed up their stuff and carried their things away. They did not have horses at that time. No dogs even. A few had a pet wolf or a coyote to carry a pack. . . . They wandered around in that way for I don't know how long. They scattered all over. We Stonies, we ran north, and all that time, as we travelled, there were hundreds of people who died, whole families. And sometimes maybe a little baby was left alone. Other parents adopted the baby. The parents left a child there, while they travelled away up north to a colder climate in the mountains. We Stonies were Sioux then. After this sickness we left them, and the disease stopped. Then the Stonies began to work their way back in the mountains.[9]

While smallpox had a hand in setting the Stoney off on their migrations, it also appears to have helped establish the conditions that led them to their final destination. Arriving on the scene so late, the Stoney migrated until they filled what was largely a vacuum along the front and in the eastern valleys of the Rockies created by the Kootenay's retreat across the mountains and a period of weakness among the Peigan, also contributed to by the disease. Another factor perhaps lay in their ability to quickly adapt to the surroundings at the Rockies' foot. One of the reasons that has been postulated for their acceptance by other tribes was their ability to make natural medicines and cures from the roots and berries

Stoneys George McLean (second right), John Hunter and their children, 1904

found in their new homeland, an essential sought out by all those natives with whom they came in contact. They also quickly learned to organize themselves somewhat differently to hunt big game animals in the mountains, while also making occasional forays to take bison on the prairies like the plains tribes. Hunting parties consisted of small bands, mainly organized along family lines, and each band eventually habituated a particular hunting area, based largely on a valley or watershed in the mountains.

A witness who provided a good description of this circumstance was the half-breed guide Peter Erasmus, who accompanied the Palliser Expedition during its explorations between 1858 and 1860. In his memoir, *Buffalo Days and Nights*, dictated to a newspaperman late in life, he recalled his earliest observations of the Stoney:

The Stoney Indians were a peaceful people. Their policy was to avoid trouble unlike the Blackfoot, Peigan, or Bloods, their nearest neighbours. They raised good mountain horses and were greatly sought after by the plainsmen. . . . The Stonies were less inclined to migratory habits and lived in selected parts of the mountain country more or less permanently for the greater portion of their lives. In my experience they were the best trackers of any of the Indian people, and they developed the use of medi-

cines to a degree unsurpassed by any of the other tribes. It was largely through their knowledge of medicine plants that the Crees looked to them as friends and never bothered them when they went after buffalo in that area bordering the North Saskatchewan River which the Cree claimed as their own hunting ground.[10]

Another distinguishing feature of the Stoney that set them apart was the degree to which they adopted the teachings of Christianity. The English Wesleyan Methodist missionary Reverend Robert Rundle was sent out to work among the tribes of the southern prairies and foothills in 1840 and despite the hostility he met from the Blackfoot and their associated tribes, he found the Stoney to be very amenable to his message. Witness, for example, his first meeting with them in April, 1841 when he visited one of their camps near Rocky Mountain House:

I met with a very warm reception, nearly the whole of the Camp, men, women & children, I believe, came out to meet me on my approach. It was a very interesting & cheering sight to behold. They all walked in their procession with their Chief at their head. The ceremony of shaking hands then, which I performed on horseback. Many of the children were brought on their Mothers backs to welcome me. I found a large place or tent arranged for my visit & shortly afterwards under the rays of a bright and unclouded sun I discoursed to them on the glories & beauties of the Son of Righteousness.[11]

Rundle's initial success with the Stoney led him to concentrate on their eternal souls for most of his missionary years up to 1848. One of his most successful innovations was to teach the gospel using a syllabic created by fellow missionary James Evans, employing symbols and figures to represent Cree words. The Stoney's good relations and relatively high degree of intermarriage with the Cree led to some familiarity with their language and resulted in this choice. Historians have often wondered why so few features in the Rockies bear Stoney names, with Cree-based words like *waputehk* (goat) and *mistaya* (bear) predominating, and although their late arrival in the region may help to explain this, the use of Cree in missionary activity may also provide part of the answer. In any event, the effectiveness of Rundle's teaching is evident in later reports of how Christian the Stoney were in their daily lives. Captain John Palliser recorded, over a decade after Rundle's departure, that he was amazed to hear them singing hymns and praying while camped with them on the Sabbath.

Despite frequently manifesting signs of Christianity in their lives, the Stoney by no means abandoned their traditional beliefs and practices, many of which related to the mountains. This has been explained in more recent times by Chief John Snow of the Wesley, himself a minister, in his appropriately titled book *These Mountains are our Sacred Places*. He explains that there were localities in the mountains and activities performed at them that were special. The hot springs around Banff, referred to as "the sacred waters of the mountains," were often visited at the direction of a medicine man or woman and used with proper preparation and prayer to maintain health and cure illnesses. Similarly, the mountains provided the site for one of the most important religious activities in a Stoney's life — the vision quest, "a tradition handed down through the centuries and practiced by us as a means of approaching the Great Spirit." Rundle had mentioned seeing a foothill south of the Highwood River on which these "abominable idolatries" took place, but it was most often performed in the mountains where "the seeker of truth" would be alone with nature seeking "wisdom and divine guidance" through a dream, a vision, or the voice of a wild animal telling him the purpose of his life.

In summing up the importance of the mountains to his people, Snow states:

Therefore the Rocky Mountains are precious and sacred to us. We knew every trail and mountain pass in the area. We had special ceremonial and religious areas in the mountains. In the olden days some of the neighbouring tribes called us the "People of the Shining Mountains." These mountains are our temples, our sanctuaries, and our resting places. They are a place of hope, a place of vision, a place of refuge, a very special place where the Great Spirit speaks with us. ***Therefore, these mountains are our sacred places.***[12]

Some of the special areas in the mountains to which Snow referred were located in the Banff-Bow Valley and had unique powers or significance attached to them. *Tatanga-mani* recalled that Stoney visiting the hot springs would sometimes hear singing or the sound of an eagle bone whistle used in the Sun Dance: "We would wait around, trying to see who it was and what was making the sounds, but we could never see anything in the waters." The people believed that the sound came from a spirit that ruled the spring: "They would bathe in the springs because of the medicine in them. Then they would drop something in as a sacrifice, as a thank-you to the spirits for the use of their water. . . ."[13] He also referred to the *makutibi*, or "little human beings" that the Stoney believed lived under the ground in some of the mountains: "Some hunters, when tracking bears or ptarmigan into caverns, have heard a great noise, and then it is as if they hear a lot of people talking. These are the little people."[14]

At the Hoodoos, the Stoney placed "little personal sacrifices" such as tobacco, pipes, and other treasured objects to propitiate an evil spirit, and this spirit would also be thanked and asked to protect them through the coming winter with sacrifices and dances at their annual Sun Dance gathering, leading to the naming of nearby Sundance Creek and Canyon. Another spirit was believed to live in the waters of Lake Minnewanka, one so frightening that "all Indians stayed away from that water." Enoch Baptiste, a Stoney from Morley, recounted the legend to an anthropologist in the 1950s:

Northeast of Lake Minnewanka is a mountain with a high, sharp peak shaped like a tower. From a long distance you can see snow on its top, but there is never any on its side. The mountain is so steep that snow does not stay on it. Because spirits lived on top of it, Indians call it Spirit Mountain.

The near-by lake they called "Minnewanka," which means "Water of the Spirits." When they travelled in the neighbourhood of the lake, they heard the voices of the spirits. As they passed by, they could see nothing that made sounds, but they could hear sounds.

One time when our people were camping near the lake, my father heard what seemed to be the beating of a drum. The noise seemed to be coming from the water. He could also hear voices down in the lake. Soon he noticed that the water was coming up on the shore. It came close to the camp and then it went back again.

Soon my father saw, near the centre of the lake, a strange creature rise out of the water. It was half fish and half human being. It had blown the water toward the shore, then it had come above the surface. As my father stood watching, the fish-person sank back into the lake.[15]

Apart from its importance as a place of spirits, the Stoney had many stories and traditions concerning the Valley as a hunting ground, some of which were related to ethnologist Marius Barbeau, the famous National Museums of Canada collector of Canadian folklore and native legends who carried out interviews with knowledgeable Stoney elders at Morley in the 1920s. Many concerned famous leaders and medicine men around whom many tales had grown, particularly Hector Crawler who was often referred to as "the old seer." One of the stories, called "Hector Crawler's Bitter Trials" as told by his nephew Dan Wildman, provides an exciting tale of a hunting trip up the Bow during starvation times and mentions the names the Stoney used for what later became Canmore and Banff:

One time I had a very narrow escape from wild animals One time in the Berries Moon (August), I went away. It was a hard time —starvation. We had not much to eat. So our children were crying for something to eat. The Bow River (Minnihsno: Cold-Water) was very cold and deep just then. We started hunting from the place now called Canmore, Tsuuptsimtsayan-kundebi. (If I shoot a little tree mistaken for enemies, I am fooled.) And we camped on the north side of Minnisni. We forded the river about six miles west of Canmore just opposite Stony Creek. . . .

The story went on to relate how Crawler and his friend Crow-Chest successfully hunted a goat on the slopes of Mount Rundle and then butchered and immediately began cooking it due to their advanced state of starvation. The smell attracted a grizzly bear and led to a fight to the death right in the bone-chilling waters of the Bow:

Hector Crawler

As soon as the grizzly saw us, he ran away towards the river. Just then I shot him. He dropped right away. I had killed him at once. Then we took off our clothes, and we had only one knife. Crow-Chest put it in his mouth, a great big knife. Just as we got to the bear, it came back to life. It was facing toward the water. We held both feet of the bear: Crow-Chest on the right hand, and myself on the left. We held both hind feet: the water was up to our shoulders. The bear was a good swimmer. We kept like that, holding him back. We cannot tell how long, because if we had let him go, he would have got the best of us. Crow-Chest took his knife out of his mouth, put it through the bear's ribs. They heard the growling of that bear through the valley. A second time he gave it a thrust. Must have been one hour we worked there in the risky river. And then the bear was dead. We tried to swim with the bear to the place where the horses were. As soon as we got to where the horses stood, we just fell down. We were that tired and stiff.

After recovering enough to cut up the bear, the two set off to the west, with Crow-Chest holding onto Crawler's horse's tail so as not to become lost in the dark, crossing and re-crossing the river. The meat fell into the water and had to be re-packed, but in the process their flints became wet and they could not start a fire, requiring them to continue on despite their exhaustion. This led to their deliverance near modern-day Banff:

We had to travel on. And it was dark, dark night. We travelled through the coulees for a little ways, no trail. And then we got into the pack trail. Then we let the horses go ahead. We travelled like that till early morning. Then I saw some light right on the trail, in the bush. I got ready to shoot. We could not tell what was in there. I asked, "Who is there?" I recognized my brother's voice. My brother was waiting there for us. We camped. It was where Banff is now (Minnehapa - water falls). That was one of the bitter sorrows I faced in my life, that trip.[16]

Other stories about Hector Crawler's experiences in the Banff area were related in Barbeau's collection, published many years later under the title of *Indian Days On The Western Prairies*. One told of the destruction of his whole herd of horses and own near-death when run-over by a railway locomotive while travelling through deep snow drifts on his return from a visit to the Kootenay. By this time the appearance of civilization had drastically changed his and all Stoney's lives, and it was this experience at the hands of the white man which led him to give up his life as a hunter and become a medicine man.

The Stoney's use of the mountains for hunting was more-or-less seasonal, they, like their enemy the Peigan tending to use them mostly at specific times of the year. In the winter, all native tribes found a protected cold-weather camping ground with good wood and water and tended to stay put, the Stoney often establishing theirs just outside the foothills area of the Bow. This was why the Reverend George McDougall, Rundle's ultimate successor as a Methodist missionary, eventually erected his mission at Morley, near this site. In his book, John Snow sums up the seasonal round of Stoney life in the mountains:

Later summer and fall were the main hunting seasons in this harsh climate. But except during the winter we spent most of our time migrating along the foothills in search of food, preparing for the cold months ahead. The tribe did not travel as a unit, but lived in several bands, usually breaking off into smaller, extended-family groups as we moved about. The elderly and sick were left at a base camp, with a few men to provide daily food. The rest of the band or family group moved for several days or weeks along the foothills or into the mountains. If the hunt was good, we might stay in one place for some time, preparing the meat for storage. If the hunt was less successful, we kept moving . . . . During the winter the band came together in protected winter camp grounds. For ceremonial and other occasions the entire tribe gathered.[17]

It is apparent from an examination of their activity in the area that, while by no means static, the situation in the Banff-Bow Valley remained stable from a first people's perspective after the Stoney had established themselves. The Peigan exerted their influence further south, also affected by the ravages of white diseases and perhaps having to go further afield in the pursuit of their buffalo economy as the numbers of the great beasts began to dwindle. The Kootenay and the Stoney, after a period during which they disputed hunting territories on either side of the divide, seem to have got along well. *Tatanga-mani* recounted that they sometimes joined together to hunt buffalo and often travelled over the divide to visit each other in their homelands. He noted that "they kept on that way for years, until the white people were thick in the country" and the Stoney were prevented by law from going over. Such comments, and the experiences of those like Hector Crawler, provide only a hint at the influence the increase in white incursion in the Stoney's mountain lands would have. By the latter part of the nineteenth century forces would be at work that would result in their extirpation from these sacred places forever.

Chapter Two
The Great River of the West

Even though the mountains of the Banff-Bow Valley had already played an integral part in the history and culture of first peoples for millennia when European fur traders appeared at their base, they would play quite a different role in the fur trade and early exploration period. This was a result of two important factors — the native situation created by the trade itself and matters of geography. These factors would combine to make the long-term influences of the fur trade on the Valley almost invisible while at the same time they were having a major effect on much of the rest of western Canada.

Essentially the Rockies were not regarded as a source of supply (fur bearing animals) for the trade, but rather as a barrier to extending it onto the Pacific slope and ultimately the Pacific Ocean itself. Competition for the control of the mouth of the Columbia River and inland areas along its course as well as New Caledonia (central British Columbia) would become a central focus of competing interests early in the nineteenth century and would provide the key element in the story of the fur trade in the Rockies.

Fur trade history in Canada began with the granting of a charter in 1670 by King Charles II to the Company of Adventurer's Trading into Hudson Bay (Hudson's Bay Company), giving to this private corporation sole rights to trade on all waters draining to the Bay. For almost a century the trade was carried on from the shores of Hudson's Bay at the mouths of the river systems flowing into it, where posts were established to trade for the furs brought down by natives from the interior. There were opposing French fur trade interests based in Montreal with which the Bay Company competed in its southern domains, but they initially posed no threat to the trade coming from the interior. However, as early as

1690 the Company had sent Henry Kelsey to report on the lands further west and in 1754 another Hudson's Bay man, Anthony Henday, entered the lands near the foothills and likely became the first trader to view *Arsinee Watchee*, "the Shining Mountains."

Beginning in the 1770s Highland Scots who had emigrated to Montreal and had begun to become involved in the trade organized themselves into the North West Company, finding their source of labour and information in the old French fur traders. The Nor'Westers were soon aggressively pushing their interests to the Lake Athabasca country and the western interior, resulting in the two fur companies beginning to build competing posts along the Saskatchewan River system. This activity culminated in the construction of the Hudson's Bay Company's Acton House and the North West Company's Rocky Mountain House near the confluence of the Clearwater and North Saskatchewan River at the foot of the Rockies in 1799.

Aggressive spirits in the North West Company took the initiative to push the trade from Rocky Mountain House onto the Pacific slope. Intent on breaking the Hudson's Bay Company monopoly, they recognized the area also represented a chance for fabulous wealth, not only because of its resources in beaver but also because it offered the opportunity to challenge the Russian-American Fur Company along the coast for the pelts of the sea-otter, prized in the Oriental trade. Alexander Mackenzie, one of the founding partners of the Nor'westers, was the individual most intent on finding the rumoured "Great River of the West," a navigable waterway connecting the mountains to the Pacific which would unlock the region's supposed riches and at the same time allow his company to steal a march on its rivals. In his quest, Mackenzie accidentally arrived on the shores of the Arctic Ocean in 1789 when he followed the river that bears his name flowing from Great Slave Lake. In 1793 he apparently succeeded in his goal when he penetrated the mountains of the Peace River and then made his way overland to the Fraser and thence by the Bella Coola River to the Pacific. However, while a major accomplishment of exploration, his achievement did not solve the problem, for the route he followed was not suitable for navigation over much of its extent.

At the same moment as Mackenzie was setting out for the Peace River in 1792, an American sea captain, Robert Gray, was probing the Oregon coast with his ship *Columbia* and found the mouth of the river that would bear his craft's name. Soon afterwards, one of the men attached to the Pacific coast explorations of Captain George Vancouver ascended the river for a hundred miles. Vancouver's book on his explorations, published in 1798, was quickly devoured by those in search of the "Great River of the West" and it became accepted that the river he described was the one they were seeking. Another of the Nor'wester partners infected with Mackenzie's spirit was Duncan McGillivray, who by the end of the century was already located at Rocky Mountain House intent on pushing the explorations forward. Under his command was David Thompson, a young surveyor in the North West Company's employ who would be the key individual involved in unravelling the mystery.

The major rivers of western Canada were the highways of the fur trade. In the case of the Rocky Mountain front, both the Hudson's Bay Company's and North West Company's decisions to utilize the Saskatchewan River system determined the development of the region. The Bow River is a tributary of the South Saskatchewan, but it was the North Saskatchewan flowing from the fur rich parkland area of Alberta and providing a staging point for the fur trade to the north that fell under the approving gaze of both fur companies. While there was some interest in the waterways of the South Saskatchewan system, they had the disadvantage of flowing through the traditional lands of the Blackfoot Nation, feared by all. When the North West Company built Rocky Mountain House it was their intention to use it as a point of trade with the Peigan as well as a jumping off point for trade on the Pacific slope. At the northern limit of the Peigan's influence, it was felt to be a safer location than anywhere to the south along the mountains' foot. For geographic and security reasons then, the Bow River watershed was all but ignored by the early fur trade.

This did not prevent occasional forays into the Banff-Bow

Rocky Mountain House, the remains of which are shown in this 1886 view, was built on the North Saskatchewan River in 1799 to capture the trade of the Peigan and Kootenay

Valley area by those engaged in the trade. Fur trade surveyors like David Thompson took every opportunity to explore, report on and map all the territory they could examine. Indeed, when still a simple clerk with the Hudson's Bay Company in 1787, one of Thompson's first assignments was to accompany a party under the guidance of James Gady from Manchester House on the Saskatchewan and proceed "in the direction of about WSW for the upper part of the Bow River near the east foot of the Rocky Mountains, where we expected to find some of the Peeagan Indians camped." As they approached the mountains, Thompson recorded his impressions, the first ever made by an European upon seeing the mountains of the Bow Valley. He said that they appeared "like shining white clouds in the horizon" from a distance, but as he drew near "they rose in height, their immense masses of snow appeared above the clouds and formed an impassible barrier, even to the Eagle." When still thirty miles from the Front Ranges, Thompson's party crossed to the south side of the river and there met the Peigan they had been searching for, and, as mentioned, he spent the following winter at their camp in the lodge of *Saukamappee.*

Thompson may well have probed upstream on the Bow during that winter, but, if so, it went unrecorded. It was not until thirteen years later, in 1800, that he provided the first detailed description of the area around Bow River Gap. By that time he was a trained surveyor, having learned "practical astronomy" in 1790 from the HBC's chief surveyor, Philip Turnor, with fellow pupil Peter Fidler. He had unceremoniously abandoned his employer in favour of the Nor'westers in 1797, partly due to his expectation they would approve explorations of the Pacific slope. By 1800 he was posted at Rocky Mountain House under Duncan McGillivray and was on the verge of achieving his goal. But in November of that year, after successfully bringing in the previously referred to band of Kootenays who had come over Howse Pass to trade, he accompanied McGillivray on a visit to a camp of Peigan on the Highwood River. As they proceeded along the front, Thompson provided his second description of the scene:

> *The latter part of this Day, the Ground became Knolly & the Surface tolerable good — all fine open Meadow with chance patches of Willows. We are on a Line parallel to the Mountain which every where is covered with Snow & seems to present an impenetrable Bank. The View is grand in a high Degree: on our right we have the Bow Hills, lofty in themselves and Brown with Woods, above them stately rises the Rocky Mountains vast and abrupt whose Tops pierce the clouds — on our left, before & behind us, a verdant Ocean.*[1]

It was clearly McGillivray's intention to penetrate the Bow Valley on his return, for Thompson mentions as much in the recording of his questions of the Peigan. He relates that they got "information of all the Brooks & Rivulets which fall into the Bow River from the Mountain southward of its Source. . . ." The last days of November found McGillivray, Thompson and the guide Dumond ascending the Bow and hunting what were described as goats (actually bighorn sheep). On November 30th they decided to ascend a mountain to determine the lay of the land, likely the modern-day Loder Peak near Exshaw. They found the ascent steep with many small stones which gave way to more solid rock as they got higher, but this had sharp points "like an enormous Rasp" which "cut our Shoes, Socks &c all to pieces in a Trice." The observant Thompson reported the rock was "of a dark Grey, with few or no Veins, very hard & Glassy and upon rubbing Two Pieces of it together for a Moment produces when hld near the Nose a strong disagreeable Smell, somewhat Sulphurous." But it was the view that held the strongest fascination — to the east "vast & unbounded" while to the west "Hills & Rocks rose to our View covered with Snow, here rising, there subsiding, but their Tops nearly of an equal Height every where."

Thompson was struck by the resemblance to waves in the ocean during a winter storm. He also cogitated on the mountains' formation, for "when looking upon them and attentively considering their wild Order and Appearance, the Imagination is apt to say, these must once have been Liquid, and the State when swelled to its greatest Agitation, suddenly congealed and made Solid by Power Omnipotent."[2] He likewise noted that there were shrubs of fir and pine almost to the summit and reported buffalo dung some two-thirds of the way up, an indication of the great beasts' presence in the mountains at relatively high altitude. The return to the horses was made some four hours after setting out, and so ended the account of the first European ascent in the Rockies, the beginning of an activity that would become one of the most enduring themes in the Valley's heritage.

When Kootenay Indians had come in to trade at Rocky Mountain House earlier in 1800, McGillivray had sent two voyageurs, LeGasse and Leblanc, to accompany them to their homeland. These were the first recorded white men to cross Howse Pass at the head of the North Saskatchewan and the following year McGillivray intended to follow it up with a more extended exploration. In June, 1801 Thompson and James Hughes accompanied by a small party were instructed to do so, but ran into problems because of the flooding river given their rather late start and as a result of the fears of their guide, a Cree, of venturing into Kootenay lands. The party turned back short of Kootenay Plains and thereafter further attempts to cross the pass were forestalled by the open hostility of the Peigan, who believed that it was the intention of the fur traders to arm their enemies, the Kootenay, in the course of the trade. Thompson described this situation and its ultimate solution in his *Travels*, a memoir written later in life:

I have already related how the Piegans waited us to prevent our crossing the mountains and arming the natives on that side, in which for a time they succeeded, and we abandoned the trading post near the mountains in the spring of 1807. The murder of two Piegan Indians in 1806, by Captain Lewis of the United States, drew the Piegans to the Missouri to revenge their deaths, and thus gave me an opportunity to cross the mountains by the defiles of the Saskatchewan River, which lead to the headwaters of the Columbia River.[3]

This matter-of-fact description belies the difficulties he and his guide Bercier had on the trip, particularly after crossing Howse Pass (named for a Hudson's Bay trader, Joseph Howse, who used it a few years later) and having to deal with the rank vegetation and the treacherous terrain of the "Portage [Blaeberry] River". Jaco Finlay, a half-breed employee of the company, had been sent ahead to prepare the way the previous year, but Thompson found his trail-blazing most unsatisfactory. However, they persevered and reached the Columbia on June 30, 1807, a momentous event even though Thompson thought it was the Kootenay River and only came to understand the difficult hydrology of the Columbia-Kootenay drainage after several more years of exploration. At that point, near modern Golden, they built canoes and ascended the Columbia to near its headwaters at "Kootanae [Windermere] Lake" where, near starvation, they built a rough post and due to the precariousness of their situation had "to lay aside all thoughts of discovery for the present and bend my whole aim to the establishment of trade & c. . . ."

Thompson returned through Howse Pass in June of 1808 after

an extensive exploration of the headwaters of the Columbia and the upper reaches of the Kootenay River across the 49th parallel. He went as far east as Rainy River near Lake of the Woods to leave his cargo of furs, the first brought out from the Pacific slope, and re-supplied to return to Kootanae House. The trip was repeated in the summer of 1809, whereupon he undertook his now famous exploration and mapping of the Columbia-Kootenay system and established several new trading houses for the North West Company in what is now the United States. When bringing the fur packs out to Rainy River in the summer of 1810, he undoubtedly felt he would be sent back to Montreal as part of the usual rotation of the wintering partners of the company and because he believed the Nor'Westers had lost interest in the exploration of the Columbia, possibly because of the high cost of moving furs and supplies over such an extended route. However, the situation was rapidly changing on the Columbia with the rumoured initiative of the American-led Pacific Fur Company under John Jacob Astor to establish a sea-supplied base at the river's mouth.

The North West Company's waning interest in exploring the Columbia to tidewater in favour of developing the trade on its upper reaches was quickly replaced with an urgency to "dispute the priority of possession with them [the Americans]." Thompson was instructed to turn back and prepare himself for a journey to the mouth of the Columbia, and made for Rocky Mountain House to do so. But he found that the Peigan, who had bothered little with the area during his use of Howse Pass from 1807 to 1810, had changed their demeanour as a result of losing a battle with some enemy Salish armed by Thompson during his trade with them during that period. Determined to no longer countenance this , the Peigan blocked Thompson's progress and he was forced to turn northward in search of another pass whose existence was rumoured by natives in the trade. Early in 1811 he made his second historic crossing of a major pass in the Rockies when he penetrated Athabasca Pass at the headwaters of a tributary of the Athabasca River, the Whirlpool, and made his way to the Big Bend, the great northern arc of the Columbia. Here some of his

Ascending Athabasca Pass, from a watercolour by H. J. Warre, 1846

men deserted and he was forced to winter with the remaining few and build boats in preparation for the spring break-up. This site was henceforth known as "Boat Encampment" and became one of the most famous locations in the fur trade.

Thompson had originally intended to run the river to the Pacific and claim possession of it for the North West Company and Great Britain before the American-led Astorians could claim it for themselves. But "being too weakly manned, instead of descending, we had to ascend the river to its source, then carry two miles to McGillivray's [Kootenay] River, descend it for several miles to the Salish Indian Road, which, through a fine country leads to the Salish [Clark's Fork] River, where I expected to find Canadian trappers and engage some of them to accompany me to the sea." This he accomplished and then proceeded to Kettle Falls to make a new canoe, embarking for the ocean on the third of July through country that was completely unexplored. He reached the Pacific on July 14th, but to his disappointment found he had lost the race as at the Columbia's mouth was "the fur trading post of Mr. J. Astor of the city of New York . . . the far famed Fort Astoria of the United States."[4]

Events would soon deliver Astoria into North West Company hands and Thompson himself would disappear from the trade, but not his legacy of maps and accounts which, when published almost a century later, became the most valuable source on the geography of the mountains and the Pacific slope for generations to come. His accomplishments were prodigious and none more so than the discovery of Athabasca Pass, for it became the main highway of the fur trade for the next half-century, particularly after the amalgamation of the Hudson's Bay Company and the North West Company in 1821. This resulted in, among other things, the development of an important post known as Jasper House and the focusing of fur trade activity on more direct routes between Fort Edmonton and the Athabasca Valley, which became the jumping off point for the Athabasca Pass and the Columbia as well as Yellowhead Pass and New Caledonia. Therefore the attention of the trade moved still further away from the Banff-Bow Valley region, and even Rocky Mountain House itself alternately opened and closed depending on the situation with the Peigan trade.

Only one direct fur trade initiative was launched in the Valley area for the remainder of the period. In 1832 the Hudson's Bay Company, reacting to competition for the trade of the Peigan by Americans on the Missouri, decided that a post closer than Rocky Mountain House to the tribes' heartland was necessary. The minutes for the Council of the Northern Department of Rupert's Land, the annual meeting of chief factors of the major posts convened to deal with company affairs, recorded the decision: "The recent defection of the Piegan tribe rendering it unnecessary to maintain the Rocky Mountain House which was originally established for their convenience, IT IS RESOLVED to abandon that post and to establish a new post to be called the Piegan Post on the borders of the 49th parallel of latitude, with a view to attract that tribe and to prevent other Indians who are in the habit of frequenting the Honble Company's Posts in the upper part of the Saskatchewan from crossing the line."[5]

The site chosen was on the north side of the Bow River near the mouth of today's Old Fort Creek on the Stoney Reserve at Morley.

Piegan Post was a substantial affair consisting of some eleven buildings surrounded by a five-sided stockade. It was placed under the command of J. E. Harriott, subsequently one of the most important Hudson's Bay men in the Saskatchewan district, but rather than gaining favour with the Peigan and their Blackfoot allies it simply increased their enmity and was abandoned in 1834. Those for whom Piegan Post had been built burned it to the ground a short time later, and the Hudson's Bay Company irreversibly abandoned the southern prairies, and with them the Bow Valley, in favour of re-opening Rocky Mountain House. The remains of what was henceforth known as "Old Bow Fort" almost rotted away before they became the main rendezvous point for later parties exploring the Rockies.

There was one other extremely brief, but important, appearance of a fur trade presence in the Bow Valley. In 1841 George Simpson, the recently-knighted Governor of the Hudson's Bay Company, was engaged in a trip around the world in the interests of the company and intended on crossing the Rockies by the now usual Athabasca Pass route. However, at Red River he met John Rowand, the chief factor of Edmonton House, who had brought with him some "Columbia guides" to escort the Governor across the prairies and through the mountains to that river. The guides suggested that the Columbia would be in full flood when he reached it and therefore extremely dangerous. He heeded their warnings and changed his plan, determining to go by horse instead of boat and to cross the mountains further south in order to connect with the headwaters of the Columbia. As the main guide for the mountain section of the trip, Rowand had engaged a well-known half-breed named Piche, or, as Simpson called him "Peechee," variously described as "a halfbreed native of the Kootonais country," and "a chief of the Mountain Cree." The route he chose was one previously untravelled by white men but a traditional path of the natives — through Devil's Gap from the Ghost River to the eastern end of Lake Minnewanka, along its shore to the vicinity of modern-day Banff. Here, at what was referred to as "the Bow River Traverse," a guide from the Columbia, Edward

Berland, was to meet the party with a relay of horses, but he did not appear. It seems from Simpson's account that Berland would likely have led the party across Vermilion Pass, but either because of Peechee's unfamiliarity with that route or his desire to reach the Columbia by the most direct course possible he led them up today's Brewster and Healy Creeks over the pass subsequently named for Simpson and down the western slope by the river similarly named for the Governor to the Kootenay River and ultimately the Windermere-Columbia Lake area.

In his account of the trip, Simpson provided an excellent description of his journey through the Lake Minnewanka region:

The path which we had been following, was a track of the Assiniboines, carried, for the sake of concealment, through the thickest forests. These Indians and Peechee were the only persons that had ever pursued this route; and we were the first whites that had attempted this pass in the mountains. In the morning we entered a defile between mountainous ridges, marching for nine hours through dense woods. This valley, which was from two to three miles in width contained four beautiful lakes, communicating with each other by small streams; and the fourth of the series, which was about fifteen miles by three, we named after Peechee as being our guide's usual home. At this place he had expected to find his family; but Madame Peechee and the children had left their encampment, probably on account of the scarcity of game. What an idea of the loneliness and precariousness of savage life does this single glimpse of the biography of the Peechees suggest.[6]

Simpson also commented on the great beauty of the area and its almost idyllic setting:

The beauty of the scenery formed some compensation for the loss of time. Our tents were pitched in a level meadow of about five hundred acres in extent, enclosed by mountains on three sides, and by Peechee's Lake on the fourth. From the very edge of the water there rose a gentle ascent of six or eight hundred feet, covered with pines and composed almost entirely of the accumulated fragments of the adamantine heights above; and on the upper border of this slope there stood perpendicular walls of granite, of three or four thousand feet, while among the dizzy altitudes of their battlemented summits the goat and sheep bounded in playful security.[7]

As he passed through the Valley, Simpson also noted some landmarks that would become famous to future generations of visitors. On viewing today's Cascade Mountain he observed "a stream of water which, though of very considerable volume, looked like a thread of silver on the grey rock." And while ascending today's Healy Creek he commented that "one peak presented a very peculiar feature in an opening of about eighty feet by fifty, which, at a distance, might have been taken for a spot of snow, but which, as we advanced nearer, assumed the appearance of the gateway of a giant's fortress," an obvious reference to the famous Goat's Eye.

On reaching the height of land, Simpson's party stopped to breakfast, and he noted that it was a level isthmus that "did not exceed fourteen paces in width." While impressed with the surrounding scenery he allowed that this pass, which would subsequently bear his name, "was inferior in grandeur to that of the Athabasca Portage" which was "little better than a succession of glaciers . . . through a region of perpetual snow." However, he was pleased to find something at the summit that gave him great delight as here he "met an unexpected reminiscence of my own native hills in the shape of a plant, which appeared to me to be the very heather of the Highlands of Scotland." Although unrecorded, he or Rowand also paused long enough to carve their initials "GS JR 1841" in a tree to mark their passage. Found sixty-three years later by a party led by Banff guide Jim Brewster in the fallen and rotting trunk, it was carefully cut out and displayed in Brewster's Banff home, where it became one of the most famous and talked about artifacts of Banff's early history (it now resides in the Banff Park Museum). Because Simpson's account was somewhat vague as to what pass he had actually penetrated, this blaze also played a key role in establishing his exact route and the course of another party (James Sinclair's) whose track Simpson mentioned in relation to his own.

Simpson's trip and his account of it are noteworthy in that they provide the earliest description of a key part of the Banff-Bow Valley area. Not only did the Governor record his impressions in his notes and diaries, he also saw to it that they were published so that others could learn of his travels and what he had witnessed during them. Few, if any, of the other fur trade personalities frequenting the mountains during these years had the reputation or the resources he did, and so his book *Narrative of a Journey Round the World in 1841 and 1842,* published in 1847, became the only contemporary account of fur trade travels in the area. In contrast, the accounts of other fur trade travellers were not published until many years later, if at all — for example none of David Thompson's writings and maps appeared until 1897. This situation would become an important factor in future explorations and would make Simpson's account all the more valuable.

The famous "Simpson blaze" recovered from Simpson Pass by Jim Brewster, 1904

One other interesting facet of Simpson's description was the obvious value that he attached to good guides. He knew better than anyone the need for knowledgeable and trustworthy men who could be relied upon to lead him safely and quickly through new and uncharted country so that he could keep up his tremendous rate of travel (he was attempting to set a record for an around-the-world trip). Guides of all types, from those attached to the fur trade brigades during the course of their entire trips from the Hudson's Bay to the Columbia, to those who provided only local knowledge and leadership in the mountains, such as Peechee, were an integral factor in the fur trade. Thus began with Peechee and some of his native and half-breed compatriots a practice of guiding in the mountains which would become one of the Rockies' most important traditions and respected occupations.

Although the fur trade itself made little impact on the Banff-Bow Valley, there were influences created by it that did. These were primarily missionary activities permitted by the Hudson's Bay Company amongst the tribes located near the mountains, mainly the Stoney, which resulted in not only successful proselytization but also in increased knowledge of the region. Primary amongst them was the Reverend Robert T. Rundle, a Wesleyan Methodist missionary from Cornwall who served the interests of his sect in the parkland and plains of present-day Alberta from 1840 to 1848. Rundle first visited a Stoney camp (he called them "Strong Wood Assiniboines") near Rocky Mountain House in March, 1841 and, as previously described, was warmly welcomed into their midst. In April, 1841 he accompanied them south to the Bow, but did not enter the mountains at this time. He did, however, provide a description that is interesting to compare with Thompson's made some forty years earlier:

On Thurs. 15th they presented the sublimest spectacle I ever expect to behold until I become an inhabitant of the "New Heaven & the New Earth." I saw them then after a recent fall of snow & they looked as beautiful as if newly risen at the call of Omnipotence & fresh from their makers smile. Their pointed & snowy summits rose high into the heavens like the lofty spires of some vast & magnificent marble temple reared by the Almighty Architect of nature to mock all the works of art. The sight seemed too grand & too glorious for reality.[8]

It was not until November, 1844 that Rundle again found himself at the foot of the peaks on the Bow, once more travelling with some of his Stoney converts. This time he was determined to investigate them and departed on the morning of November 7th from a camp near the "Dead [Ghost] River," passing Old Bow Fort and penetrating the mountains only a little as "the road was shut up & there was much snow." The entry in his diary for Saturday, November 9th recorded an unforgettable day:

Am now climbing a mountain. There are two veins, perhaps of spar in the bed of rock where I am sitting. I became quite ill thro' fatigue &c. but was in good spirits when climbing, until I was very high up. I made two attempts to get up an elevation but could not succeed. Rocks very steep — felt very weak, so weak, that at last I was near fainting whilst passing over a projecting ledge of rock. What a moment of anxiety. I have some recollection of calling to the Almighty to assist me & praised by His name, my prayer was heard. I descended to the next stage. It was presumptuous of me I know but I began again to see if I could not find a way to scale higher but I could not succeed so I now abandoned my design & commenced descending. I was very weak from want of food, having left without breakfast, & I began to feel afraid ever & anon too I heard the moving stones which terrified me. How hard too, to pass along the steep sloping sides sloping away to fearful descent. At length, however, I reached the bottom, but how was I to get to the encampment as I had lost the road. Very tired, weak, & unwell. Heard gun fired! so guided!! Reached at last thanks to Providence. Took some medicine and had breakfast about sunset.[9]

While Thompson's prosaic description of climbing Loder Peak had been the initial recorded account of an ascent in the Rockies, certainly Rundle's was the first report of a climbing adventure. It was later held that this ascent had been on Mount Rundle, which would have made it impressive indeed, but it was more likely Grotto Mountain or some other lesser peak on the north side of the Bow. This is attested to in Rundle's account of a further visit to the area in 1847 when he almost drowned while crossing the Bow on his horse some miles below Old Bow Fort. He recorded in a memo written at Edmonton House upon his return from this trip that "this was my first crossing of the Bow River but I had before been near it first in 1842 and in 1841(1844)."[10] However, the account of his supposed climb of Mount Rundle, presented in 1911 in a Methodist missionary magazine *The Foreign Field*, added much to the later interest in his activities in the area and, like many stories associated with the mountains that were not altogether true, became imbedded in the Valley's lore.

While apparently not having ascended Mount Rundle, which nonetheless was named in his honour by Captain John Palliser in 1859, the missionary did perform some interesting explorations in the Valley. In late June, 1847, shortly after his mishap crossing the Bow, he found himself in the mountains proper and exploring up the river. Accompanied by guides, he was shown "the most interesting lake I ever saw" which he described as "several miles in length, embedded in the mountain which rise in grandeur." He also made the first mention of the lake's subsequently famous fishery, stating that "Mr. Munro told me there are most beautiful salmon trout in it." He too was describing Lake Minnewanka (he called it Wildcat Lake after the Indian name for Peechee) and as his party proceeded along its shore he noted the oblique strata on both sides of the lake that seemed to correspond to one another. At the east end of the lake, before leaving it to proceed through the gap at the foot of the Devil's Head and into the valley of the Ghost River, he too recorded his passage by blazing "RTR July 1, 1847" in a tree.

During the period that Rundle was attempting to secure the loyalties of the first peoples at the Rockies' foot to the cause of the Wesleyan gospel, a rival Jesuit missionary, Father Pierre J. de Smet, was actively trying to convince them of the alternative message of Roman Catholicism. De Smet had spent several years toiling amongst the Kootenay in the Oregon Territory missions of his church prior to 1845, when he was instructed to try extend his work over the mountains among the feared Blackfoot tribes of the plains. This required him to travel to his field of endeavour from the Columbia River, providing a description of the west side of the

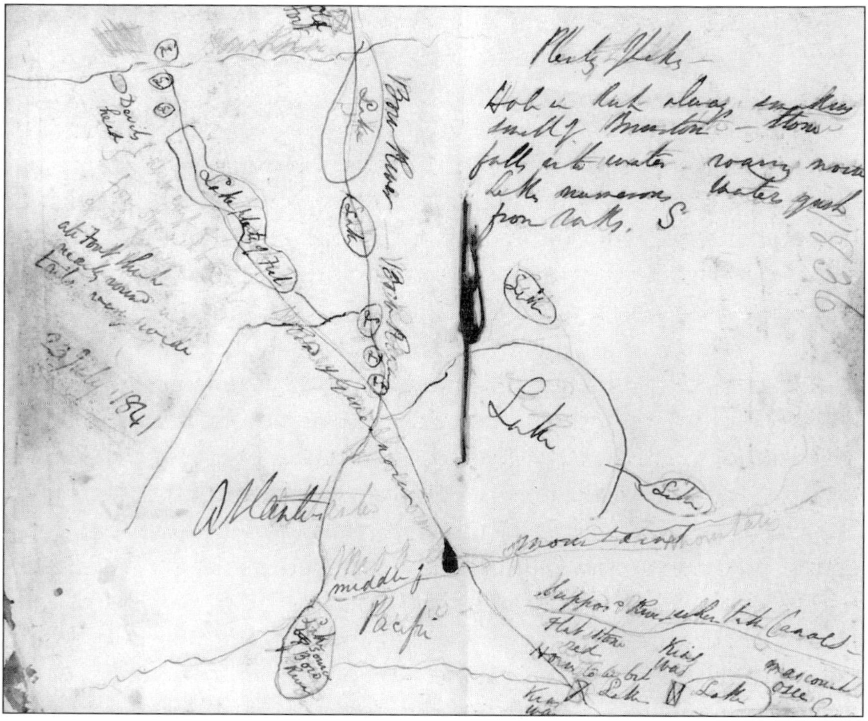

Rundle drew a rough map of the Bow River and Lake Minnewanka in his journal in July, 1847

Rockies and the approaches to the Banff-Bow Valley region from that aspect. De Smet was a diligent recorder of his observations (these were in the form of letters to his superior) and mentioned a good deal about the landscape, the vegetation, the wildlife and even such phenomena as the borealis during his travels.

De Smet crossed to the eastern side of the mountains from the headwaters of the Columbia through the area of the Cross and Mitchell River systems, the former which he provided with its name in his efforts to spread his message:

After much fatigue, labor and admirtion, on the 15th we traversed the high lands separating the waters of Oregon from those of the south branch of the Sascatshawin, or the ancient Bourbon river, so called before the Canadian conquest by the British. . . . The Christian's standard, the cross, has been reared at the sources of these two rivers: may it be a sign of salvation and peace to all the scattered and itinerant tribes east and west of these gigantic and lurid mountains."[11]

Passing on to the northeastward, de Smet probably became the first white person to see Mount Assiniboine, mentioning that "the far-famed Egyptian monuments of Cheops and Cephren dwindle into naught before this gigantic architectural cliff of nature." He then proceeded on to the Bow, likely by way of Whiteman's Pass and down past today's Spray Lakes. On reaching the river he saw the remains of an Indian camp and "was beset by a thousand disquietudes concerning the fate that awaited me," believing them to be the ferocious Blackfoot. To his relief, de Smet found the natives whose camp he discovered were Stoney, and although he had a rather low opinion of them, he spent some time travelling in their company in the Bow Valley. He too commented on Cascade Mountain, noting "a beautiful crystalline fountain issues from the centre of a perpendicular rock about five hundred feet high, and then pours its waters over the plain in foam and mist." But he spent little time in the Valley, travelling to Rocky Mountain House, where he had an interesting encounter with the Reverend Rundle, before proceeding on to Edmonton House to spend the winter. In the spring, he made for Athabasca Pass to return to his missions in the Oregon Territory, where major events were unfolding that would affect the entire future of the fur trade in the Rockies.

At the time of the amalgamation of the North West and Hudson's Bay Companies in 1821, the British government had awarded the new company an extension to its trading monopoly for twenty-one years for all that part of British North America between Rupert's Land and the mountains, as well as sole British rights of trade in the area near the Columbia River in what is now the U. S. Pacific Northwest. The Columbia Department, as it was known, became a hotbed of dispute with American authorities who also claimed the territory, and from 1818 to 1828 a treaty was in place that allowed the nationals of both governments to trade in the area. As part of that treaty, discussions took place between the

American and British governments as to the ultimate partition of the area, the Americans proposing the 49th parallel drawn from the mountains to the sea and the British holding out for the 49th parallel to the point where it intersected the Columbia and thence following its course to the mouth. Simpson's ability to reorganize and make a profit from the trade in the district made it a bone of contention worth fighting for and the dispute continued in deadlock until the growth in American settlement in the area swung the balance in their favour. The Hudson's Bay Company took the fateful step in 1845 of shifting its base of operations from Fort George (formerly Astoria) at the mouth of the Columbia to Vancouver Island, where a British crown colony was created around Victoria, all but abandoning the lower Columbia. This paved the way for the Oregon Treaty of 1846 which fixed the boundary at the 49th parallel and effectively ended the company's influence and trade in the area. In the circumstances, the need for the annual fur brigades over Athabasca Pass would soon disappear and, in a short time, so would the company's role in the Rockies.

It is somewhat ironic that while the Banff-Bow Valley was largely bypassed by the fur trade, one of the major decisions taken by the Hudson's Bay Company in the waning days of the period would affect its future in fundamental ways. The decision to move the company's base of operations to Vancouver Island and abandon the "Great River of the West" would seemingly have ended the role of the mountains in the history of western Canada, but instead it ensured a continued one. A new engine of history would soon enter the scene which would have a more profound and lasting influence than the fur trade, and this time the focus would be on the southern Bow Valley and its defiles rather than the more northerly passes of the Rockies.

Chapter Three
The Amazing Dr. Hector

In the story of any country or region, there is always one or two individuals who stand out from the crowd. The Banff-Bow Valley is no exception, as throughout its history there have been those who have left enduring legacies with which we can still identify. Several of those who are key to the area's heritage will be met in these pages, but one of the first, and interestingly one whose contact would be very brief, set the trend in adding to our knowledge. And, of telling importance in establishing the tone of the Valley's future, he was neither politician, businessman, nor military leader, but rather an active and inquiring scientist. Dr. James Hector was the man who provided the real starting point for our understanding of the geology, geography and natural life of the Valley.

During the final stages of the fur trade period in the mountains, parties appearing in the Valley were infrequent but interesting. They were mainly associated with the dispute over the Oregon Territory, which in the 1840s added some impetus for further use of passes leading to the Pacific slope. Simpson had fought hard to retain the territory for the company's interests and had instigated several initiatives in his efforts, including the promotion of settlement of British subjects in the Oregon region to combat the growing influence of American settlers and arranging for a British military reconnaissance to determine if the territory could be defended. The parties involved in these enterprises provided the first record of the crossings of Whiteman's and Kananaskis Passes.

Credit for these feats largely belongs to James Sinclair, a University of Edinburgh trained leader of the Red River Metis who was among those challenging the Hudson's Bay Company's monopoly in the fur trade. Despite this, Simpson was able to convince him to escort a group of Metis to Oregon in 1841, at once getting rid of an irritant in the Red River Colony and at the same time taking a step towards achieving his strategic objectives in the Oregon Territory. The party consisted of twenty-three families comprising 121 souls, most of whom had been promised land and other assistance by the Hudson's Bay Company, travelling in a cavalcade of fifty-five Red River carts and accompanied by 200 head of cattle. Simpson encountered Sinclair's group during his own trip from Fort Garry to Fort Edmonton in 1841 and when he reached Edmonton made arrangements for them to follow the usual Athabasca Pass route. But the free-thinking Sinclair had ideas of his own and instead struck off to the south under the guidance of the noted Cree chief "Mackipictoon" (*Maskepetoon*), or "Broken Arm," who knew of a new pass as yet untravelled by white men. The party followed Sir George's footsteps through the Lake Minnewanka region but then diverted to the Bow by today's Carrot Creek and headed downstream instead of up, fording the river opposite today's Three Sisters. Here they abandoned their carts and followed the Spray River to the pass, from where they made their way to the Cross River and down to the Kootenay, the reverse route that de Smet would follow a few years later, and finally through the narrow defile named for Sinclair into the Columbia Valley. Although the majority of the party were Metis, a few men from the Maritimes had joined them prior to departure and seem to account for the name "Whiteman's" attached to the new pass.

After enduring severe hardships, Sinclair's party ultimately arrived at Fort Colvile on the Columbia in today's Washington State late in the autumn, only to find that there were doubts about the British government's right to grant them lands in the disputed territory. In spite of Sinclair's disobedience, Simpson later had to admit that his pass was superior to the one he himself employed, noting it was "not only shorter but better in every respect, so that even with families, and encumbered with baggage as they were, they effected the passage of the Mountains with infinitely less labour, & in a shorter time than we accomplished it."[1] As to the fate of the Metis, most of them quickly became disillusioned with the treatment they received at the hands of the Hudson's Bay Company and, just the opposite of what Simpson had hoped, ultimately became strong supporters of the American claims to the territory. In Sinclair's case, the mountains were to see him again.

In 1845, a few years after Sinclair's journey, a military reconnaissance party was arranged by Simpson, consisting of two officers, Lieutenants Henry J. Warre of the 14th Regiment, nephew and aide-de camp of Sir R. Downes Jackson, Commander of the Forces in British North America, and Mervin Vavasour of the Royal Engineers. They were ordered by Jackson, on the expressed instructions of the Governor-General, to cross the Rockies disguised as private adventurers to report on "the capabilities of the Oregon Territory in a Military point of view." Governor Simpson directed one of his chief factors, Peter Skene Ogden, to "conduct these gentlemen from Red River to their destination, crossing the Rocky Mountains at the Bow River Pass." Elsewhere Simpson identified the pass to be used as "lately passed by a large body of emigrant families from the Red River Settlement" and so it appears to be Whiteman's Pass they utilized.[2] Because the party was relatively small and vulnerable to Indians, it hugged the Rocky Mountain front in its journey south from Edmonton House and rather than following the normal route up the Ghost River and through Devil's Gap instead continued south and fell upon the Bow River and the site where "they [Sinclair's party] were obliged to leave their Waggons etc."

Warre recorded the journey in a journal, later published as *Sketches in North America and the Oregon Territory*, but did not provide a great deal of written detail. He did, however, indicate that the trip through the mountains was a trying one:

Our passage over the magnificent range of the lofty mountains was not accomplished without much difficulty, and a fearful sacrifice of the noble animals that aided us in the transport. We left Edmonton with sixty horses; on our arrival at Fort Colville, on the Columbia River, we had only twenty-seven, and several of these so exhausted they could not

Warre's watercolour sketch entitled "The Rocky Mountains, 1845" was the first painting showing identifiable features in the Banff-Bow Valley

have continued many more days. The steepness of the mountain passes, the want of proper nourishment, the fearful falls that some of the animals sustained, rolling in some instances many hundred feet into the foaming torrent beneath, combined to cause this great loss. The scenery was grand in the extreme; similar in form to the Alps of Switzerland, you felt that you were in the midst of desolation: no habitations, save those of the wild Indians were within hundreds of miles; but few civilized beings had ever even viewed this.[3]

Fortunately, Warre amplified these descriptions with a series of sketches of his party and the scenery along the way. While other early explorers, such as Thompson and Rundle, had made rough sketches of the mountains, Warre's would be the first real art that depicted identifiable scenes in detail, including one that clearly shows the shoulder of Mount Rundle and Cascade Mountain, thereby beginning the henceforth important tradition of art and artists in Banff-Bow Valley culture. Ultimately, the lieutenants determined that the mountains presented an impossible barrier to military accessibility and reported that "without attempting to describe the numerous Defiles through which we passed, or the difficulty in forcing a passage through the burnt Forests, and over the high land, we may venture to assert, that Sir George Simpson's idea of transporting troops . . . with their stores, etc. through such an extent of uncultivated Country and over such impracticable Mountains would appear to Us quite infeasible."[4]

Meanwhile, James Sinclair had returned to Red River after his 1841 trip and after once more making the round trip through Whiteman's Pass in 1850 was convinced by Simpson, with a promise of chief trader status in the company and land and livestock suitable for starting a ranch, to take a second group of emigrants through the mountains in 1854. In this case the party consisted of some 100 people with carts drawn by oxen, and it is likely that Sinclair intended to go by his now customary route until he once more met Broken Arm and was convinced to follow a different track. This involved going directly to the Bow along the mountain front from Edmonton House as had Warre and Vavasour, but then taking the first tributary coming from the southwest, the Kananaskis. This trip proved to be one of the few early expeditions passing through the Valley that has survived in accounts provided by both white and native participants.

Sinclair charged his young brother-in-law, John Campbell, with keeping a log of the journey, and while the party was making its way up the Bow he recorded an attack by a band of Blackfeet:

The Crees acted as escort to our party, stood guard at night, and kept with us until we came to a camp of Stony Indians on the Bow River. There was something I missed telling you. When we were encamped at the Bow River. . . we were followed by Indians for eight days. . . . Although we did not see them, we knew they were near. One terrible night we spent in momentary expectation of attack. All waited in suspense. But the night passed without any disturbance till towards day break when some of the cattle came running with poisoned arrows sticking in their bodies. . . . That was how we happened to find out about the Indians being around. . . . As soon as it was light some of the men ascend-

ed the high hill, but the renegades got away with three horses. . . . They could see no Indians. They, however, found they had killed two animals and carried off the meat.[5]

When ethnologist Marius Barbeau was carrying out his research at Morley in 1926, Isaac-Rolling-in-the-Mud told him the story of "Cattle Crossing the Rockies" that was well-known to the natives. It source was a Stoney named "Wolf-Viewing-on-a-Hill," or "Mark," who was in his twenties when a man "who bought a lot of cattle east of here" hired him and four or five half-breeds to take his herd across the Rockies into British Columbia. Mark knew the way through the Kananaskis, but while they were driving the cattle up the Bow near "Osade," the forks of the Bow and Kananaskis, they were attacked by two hundred enemy Blackfoot and Sarcee who had been following them:

Toward evening the marauders spread round. When the cattle were gathered in one place at dusk, the first thing they heard was the bawling. The chief white man asked his men to go and see what was wrong. And they got on horseback, those wild cowboys, and before they went any distance, they met their cattle stampeding towards camp. They saw animals running and falling head-over-heels Some ran into camp and fell, with arrows in their bodies. It was the arrows that the enemies had shot them with. When the boss found out that there were enemies killing off his cattle, he was sure he himself would not be spared. So he told the Stony, Mark: "Look after me, and save me. . . ."

Mark knew that plains Indians did not like to go into country with heavy timber, so he had the party take refuge along the Kananaskis River while he stood watch all night. His hunch was right, as the enemy did not attack, and in the morning, after the party broke up their Red River carts and packed their belongings on the remaining cattle, he led them up the river to the area of today's Ribbon Creek. There he left them, making his way as quickly as possible to Rocky Mountain House, and boasted of his enemy's decision not to attack despite their superior numbers by explaining that "when there were Stonies, they were sure that most of themselves would be killed off before they killed the Stonies." Mark also related, in telling the story in later years, he had heard that twenty of the 150 cattle had been killed in the attack but only ten survived the remainder of their journey over the mountains.[6]

The two version of events concur in that this was the first recorded white crossing of a pass in the Kananaskis and that it proved extremely difficult. According to Campbell, they broke up their carts to make pack saddles for their oxen at Old Bow Fort, and then Broken Arm led them up a stream he called "Strong Current River" assisted by two Stoney guides that Sinclair had hired. The going was hard on the animal's feet and the emigrants soon began to show signs of nervous strain, leading Sinclair to curse his Cree guide for taking them this way when the comparatively easy and well-known route over Whiteman's Pass was so close by. Because of the difficulties of travel and the lack of game, some of the oxen had to be slaughtered for food and Sinclair was himself forced to take over leadership when it became obvious that Broken Arm was lost. Eventually, in late October, they found their way out of the morass by way of the South Kananaskis Pass, the entire party being so exhausted that they could not ride and had to cross the pass on foot in three-foot-deep snow. Campbell summed up the experience by stating that "our mountain guide took a new route across the mountains which took us thirty days whereas we could have gone by Mr. Sinclair's old route in ten days."[7]

Perhaps noting the Sinclair parties' abandonment of their carts, Simpson concurred with Warre that the route he had followed was impracticable for wheeled carriages, but he did feel it should not be difficult on horseback. However, within a few years his assumption that wheeled vehicles could not be taken over the mountains was beginning to be examined. It was a challenge born of expediency resulting from the growth of British North America and the need for better transportation, not the least of which was to the now growing crown colony which the Hudson's Bay Company had begun on Vancouver Island when it abandoned the mouth of the Columbia. The examination of these possibilities resulted in the appearance of one the most important groups of individuals ever to penetrate the Valley — the members of the Palliser Expedition, and in particular its geologist-naturalist, Dr. James Hector.

Captain John Palliser, the wealthy Irish landowner who would lead the expedition, was an avid outdoorsman and had participated in a buffalo hunt on the upper Missouri River in 1848. There he met James Sinclair, who told him of his 1841 trip and described to him another pass he hoped to try some day. Palliser remembered the discussion and in 1857 when questions about the north-west of British North America were being raised in England he decided to make himself a one-man expedition to the British-held prairies and mountains north of the 49th parallel and determine if there were passes practical for a transportation route to the Pacific. Eventually his idea was supported by the Royal Geographic Society and the British government and he was appointed the head of the British North American Exploring Expedition, assisted by some of the best scientists available. His instructions, as issued by the British government, directed: "At the commencement of the season of 1858 you will start, as soon as the weather is sufficiently open and favourable, to explore the country between the two branches of the Saskatchewan River, and south of the southern branch, and thence, proceeding westward to the head waters of that river, you will endeavour, from the best information you can collect to ascertain whether one or more practicable passes exist over the Rocky Mountains within the British territory, and south of that known to exist between Mount Brown and Hooker [Athabasca Pass]."[8]

As previously mentioned, while a substantial number of first peoples, half-breed guides, white fur traders and missionaries had by this time become familiar with the Rockies and their passes, virtually nothing was known of those between Athabasca Pass on the north and the passes at the head of the Missouri on the south to the world at large. This was due to the fact that information resided mainly in the oral traditions of the native peoples or the cryptic diaries and journals of the fur traders, few of which would come to light until many decades later (only Simpson's and de Smet's recollections were in print by 1850). Athabasca Pass, as is evident in Palliser's instructions, was acknowledged, but the information on it was grossly exaggerated. This was a result of the report of botanist David Douglas, who crossed the pass with a fur brigade in April, 1827 and climbed a peak at the divide, naming it Mount Brown and recording that "its height does not appear to be less than 16,000 or 17,000 feet above the level of the sea." Douglas's fantastic description appeared in print in 1836 in an article on his journey from the Columbia to Hudson Bay in the *Companion to the Botanical Magazine*, and thereafter his altitude was adopted as gospel. The great map publishers of the era, Aaron Arrowsmith and his nephew John Arrowsmith, who had begun producing maps of North America in 1796 and had printed their most recent version in 1854, were very unsure of their accuracy in this region due to "the want of information respecting this country." Indeed, Black's Atlas of 1856, used by the British Colonial Office when Palliser was sent out, showed no passes between the Athabasca and the Missouri, which by this time had been well explored and reported on by the Americans. Even the prestigious Royal Geographic Society in London reported in 1857 that "it is distinctly asserted by those who ought to know that there is no practicable pass in the Rocky Mountains for about 180 miles from the Kootonais Pass to that between Mounts Brown and Marker [Hooker]." Palliser himself would subsequently complain in his report that even at the foot of the mountains he could not find guides who knew much about them.

The scientists who accompanied Palliser included John Sullivan, astronomical observer and secretary, Thomas Blakiston, magnetic observer, Eugene Bourgeau, botanical collector and James Hector, geologist-naturalist and medical doctor. It would be the latter two, and, in particular Hector, who would have the greatest interaction with the Banff-Bow Valley region, exploring and reporting on its resources in great detail. This was due to a decision Palliser made to split the party in three during his approach to the Rockies' foot in August, 1858 after a summer spent trekking across the plains:

Captain John Palliser (left) and Doctor James Hector

Being unwilling to cross the mountains without previously knowing something further of the British territory to the south, and also being anxious to see what kind of land or what the quality of the land was in the neighbourhood of the international line from the base of the Rocky Mountains towards the east, I determined to make a rapid journey to the boundary line, distant about 170 miles. I arranged that Dr. Hector should ascend into the mountains in any direction which he thought most conducive to the interests of geological and geographical science; that Captain Blakiston should explore the passes generally used by the Coutanies, crossing the mountains by the more northerly pass and returning by the more southerly (near the International Boundary). I gave Mons. Bourgeau instructions to penetrate into the mountains as far as he thought conducive to the interest of botanical science. And to myself I reserved the exploration of a pass, the existence of which I had heard of when in the American Indian country in the year 1848, from Mr. James Sinclair, a very intelligent half-breed, well known and deeply regretted.[9]

In late August, Palliser rendezvoused with his hunters at Old Bow Fort after his dash to the International Boundary and set off to cross the mountains by Sinclair's supposed pass. Of this route Palliser stated, "this pass I have called the Kananaskis pass, after the name of an Indian, of whom there is a legend, giving an account of his most wonderful recovery from the blow of an axe, which had stunned but had failed to kill him, and the river which flows through this gorge also bears his name." His account provided a very complete description of this valley before he passed out of it by what is likely today's Elk Pass onto the headwaters of the river that would bear his name and ultimately by way of the Kootenay to the headwaters of the Columbia River. Likewise, Blakiston following his instructions, proceeded to the south and crossed the mountains by the North Kootenay Pass. On his return by way of the Waterton River, which he named, he discovered another famous Rockies beauty spot, the Waterton Lakes.

Hector and Bourgeau, free to determine which route would be "conducive" to their interests, chose the Bow, as it allowed them to enter the mountains quickly. They were accompanied by Hector's hand-picked Stoney guide whose tongue-twisting name meant "the one with the thumb like a blunt arrow," and so was simply called "Nimrod," as well as an educated half-breed guide named Peter Erasmus and two other Metis, Brown and Sutherland. Immediately upon passing through Bow River Gap both scientists were overwhelmed by the scenery and the fertile field in which to indulge their interests and quickly decided to ascend a peak. On their climb they discovered a cave which Hector described as "like Robinson Crusoe's one, with its old goat for a tenant, but in this case had long been dead. . . the floor was quite battered hard by the tracks of sheep and goats." The peak was appropriately named Grotto Mountain and after descending it they "camped by some old Indian wigwams where the valley is wide and flat," an obvious reference to Indian Flats at Canmore. Opposite the camp he described "a mountain with three peaks which form a striking group," the first recorded description of the Three Sisters. The following day, not wishing to travel in order that Nimrod could procure some game, he climbed the range to the north-east which he named after Palliser's brother-in-law, William Fairholme.

Leaving Bourgeau to continue his botanical pursuits in this area, Hector and his guides pushed further on up the Valley. On August 15th they arrived at a well-known Stoney camping area, noting that "we reached a beautiful little prairie at the base of the 'Mountain where the water falls,' as the Indian name has it, or the Cascade Mountain." Again he concluded this peak must be ascended to gain a proper understanding of its geology and while doing so also noted some of its natural life, including sheep, pica, marmot and even a hummingbird. Meanwhile, his men were busy clearing a trail to the west and on August 17th they set out over it. However, at camp Hector was informed of one of the beauty spots in the Valley and decided to visit it before joining them. This little side trip elicited the first recorded description of one of Banff's most noted landmarks, Bow Falls, as well as the Vermilion Lakes:

The men with the pack-horses followed the track which they had cleared the previous day, while with Nimrod I set off to see a fine fall on the river, which lay about three miles out of the direct course. A high hill stands out in the centre of the valley, and it is in breaking past this that the river is compressed into a very narrow spout-like channel, and then leaps over a ledge of rocks about 40 feet in height. . . . Above the rocky contraction of the channel the river is dilated and sluggish, and the valley is filled up with large swampy lakes, just like those in the canon through the first range. . . .[10]

Continuing upstream he looked up the first valley to the southwestward and saw "a truncated mountain evidently composed of massive horizontal strata, and which I named Mount Bourgeau." He knew that Simpson's pass was up this valley and considered following it, but the water in the stream was high and an old Stoney travelling with them stated he would fail to get through that way, so he "determined to continue up the same side of Bow River, until opposite an old neglected pass that used to be used by Cree war parties, and known as the Vermilion Pass." As he proceeded to this location, he passed and named the Sawback Range and saw ahead of him in the centre of the valley "a very remarkable mountain . . . which looks exactly like a gigantic castle." Upon reaching its location, he again decided an ascent was in order to study its geology, and, following his initial impression, named it Castle Mountain. The next day, August 20th, he began to ascend to the Vermilion Pass and was surprised how close he found it to the main Bow Valley. Next he visited the Paint Pots, stating "the Kootanie Indians come to this place sometimes, and we found the remains of a camp and of a large fire which they had used to convert the ochre into the red oxide which they take away to trade to the Indians of the low country, and also to the Blackfeet, as a pigment, calling it vermilion."

Hector carried his journey to the headwaters of the Kootenay River and over the pass to a river he named the Kicking Horse after his horse almost killed him by kicking him in the chest at one of his camps near today's Wapta Falls. Facing hardships and hunger due to a complete lack of success at hunting, his now ragged party crossed back into the Bow Valley over the rugged Kicking Horse Pass and began to once more ascend the Bow. Under the steep slopes of the peak that would later be named for him by another famous geologist, George M. Dawson, they fell in with a Stoney camp and replenished their larder with moose meat, allowing them to continue their explorations. On September 9th they reached the shores of Bow Lake and provided the first recorded description of the river's source:

An hour's ride brought us to where Bow River dilates to form a narrow lake, the water of which was of a bright green colour. Two miles further we reached a second and larger lake, being two miles long and one broad. Along its western shore the mountains rise precipitously, except at one point where a narrow valley allows a short glacier to reach the water's edge, being fed by the perpetual ice and snow that mantle the mountains in that direction. We kept along the east shore of the lake till it was terminated by an open prairie with a considerable slope, the surface of which is mossy, with many springs, from which the first waters of the Bow River rise.[11]

Hector continued on through Bow Pass and explored the approaches to Howse Pass, commenting "up this river there is said to be a pass direct to the Columbia, which was the one first used by trappers in the time of the North-West Company, as far as I could make out from the accounts of the Indians," illustrating just how little information the expedition had with respect to the earlier fur trade history of the mountains. While attempting to find the entry to the pass, he took a wrong turn and discovered the Lyell Glacier, which he decided to explore. Despite his insistence, he could not get Nimrod to accompany him, the guide relating "all sorts of stories of sad disasters that had befallen those Indians that ever did so" and expressing the belief that if he did not fall in a crevasse he was at least sure to be unlucky in hunting afterwards. He was therefore forced to take Sutherland with him and had an extremely interesting day, observing and naming one of the great peaks of the Rockies, Mount Forbes, after his professor Edward Forbes, during the exploration of which his way was almost blocked by a tremendous bergschrund. In typical matter-of-fact Hector style he described the solution, which turned out to be a remarkable feat of mountaineering:

At one point we thought at first we should require to turn back, and gain the surface of the glacier, as we came to a precipice that was closely hemmed in between a wall of ice and one of rock. However, by knotting our leather shirts together, and taking off our moccasins, which were now frozen, we managed to get past the difficulty, and pushing on rapidly reaching our camp at eight o'clock.[12]

Unfortunately, due to the late season and short rations, he was forced to abandon his effort to penetrate the pass that year and headed downstream towards Rocky Mountain House and ultimately the expedition's winter headquarters at Edmonton House. The fact remained that in a period of almost exactly a month he had explored the entire main Bow Valley, with the exception of the stretch between Castle Mountain and Lake Louise, and had recorded more observations than all those who had preceded him combined. The information he gathered, in concert with that of other members of the expedition, would be critical to decisions made in the years ahead affecting the development of the Bow Valley and the entire Canadian Rockies. Palliser was already writing to the Secretary of State on October 7, 1858 — even before hearing of Hector's discoveries— that "I have completely succeeded in discovering not only a pass practicable for horse, but one which, with but little expense, could be rendered available for carts also." He also noted "this pass will connect the prairies of Saskatchewan with Her Majesty's possessions on the west side of the Rocky Mountains."[13] Hector himself would soon write that "we now know that this chain does not present any bar to the construction of a railway, as there are several passes which will admit of easy gradients through valleys so wide as to afford great variety in the choice of ground for locating the line."[14]

Hector was to visit the Bow Valley again. The following summer after investigating the prairies eastward to the Cypress Hills, Palliser ordered him to "proceed from this to Old Bow Fort, enter the mountains again by the pass you explored last year, and endeavour to explore a route practicable for horses to the westward, as far as ever it lies in your power, proceeding by the valley of Fraser and Thompson Rivers, and avoiding the valley of the Columbia." This time he moved more quickly, but did pause long enough in the Banff area to record that "to the right of the trail I observed some warm mineral springs which deposited iron and sulphur, and seemed to escape from beds of limestone," an observation that would have huge implications for the later history of the Valley. Discounting Vermilion Pass as a route of travel due to the previous year's difficulties, he took the advice of his Stoney guide William who said "that if we left the Bow River and went by Pipe Stone Pass, which is more to the east, and leads from Bow River to the North Saskatchewan, at Kootanie plain we should get plenty of sheep, and besides have a better trail. . . ." It also allowed Hector to fill in the gap in his Bow Valley explorations between Castle Mountain and Lake Louise.

Travelling that route and approaching the North

Saskatchewan, he noted a peak that he had seen the previous year that Nimrod had told him was the highest known to the natives and he had named for one of the expedition's sponsors, Sir Roderick Murchison. This time he lowered his previous 16,000 foot estimate of its height stating, undoubtedly with an eye to David Douglas' claim, "I am inclined to think that none of the Rocky Mountains rise above 13,000 to 13,500 feet." On reaching the Kootenay Plains at the end of August, his party was able to successfully hunt sheep and restore the larder. But here his until now faithful guide Nimrod deserted him and headed south towards the Bow. Hector related in his subsequently published account that "I have since heard of after movements from the Earl of Southesk, who met him ten days afterwards in the mountains of the Bow River." He was referring to the other noteworthy journey through the region at the time by James Carnegie, the Earl of Southesk, who was out in the mountains aided by the good graces of Governor Simpson in his "desire to travel in some part of the world where good sport could be met with among the larger animals, and where, at the same time, I might recruit my health by an active open-air life in a healthy climate."[15] His quest had led him through the heavily wooded country to the west of Edmonton House, entering the mountains by the McLeod River and then following south-east along the Cline River to Kootenay Plains. He then crossed the Saskatchewan and followed a route through the Pipestone Pass to the south, observing a date and latitude mark that Hector had blazed only ten days earlier. As Hector himself noted, it was a remarkable coincidence that "the only two travellers, excepting Indians and a few employees of the fur companies, that have ever been in this district of the mountains, should have so nearly met, and without the least knowledge of each other's proximity."

Nimrod's desertion forced Hector to become his own guide — "I was now not only the directing but the actual explorer of the country; and I needed all the little experience I had picked up of the Indian's tact in threading through forest country in a given direction" — but he succeeded in leading his party over Howse

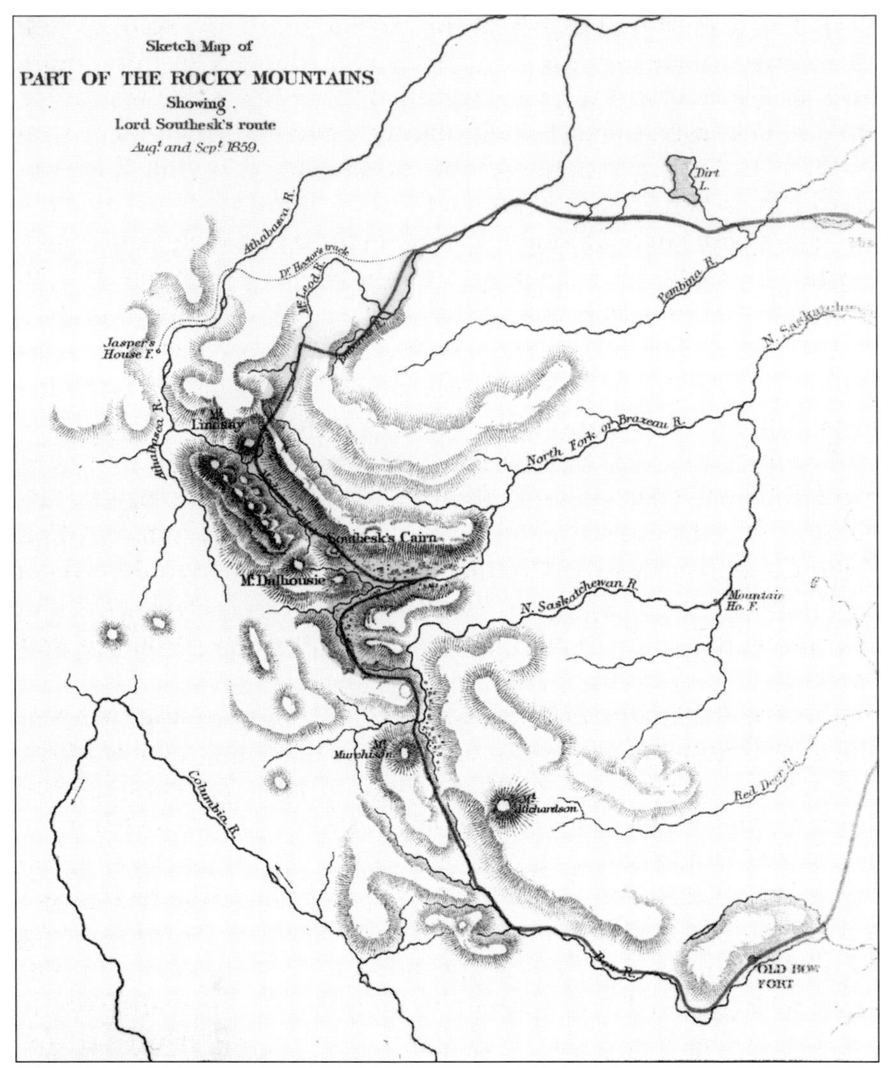

The map in Southesk's book, **Saskatchewan and the Rocky Mountains,** *was the first in a publication that depicted the Banff-Bow Valley*

Pass and down to the Columbia. Here he turned north, hoping to follow Palliser's instructions to find a way through the Selkirks to the Fraser and Thompson Rivers. The travel in this range proved more difficult than anything he had previously encountered, with continual rain rotting their pemmican and vegetation so thick that there was virtually no pasturage for the horses at night. Eventually they met a Shuswap Indian who told them it was too late in the season to reach their objective and he turned back, proceeding to Lake Windermere and ultimately following the standard fur trade route to the Pacific.

The optimism of 1858 about there being a relatively easy transportation route to tidewater would now be tempered with Hector's experiences in the Selkirks, which made it apparent that it was in this range where the real obstacles would have to be overcome. Palliser himself would ultimately report that although the expedition had successfully made a connection between the Saskatchewan River and British Columbia without entering United States territory, "still the knowledge of the country on the whole, would never lead me to advise a line of communication from Canada across the Continent." These words would have a profound effect on helping to hold back the tide of development in the mountains of the Banff-Bow Valley for almost another quarter century.

Before leaving the Palliser Expedition, it is interesting to examine their comments on the game in the Bow Valley and the Rockies, as their explorations were taking place at what appears to have been a critical moment in mountain ecology. It is clear from the records of Thompson and other fur traders that big game was relatively plentiful in the mountains at the turn of the nineteenth century. Thompson commented on the habit of the Peigan to hunt big horn sheep in the Bow Valley and himself found evidence of buffalo ranging as high as half way up Loder Peak. The valley of the North Saskatchewan seems to have been particularly good for hunting the larger, darker mountain bison more akin to today's wood bison, with the area around Kootenay Plains being noted for its excellent sheep hunting as well. Moose were particularly plentiful and Hector reported that his guide Nimrod "is said to be the best hunter among the 'Stoneys' and once, in a single season to have killed 57 moose-deer."

Palliser expected expedition members to be able to supplement the few provisions they carried with game shot en route, but all members found this to be difficult. Hector, on setting off up the Bow, "had with me eight horses, three of which served to carry all the little baggage I cared to take, consisting principally of instruments, bedding, ammunition, and tobacco; for as I was assured that in the part of the mountains I intended to explore, there was abundance of game, I did not take any provisions excepting a little tea and few pounds of grease." His experiences over the next month, during which his party at one point went for three days without any food and may well have started to eat their horses had they not succeeded in killing a small doe moose and then been taken in at the Stoney camp near Mount Hector, gave the lie to these predictions. Hector perceived that the matter of game populations was in flux and noted in his journal what he could learn of them. Some of his comments bore out the fact that until recent times their numbers had been healthy. In speaking of Cascade Mountain, he reported "the Indians often get the white goat on it and the grey sheep is common" and also indicated that the Indians said the goat was "the hardest to kill of all animals." But he found sheep anything but abundant as it was not until almost a month later that he saw his first one near Glacier Lake while ascending the Howse River, and noted that Nimrod held "this is the only place where these are to be seen so far in the mountains." It was not long afterwards, while descending the Howse River near present-day Saskatchewan Crossing, that Hector made a key entry in his journal reporting on what had occurred with respect to game in the mountains:

Near our camp we found some old buffalo dung, and the Indians told us that not many years ago there were many of these animals along the valley of the North Saskatchewan, within the mountains. Eleven years ago, they say, there were great fires all through the mountains, and in the woods along their eastern base; and after that a disease broke out among all the animals, so that they used to find wapiti, moose, and other deer, as well as buffalo, lying dead in numbers. Before that time (somewhere about 1847 or 1848) there was abundance of game in all parts of the coun-

try; but since then there has been great scarcity of animals, and only the best hunters can make sure of killing.[16]

Dr. Hector (seated) returned to the Rockies in 1905 and was photographed with the world's most noted mountaineer, Edward Whymper

Obviously, changes other than those brought about by increased exploration were already affecting the Rockies.

In examining the importance of the Palliser Expedition, and particularly James Hector, we must return to the almost complete lack of knowledge of the world-at-large of the Rocky Mountains at the point in Canadian history on the very eve of Confederation. For the Valley, Hector changed that, recording the first geological observations of the area, supplying a large number of the names of geographic features, providing significant information on animals, birds and other fauna, and, equally important, doing so when the Valley was still a virgin wilderness. Perhaps no other individual, apart from David Thompson a generation earlier, provided more foundation for the subsequent history and culture of the Rockies. Although not readily available and well circulated until many years afterwards, virtually all subsequent natural science would be based upon his reports and those of his confreres on the expedition.

Chapter Four
Steel Through the Wilderness

By the time the Palliser Expedition report was printed as a government "blue book" in 1863, there was little attention being focused on the western part of British North America. The Hudson's Bay Company was nearing the end of its two hundred year domination of Rupert's Land (it would transfer ownership to the new Dominion in 1869), and the British colony on Vancouver Island was busy preparing to amalgamate with one on the mainland, created after the 1857 discovery of gold on the Fraser River, to form the new colony of British Columbia. To the east, attention during the whole decade starting in 1857 was devoted to gaining the political union that would achieve Confederation and the creation of the Dominion of Canada in 1867. In the mountain fastnesses of the Bow Valley, it remained a time of little activity — indeed it would not be until the decade of the eighteen-seventies that any significant attention would again be paid to the passes of the Rockies. By that time, the desire of the new Canadian government to add the coastal colony of British Columbia as a new province had led in 1871 to a promise of a railroad to connect it with central Canada within ten years. And fulfilling that commitment would lead, through one of the most remarkable and least understood twists in Canadian history, to bringing the Valley into national prominence.

As mentioned, after the Palliser Expedition the Banff-Bow Valley essentially went back to sleep for a quarter century. The occasional party made its way through some part of it, particularly its lower end where the Kananaskis seemed to be somewhat of a focus. The discovery in the early 1860s of gold on Wild Horse Creek, a tributary of the Kootenay River near today's Fort Steele, saw a significant rush to that area from the United States, leading some prospectors through passes in the Kananaskis and over Whiteman's Pass in an ever-widening search for minerals. But while a few prospectors and trappers, such as Joe Healy and Willard Young, appear to have been in the Banff area before the 1880s, they were certainly the exception rather than the rule. To a great degree, it remained the Stoney who most consistently frequented the Valley in this period, often joined in their sojourns by a new generation of missionaries, the McDougall family, who would be an important element in its story.

As the earliest and most frequently associated with missionary work among the southern tribes, and particularly the Stoney, it is not surprising that the Methodists, following in Robert Rundle's footsteps, would re-appear on the Bow. Reverend George McDougall and his son Reverend John McDougall had already been active for several years among the Cree in the Edmonton and Pigeon Lake areas when they were called upon by the church to extend their work to the Stoney. The Reverend John McDougall described the circumstances to fellow cleric Reverend George Grant when they met in 1883:

My father and I started this mission in 1873. He always liked the Stonies, for they were Indians of the best type, and braver than even the Blackfeet. That, you would expect, for you know they are Highlanders. Ten years ago they were scattered in small bands, up and down both sides of the Bow, and as far south as the boundary, and north to the Athabaska. This spot that we named Morley, although the name is sometimes lengthened out to Morleyville — was one of their favourite headquarters; and, as it was a good centre geographically and for hunting, we determined to try and gather them in a settlement here, for while they continued their nomadic habits it was impossible to do much, either in the way of civilizing or teaching them. We got about five hundred to look on the place as their home, though at first they might be absent hunting for the greater part of the year.[1]

Treaty Number Seven, to which the Stoney adhered, created a reserve at Morley in 1877 and the fact that rations were to be available as part of the treaty agreement should have meant that there would be less desire for the natives to leave to hunt. But, according to John Snow, the Indian agents recognized that the Stoney were good hunters and actually encouraged their efforts in an attempt to save on the cost of rations. This meant that they continued to habituate the mountains, even though the hunting became progressively more difficult. In turn, the McDougalls were forced to follow the Stoney to administer to their spiritual needs, and, as John McDougall's brother David had set up a trading business near Morley, he too often accompanied them in their mountain travels in search of meat, hides and heads. Over the years his collection of trophies and artifacts grew, making his trading store, located just east of today's McDougall Church near Morley, a place of wonder according to a visitor who described it in the summer of 1883:

His store was a veritable trophy room, with the assortment of big and small game hides. Grizzly, cinnamon, brown and black bear hides were there in abundance, in all sizes and ages. Many of them had been bought from the Indians, but there were numerous hides representing animals he had killed himself. These were the grim evidence of what sport the Rocky Mountains afforded in the early days, in unexplored regions, unknown valleys threading their way up amongst the towering craggy sentinels that reared their heights into the azure blue.[2]

Part of John McDougall's activities included accompanying the Stoney on their sojourns over the mountains to visit the Kootenay in the Columbia Valley. The same observer who had visited David McDougall's trading store continued west and stopped at what was to become known as Hillsdale, opposite Pilot Mountain, one of the Stoney's traditional camping grounds in the Bow Valley. There he met the Reverend John with some of his flock returning from one of their transmontane trips, and many years later recalled the event:

The Missionary advised that they had just returned from a visit to the

Indians near Windermere, B. C. and they had done some trading as well as some hunting and fishing on the way there and back. . . . They were trying to make the pasture lands in our vicinity since the missionary and his followers had used this as a camping spot for many years. . . . The missionary claimed that this was so long ago, that his Indians had no traditions or even legends as to how long ago their Red ancestors had used it as a camping ground. Anyway there were teepee lodge poles scattered all through the meadow and from this it was quite evident it was one of the favorite Indian campgrounds. There was beautiful pasture and grazing for the horses as well as good water for cooking purposes. There were signs evident around the locality that the Indians had dried fish as well as converting their venison into pemmican that kept so well for an emergency and trail ration.[3]

Later, John McDougall would play an important role in mediating the dispute that arose between the Kootenay and Stoney concerning hunting territories, serving as a negotiator with Chief Chiniki at meetings held in Golden in 1893 which settled on the Great Divide as the demarcation line. Little could he and his Stoney disciples have imagined that within a few months the natives' traditional campground would become a major mountain commissary for railway locating engineers. This development was rooted in a decision made about the route for the proposed line to link the eastern provinces of the Dominion of Canada with the new province of British Columbia.

The man placed in charge of the surveys for the railway by the Canadian government in 1871 was the former chief engineer of the Intercolonial Railway running from Halifax to Quebec City, Sandford Fleming. Fleming, who would later be called "Canada's foremost railway surveyor and construction engineer of the nineteenth century" and was the inventor of standard time, was given the task of determining the best route across the prairies and mountains for the nation-binding line. He gave the challenge of finding suitable passes through the Rockies and Selkirks to Walter Moberly, a veteran wilderness traveller who had first arrived in British Columbia in 1858 and had worked as a surveyor for the colony. One of his primary tasks had been to find a pass through the Gold (Monashee) Range, west of the Columbia River, and despite meeting Palliser in 1859 when the erstwhile Captain stated that these mountains "present an unbroken and impassable barrier," he persisted. In 1864, while following the flight of an eagle into a valley running eastward from Shuswap Lake, he discovered the key to the route and named it Eagle Pass. By 1866 he was attempting to find a way through the Selkirk Range and noted in his diary that one of his men, Albert Perry, had been following a hopeful-looking valley up the east fork of the Illecillewaet River and, although he had not reached the divide, reported that there was a low, wide valley as far as he proceeded.

When he went to work for Fleming in 1871, Moberly was tasked with finding the best railway passage through the Rockies and established his headquarters at the confluence of the Blaeberry and Columbia Rivers, intent on examining David Thompson's old Howse Pass route. But Fleming, having read the Palliser Report, knew that while it stated there were passes suitable for railways through the southern Rockies, it had nothing good to say about the prospects of the southern prairies, finding them arid and unsuitable for agriculture. As well, the Palliser Expedition had not done any exploration north of Athabasca Pass and a preliminary reconnaissance Fleming had ordered of the Yellowhead Pass area in 1871 had shown some interesting results. Based on these premises, and despite the fact that Moberly's work was already well advanced on Howse Pass, Fleming summarily ordered him north to the Yellowhead Pass in 1872. There the surveyor was visited by Fleming and his travelling companion, the Reverend George Grant, and they personally explored the trail up the Miette River, over the Yellowhead Pass and onto the rugged North Thompson River. Despite the difficulties of building a line along this route, Fleming continued to favour its low elevation and by the end of the decade surveyors had laid out a preliminary location line for the railway all the way from the Lakehead at Fort William, across the prairies by the old Carlton Trail to Fort Edmonton, westward through Yellowhead Pass and down the Thompson to where the

Pacific section of the line was already under construction by government contractor Andrew Onderdonk.

Once again, as it had during the fur trade period, it seemed as though the Athabasca Valley would carry the major transportation route through the mountains rather than the North Saskatchewan or the Bow. But in one of the most momentous and least understood decisions in Canadian history, all that changed at a meeting held in Saint Paul, Minnesota in May, 1881. The meeting was occasioned by the fact that the Conservative government of Sir John A. Macdonald had been returned to power in 1878 and, in order to get the waning railway to the Pacific built, had convinced Parliament to turn it over to private enterprise. The Canadian Pacific Railway Syndicate, as it became known, was headed by three men who had been instrumental in resurrecting a failing American line, the Saint Paul and Pacific, and making a fortune from it. They were George Stephen, the president of the Bank of Montreal, his cousin Donald Smith, chief commissioner of the Hudson's Bay Company, and James J. Hill, a former Canadian businessman living in St. Paul who had brought the other two into the St. Paul and Pacific deal.

The new Canadian Pacific Railway Company was incorporated on February 15, 1881 and the meeting of its executive committee was being held in Saint Paul to discuss the matter of routes and hear from a noted Canadian naturalist, John Macoun. Macoun had accompanied Fleming on his trip to the Yellowhead in 1872 and had then explored the southern prairies as far as the Bow River for the Canadian government in 1879 and 1880. These explorations had convinced him that the plains were not the arid place that Palliser and others had reported (he apparently visited them in a very wet period) and he made it his mission to persuade authorities that their agricultural potential should be re-assessed. This included attempting to convince the Syndicate that a more southerly rail route was possible and that the Bow Valley was an excellent approach to the divide. He appears to have been a very effective spokesman. In his memoirs, Macoun recorded that the members of the Syndicate discussed the matter for a short time, whereupon Hill raised his hands and banged them down on the table, announcing "Gentlemen, we will cross the prairie and go by the Bow Pass if we can get that way."[4] With this gesture, the fate of the Banff-Bow Valley was sealed.

The "Bow Pass" Hill was referring to was Hector's Kicking Horse Pass, which Macoun informed the Syndicate members he had given a cursory examination to two years previously and had seen "a wide open valley." However, since his famous exclamation included the phrase "if we can get that way," it appears Hill was depending on location engineers to determine the exact route, his knowledge of the geography of the area undoubtedly being very limited. Of interest was the reason why all the work carried out on the well-examined northern route would be abandoned at such a late date in favour of an obviously more tentative southern one. Numerous reasons have been postulated by historians for this decision — the fact that the line was shorter, that it would prevent competition coming into Canada from U. S. railroads, and that it would allow the CPR to better control land development than along the proposed northern route where land speculation had already begun (the CPR's agreement included a subsidy of $25 million and 25 million acres of land). Evidence of the most compelling factor has yet to be unearthed, but whatever the reason it is apparent that the idea was already afoot before the St. Paul meeting.

One of the first thing Hill had done after the company was created in February, 1881 was to hire Major A. B. Rogers, an American locating engineer, and send him off to the west with instructions to examine four Palliser Expedition passes — the Kicking Horse, Vermilion, Kootenay and Howse — which, with the exception of Moberly's work on the latter, had not hitherto been given attention by the railroad survey. He was also instructed to attempt to find a pass through the Selkirks, being offered a five thousand dollar bonus and the honour of having his name attached to the pass as an inducement. Rogers cared little about the money, but, like many surveyors, wanted very much to be memorialized. He was a tough-talking, hard-riding, tobacco-spitting, pepper-pot of an individual who was just as hard on himself as his men, earning him the nickname "Hell's Bells" Rogers. He was to leave an indelible imprint on the lore of the area.

Major A. B. "Hell's Bells" Rogers

Major Rogers and his nephew Albert Rogers set off in April from San Francisco to Victoria and then travelled overland to Fort Kamloops, the closest settlement to the Selkirks. There, armed with the passage from Moberly's journal of 1866 concerning Perry's abbreviated exploration of the Illecillewaet River, he hired ten natives and set off across the Gold Range and down the Columbia by raft (with the Indians swimming alongside) until he reached the mouth of the Illecillewaet. The trip up the river was made under terrible conditions, as the snow was just beginning to melt and Rogers was notoriously stingy with the rations, but they managed to reach what appeared to be the summit and hoped-for pass. Unfortunately, in the conditions they could not be entirely sure and after climbing a nearby peak to ascertain if it were, they were forced to bivouac on its slopes overnight. Exhausted and weak from hunger, the next day they retreated back down the valley. Rogers was almost certain that he had found the pass that would eventually bear his name, but he could not be sure until the next year when he actually reached the height of land after ascending up the Beaver River from the east.

Events had now all but overtaken Rogers, as the St. Paul decision had determined that the western approach to the Selkirks would be by way of the Bow Valley, and he had yet to lay eyes on it. Ordering his young nephew Albert to take a packtrain to the confluence of the Kicking Horse with the Columbia and then explore up it from the western side, he himself made his way across the Brisco Range by way of the Kootenay River and then over Whiteman's Pass to the Bow. Here he was to meet a party of surveyors that had been dispatched up the Missouri River from St. Paul to Fort Benton, Montana, the closest point of supply linked to ready transportation for a penetration of the Rockies from the east. One of the packers who had signed on to move the surveyors' goods and equipment was Tom Wilson, a young man from near Barrie, Ontario who had recently resigned his position in the North West Mounted Police at Fort Walsh to participate in the adventure. Unbeknownst to Wilson, he was on the verge of becoming a key individual in the early history of the Banff-Bow Valley and one of its true pioneers. But all that was in the future when he joined with the 100 man crew under Rogers' assistant P. K. Hyndman, who had just disembarked from a Missouri steamer and prepared to head for the mountains. For the first time since the Sinclair contingents had made their way through its environs in 1841 and 1854, the Bow Valley was about to see a large party descend upon it.

The outfit was hauled by the freighters of Fort Benton's I. G. Baker Company using eight wagons drawn by twenty-four teams of horses and accompanied by eighty pack animals under the care of Wilson and his fellow packers. They followed a route up the Fort Benton trail through the Mounted Police posts of Fort Macleod and Fort Calgary and thence up the Bow to the site of Old Bow Fort, where the Baker company's contract ended. However, it was determined that the survey headquarters needed to be further west and David McDougall was hired to freight the supplies and equipment to the mouth of the Kananaskis River, the place referred to by the Stoney as "Osade," where a commissariat was established. This, the first spot that could be considered a permanent human habitation on the upper Bow River, was named

Padmore after F. W. "Paddy" Padmore, the Assistant Commissary, who, Wilson noted, "was sincerely liked by all the men." It was a simple affair, consisting of one log building with accompanying corrals, but it would well serve the needs of railway construction for the next several years. There the surveyors awaited Rogers' arrival and he appeared on July 15th, presenting quite a sight in Wilson's memory as "his voluminous side-burns waved like flags in a breeze; his piercing eyes seemed to look and see through everything at once" and "every few moments a stream of tobacco juice erupted from between his sideburns."[5]

With the season already well-advanced, Rogers wanted to assure himself that the Kicking Horse Pass, which he had instructed Albert Rogers to explore, was indeed the best route. He quickly ordered one survey party to run a preliminary line from the Bow to the Kananaskis summit and other parties were assigned location work as they ascended the Bow. Rogers soon announced his intention to go off and explore on his own, asking for a volunteer to accompany him. Given his reputation for being hard on his men, no-one was eager to accept, and finally Tom Wilson stepped forward to take on the challenge. It was a momentous decision for the young packer, since as Rogers's assistant he would get the opportunity to explore a great deal more of the Valley than otherwise would have been the case, something that would pay excellent dividends later in his career.

Their first task was to make directly for the upper reaches of the river and try find Albert Rogers, who was at this point toiling his way up the rugged Kicking Horse. During their search, the main tributary of the Bow near Kicking Horse Pass received its name when they reached its banks late in the afternoon and found it swelled with meltwater. Despite Wilson's recommendation that they await until the water subsided in the morning to cross, the hard-driving Major swore a few oaths and ignored his advice. Plunging in, he was immediately swept from his horse into the boiling, bone-chilling water and Tom was forced to rescue him with a limb conveniently found close at hand. Thereafter, whenever the stream was running high and dirty the men on the survey would quip, "the Major must be taking another bath," and it soon became known to all and sundry as Bath Creek. Two days later Wilson and another packer found the near-starving Albert Rogers near the confluence of the Kicking Horse and Yoho Rivers. From his report, the Major determined that while difficult and requiring steep grades, the Kicking Horse could be used for the line.

Tom Wilson spent the remainder of the summer packing supplies from Padmore to the various survey camps spread throughout the Valley. One of these he particularly well-remembered was near the future site of Banff, located on the banks of a small creek, and was called "Aylmer Park" after Fred Aylmer, the chief of the survey crew located there. The creek was subsequently referred to as Whiskey Creek because of the activities of an individual named Gosling who made a "snake bite cure" from potato peelings near its head. Tom later recalled, "two drinks and the snake died if it bit you."[6] The memoir of his activities working on the survey, later published as *Trail Blazer of the Canadian Rockies*, provides one of the few views of the survey's impact on the Bow Valley. It is apparent from his descriptions that this previously lonely, practically untouched wilderness was virtually overnight heavily impacted and turned into a beehive of activity with survey crews working throughout its length and breadth, initially performing exploratory work but before long blazing and cutting location lines for the rails. Likewise, pack trails and tote roads were cleared to allow Wilson and his confreres to supply the various survey crews, from those probing the Kananaskis to those engaged in exploring towards Bow Pass, with equipment and supplies.

Wilson was quickly gaining a mountain education, and one of the most important aspects of it would occur early in the 1882 season when he returned to the survey after a winter of trapping in the Little Snowy Mountains of Montana. Following the packing in of his second load of supplies to a survey camp near the Divide, he camped near the confluence of the Pipestone and Bow Rivers. While sitting around the fire that evening with a group of Stoney camped at the same spot, Tom used his limited Indian vocabulary and sign language to ask one of the natives where the sound of

Tom Wilson in later years beside Lake Louise, his most famous "discovery"

avalanches they could hear nearby was coming from. The Stoney, whose name was Edwin Hunter or "Gold Seeker," indicated that the source was the "snow mountain above the lake of the little fishes" to the southwest. As the next day was wet and unsuitable for travel, he asked "Gold Seeker" to take him to the spot. It would be a momentous visit. When they emerged on the shore of the lake Tom was awestruck with the view and, given packers' usually colourful language, probably uttered something along the lines of "Sonofabitch, that's beautiful!" But, because of his later fame for this discovery and the frequent requests of tourists to tell them what he thought at that moment, he came up with a more discriminating description:

As God is my judge I never in all my explorations saw such a matchless scene. On the right and left the forests that had never known the axe came down to the shores apparently growing out of the blue and green waters. The background, a mile and a half away, was divided into three tones of white, opal and brown where the glacier ceased and merged with the shining water. The sun, high in the noon hour, poured into the pool, which reflected the whole landscape that formed the horseshoe.[7]

He named his "discovery" Emerald Lake, but it was later changed to Lake Louise to honour Princess Louise, the wife of the Marquis of Lorne, Governor-General of Canada. Regardless, it would become the most famous and oft-visited locale in the whole Banff-Bow Valley and one of the true icons of the Canadian Rockies. As mentioned, Tom himself would later gain much notoriety from this event and become somewhat of an archetype "mountain man," reminiscing to the thousands of visitors to his lake. The name Emerald Lake did survive, however, as later that summer while following some lost horses from a camp near the Natural Bridge on the Kicking Horse, he visited another subsequently well-known beauty spot that eventually became known by that name.

That summer Major Rogers also made his trip to Rogers Pass from the east side up the Beaver River, assuring himself of both its existence and suitability for railroad construction. Nevertheless, there would prove to be some doubters, among them William Cornelius Van Horne, a fellow American railroader who had become the new general manager of the CPR in January, 1882 and would be an important influence on the Valley's heritage. Only thirty-eight when he was hired by Hill to carry out the gargantuan task of completing the line, he already had a considerable reputation from twenty-five years of experience in the railway business in Illinois and Wisconsin, having mastered everything from telegraphy to finance. Indeed, in writing to Stephen to inform him of Van Horne's appointment, Hill offered "I have never met anyone who is better informed in the various departments, machinery, cars, operation, train services, construction and general policy which with untiring energy and good vigorous body should give us good results."[8] Indeed he did, for Van Horne would defy all odds and complete the line on a shoestring budget by 1885 and would then successfully operate it as general manager until 1888 and as president until 1899. During this period his effects on the

Valley would run the gamut from hotel design to its artistic interpretation.

Van Horne's immediate responsibility in 1882 was to complete the construction of the line as quickly and economically as possible, but he also looked ahead to operational concerns and believed that railways must reach their destinations by the shortest route feasible. His doubts were shared by George Stephen, and in the summer of 1883, even as the rails were being pushed across the prairies towards Bow River Gap, they both dispatched their chosen experts to assess the Kicking Horse situation. Stephen's choice fell on the line's former engineer-in-chief, Sandford Fleming, who had retired to England in 1880, while Van Horne's rested upon two veteran surveyors, Charles Aeneas Shaw, who possessed thirty years experience, and James Hogg, a cousin of the man in charge of mountain construction, James Ross.

Acting on Ross's instructions, Shaw was already at work in the Bow Valley west of Calgary in the spring of 1883 trying to find a better location than Rogers's proposed line to eliminate a mud tunnel that would have been half a mile long. His success in relocating the line, mainly to the south side of the river between Calgary and the Gap, saved the company over a million dollars (according to Shaw). It also earned him Ross's confidence and he was asked to continue his work all the way to the summit. One of the problems of the original line was the fact that it foresaw a half-mile tunnel on the lower reaches of the Cascade River (which he called Devil's Head Creek) through what was being called Tunnel Mountain. This Shaw felt was unnecessary:

On examination, I found that Tunnel Mountain was an island with a valley to the west of it joining the valley of Devil's Head Creek. So I located the line up this creek and around Tunnel Mountain to the main Bow Valley, shortening the line by a mile, avoiding two long grades, and above all, eliminating the tunnel.

On reflecting on the switch-back pack trail often used by locating engineers to pass over Tunnel Mountain, Shaw expressed dismay

A CPR survey party near the summit of Kicking Horse Pass, 1883

that they had not investigated the route he himself found and called Rogers's location "the most extraordinary blunder I have ever known in the way of engineering."[9]

Sandford Fleming responded to Stephen's call for an examination of the route through the Kicking Horse and Rogers Passes, and appeared in the mountains accompanied by his son Frank and his old travelling companion of 1872 the Reverend George Grant, by this time principal of Queen's University. The now middle-aged explorers found the going difficult, as they were not in the best physical condition and the route was severe, particularly in the lower Kicking Horse and on the west side of the Selkirks. But their observations, Fleming's published in a book in 1884 under the title *England and Canada. A Summer Tour Between Old and New Westminster* and Grant's as a series in the periodical *The Week* entitled "The C.P.R. By The Kicking Horse Pass And The Selkirks," provide some interesting information on the progress of railway construction in the Bow Valley in August, 1883.

When the Fleming-Grant party reached Calgary on the newly laid rails in August, they sought out James Ross, who had sent out couriers to ascertain the state of the route they intended to follow.

One courier reported Major Rogers headquartered at the mouth of the Kicking Horse and indicated he had experienced difficulty and danger getting through to Calgary from the Major's camp, occasioned by the bad state of the trail in the Kicking Horse and the forest fires that were burning at various points in the mountains. The courier carried a letter from Rogers stating that there was no doubt of a pass through the Selkirks and that two parties of his men had been engaged in preliminary surveys and making a trail, the said path now extending some distance down the west side of the pass. Although Rogers recommended that they head south to the United States and then to the Pacific coast to approach the pass from the west, Fleming very much wanted to be the first to travel the route of the new line from Lake Superior to the Pacific. Ross informed them "that we could take wheels nearly to the summit of the first range, as parties were engaged on construction work all the way up the valley of the Bow. . ." and provided them with two wagons with teams to transport themselves, their baggage and the supplies they would require. The wheels on these wagons proved problematic on their journey up the Bow but fortunately they were accompanied from Calgary to Morley by David McDougall, described by Grant as "merchant, trader, stockman, farmer and anything else that may be required," who repaired them on two or three occasions using willow sticks, boiling water, rope and shaganappi (buffalo hide).

Upon leaving Morley they soon reached "Padmore's," which Grant described as the spot which "bears the name of a gentleman who settled here, apparently actuated by love of solitude and love of the beautiful combined." Just beyond it they passed through the Gap and Fleming was struck by the dichotomy as "on every side the sound of the hammer and drill was heard, and every turn of the road revealed new views of the grandest mountain scenery." Fleming noted that as they advanced their eye fell constantly on these mighty heights "when they are not concealed from view by the hazy atmosphere," alluding to the numerous fires that had but recently been extinguished by rains. Grant was moved to a more poetic description of the scenery:

These mountains forms are superb; so varied and clearly defined, and on so gigantic a scale. Here is a great sphinx face, a thousand feet long, there a Brobdignanian baby sleeping peacefully, its face upturned to the open heavens. A gigantic leopard couchant is succeeded by a lion rampant. Single peaks, then a Parnassus, then a group of sisters, and then a serrated range; every possible form, all alike beautiful and on the grandest scale.[10]

As they proceeded up the Bow to the base of Cascade Mountain, both men mentioned reports of mineral claims that had been made near-by. Grant postulated that "if it be true that a vein of good anthracite coal has been discovered at Cascade Mountain, the realistic settlers will probably change the name to Mount Anthracite." Fleming's passage, written the following year, noted "discoveries of anthracite coal have been made in the flanks of this mountain, and since my visit mining operations have commenced." Eventually the wagons arrived at Hillsdale, the traditional campsite of the Stoneys that McDougall had described only a few months previously, but was now the main supply camp for location and construction in the upper Bow Valley. Grant described the camp as "the most beautifully situated of any that we had yet seen," and noted that on the five or six acres of grassy park "our teams and the teams of half a dozen other parties, and cattle intended for speedy conversion into beef, were quietly grazing." From its vicinity, they had a good view of Castle Mountain, which Grant described as looking like it had been "piled up by masons, and chiselled and sculptured by artists," moving him to state that "in their singular multiplicity and finish of detail the mountains of the Bow River certainly excel the Alps." He also commented on the parties of prospectors who were seen searching for silver and gold and spoke of talking to a few who believed the area was another Colorado. However, he reported that there was some skepticism and that "it is difficult to know whether or not the specimens were carried to the spot in the pockets of speculators, and people have been bitten so often, that average credulity is not so great on the nugget and bonanza business as it once was." His

Corry Brothers construction supply team on the CPR tote road, 1883

words would prove prophetic in the period of the booming of Silver City just ahead.

The wagon road, such as it was, ended twelve miles west of Hillsdale and the Fleming-Grant party had to switch to saddle and pack horses for the remainder of their journey. As they proceeded, Fleming again mentioned the effects of forest fires on the valley, as one had swept through the area only three days earlier. At night the flames ran up the mountainside and "gleam with a weird light" while during the day as they rode along they often passed through burnt woods or "brules," which Fleming described as "an ominous word to any one who has to make his way through the bush." Grant described the country beyond Castle Mountain as having "a desolate appearance" because of the "blackened poles, that the fires had left as grim monuments of their fury." When they reached the divide at Summit (Wapta) Lake, they found that preparations for the line had ceased about a month earlier at the point where Bath Creek joined the Bow, in order that James Hogg could make one last investigation of Howse Pass to determine if it was preferable to the steep grades of the Kicking Horse. At this point, Fleming's and Grant's path passed out of the Bow Valley, but their journey only became more difficult and, in fact, downright terrifying as they made their way down the narrow, cliff-hugging trail of the Kicking Horse, known as the "Golden Stairs." This was only superceded by their experiences on the west side of the Selkirks, after enjoying a day with Major Rogers at Rogers Pass, where they were forced to find their own route and blaze their own trail. Their brief sojourn with Rogers, during which they smoked cigars, played leap-frog and decided to create a Canadian alpine club, provides convincing evidence that they felt his pass was entirely practical.

The Fleming-Grant accounts give a good picture of the effects of construction activities on the Banff-Bow Valley. It was obvious that much of the terrain in proximity to the line had been burned over due to carelessness of work crews or prospectors and that the game populations had suffered from both hunting and fire. Other recorders of the scene also provide clues to the scope of the devastation. Charles Shaw observed an incident in 1883 that was all too common:

We had completed the location nearly to the Great Divide when some of the men who were clearing the right of way started a bush fire. It had been a very dry season, and there were piles of brush and timber all along the line; the whole valley was soon in a blaze. Our camp was in a small open spot near the Bow River, which at this point was quite wide and had a small island in it.

So we made a raft and ferried over our blankets, some supplies and cooking utensils. Everything else at the camp site we piled in a heap, with wet tents and some earth on top. Then we swam to the island. The fire burned for days. It was pretty hot, and the smoke was bad for a time, but we, our camp outfit and supplies came through safely, also our horses, which we had driven to a small meadow close to the river. But some of the men and teams working on the line were burned.[11]

The appearance of the crews grading the roadbed and actually laying the rails would only add to the impacts already in evidence. An account by British novelist and adventurer Morley Roberts, who worked on the construction of the line in the spring of 1884 and published his reminiscences in a work with the telling title *The Western Avernus*, provides a good picture. After riding on top of one of the cars on the work train heading into the mountains and enjoying the scenery "spite of choking smoke, cinder and ash," Roberts was forced to retire after dark. When he awoke the next morning near The Summit (Holt City as it was then known, after one of the main contractors Herbert Holt, later Laggan and now Lake Louise), he commented on the scene:

On the morning when we woke in the Rockies we found ourselves at the end of the track. We had come nearly as far as the rails were laid, and quite as far as the passenger-cars were allowed to run. Round me I saw the primeval forest torn down, cut and hewed and hacked, pine and cedar and hemlock. Here and there lay piles of ties, and near them, closely stacked, thousands of rails. The brute power of man's organized civilization had fought with Nature and had for the time vanquished her. Here lay the trophies of the battle.[12]

The devastation that Roberts described was the product of the work of some 500 men who had been kept on over the winter at the end of track to cut half a million ties and 20,000 cords of wood to fuel the locomotives for the 1884 work. Roberts's train carried about 100 navies, but they were just a drop in the bucket, for James Ross had announced that he would need some 12,000 men to work in the mountains that summer.

While there are numerous references to the effects of fire on the forests of the Valley during the construction period, those reflecting on the situation with respect to game are more scant. Grant commented on the effect that all the activity was having on game populations while near Aylmer Park when he noted that "a party that wished to hunt would require to engage, at Morley, Indians who know the mountains, for between the Stonies and the work connected with tracklaying and prospecting of miners, every kind of game must have been driven out of the valley of the Bow; but to the north and the south good sport can still be had." Apart from this comment, Peter Turner Bone, one of the construction engineers, made some comments about bears in his memoirs:

The great ambition of many of us coming to the mountains, was to shoot a bear; and with this end in view, Stuart and I set out one evening and climbed well up the thickly wooded side of the mountain adjacent to our camp. We lay out on this mountain side all night in the hope of getting a bear in the early morning. But we had no luck; the bears were too wary. One day, however, while we were busy in camp preparing our monthly estimates, we heard the sudden crack of a rifle. Greatly excited, we grabbed our rifles and rushed out, eager to get into the fray, whatever it was. We found that the rifle shot we had heard had come from the cook's rifle; and that with the shot he had killed a bear which had come close to the camp. After the excitement had died down, the bear was skinned and the skin stretched on an improvised frame to dry. The best parts of the carcass were later served by the cook for dinner.[13]

Undoubtedly, with Ross's intention to have 12,000 men at work in the mountains, these comments show only the tip of the iceberg of the impact of construction on game populations of all types.

The rails over which Shaw and Roberts reached their destination at The Summit had been laid the previous October. Track-laying had left Calgary in August and had sped up the relatively easy incline of the lower Bow Valley — in fact, one of the track-laying crews accomplished a short-distance record near Bow River Gap when they laid 600 feet of track in six-and-a-half minutes. End of steel arrived at Siding 27, soon to be named Canmore after Scottish King Malcolm of Canmore, in early October and construction began on a round-house, since this siding had been chosen as a divisional point. Each divisional point was the location where service was to be performed on the locomotives and other rolling stock and where railway operating crews would be changed, requiring railway facilities as well as boarding and restaurant amenities. A couple of days later at the foot of Cascade Mountain another siding, Siding 29 (the 29th siding west of Medicine Hat), was laid out near the waterfall that had been of such interest to generations of earlier explorers. A few tents and rough shacks soon sprang up at the siding, and it was quickly renamed Banff to recognize the birthplace of president George Stephen at Dufftown, Banffshire, Scotland.[14]

Part of Siding 29, or "Old Banff," as it appeared in 1885

The track-laying crews sped on to the westward, leaving the fledgling new settlements in their wake. But even though it would be November, 1885 before the last spike was driven, and June, 1886 before the first transcontinental passenger train chugged up the Valley's grade, the die had been cast. In three short years, the Valley had gone from a virtually untouched wilderness to become an integral part of the nation's main transportation route. Impacts of construction and related activities on its ecology were enormous, beginning a transformation that would never be reversed. It is important to realize that these events had consequences literally beyond the power of those entering the Valley at later times to reverse. Perhaps more than any other event in its early history, the driving of steel through the heart of the Rockies set the course for what the Banff-Bow Valley would become.

Chapter Five
The Vision of Sir John A.

One is sometimes left with the impression, when they read accounts of the history of the Canadian Rockies, that as soon as the CPR line was completed the age of tourism began in earnest. This is an oversimplification, as it was almost three years after Siding 29 was created before the first fare-paying tourist stepped off a west-bound train at the boxcar Banff station. While tourism would become the most powerful economic force in the Valley, it was originally not the most important, nor would it have the field entirely to itself. In fact, other economic generators were at work that would greatly affect the situation in the Banff-Bow Valley with respect to its development and future potential before tourism hit its stride in the 1890s. And, as with other factors such as the fur trade and railway construction which affected what the Valley would become, these influences were part of a much larger story unfolding on a national scale.

There can be little argument that the most compelling aspect of Canada's history from the election of 1878 until well after the turn-of-the century was Sir John A. Macdonald's "national policy." As Canada's first prime minister, Macdonald had used all means at his disposal to make good on his promise of 1871 to link British Columbia to central Canada with a railway within ten years. This had, unfortunately, involved him in the famous "Pacific Scandal" evolving from the 1872 election campaign, when he and his colleagues in the Conservative Party were accused of receiving campaign contributions from Sir Hugh Allan, who, it was claimed, had thereby bought the right to build the line. Macdonald won the election but was forced to resign when the scandal broke and in an attempt to formulate a new policy upon which to fight the next campaign became involved in the question of Canadian tariffs.

Support for raising tariffs to bolster Canadian manufacturing helped to get him elected in 1878, and thereafter the protective tariff, with its latent anti-Americanism, became the central tenet of his new "national policy." But, as time went on, it was not the only one, for the policy extended to all matters that were seen to support the Canadian economy and provide confidence for Canadians in the future of their country. The building of the Canadian Pacific Railway itself, although carried out by private enterprise, was largely subsidized by government and was embraced in the national policy concept as helping to achieve the great Canadian dream. Likewise, it encompassed the whole development of western Canada, both in terms of immigration and agricultural settlement and the exploitation of natural resources such as minerals, timber and, ultimately, scenery.

It has been said that if there is one phrase that summed up Sir. John A.'s goal for Canada it was delivered in an 1860 speech — "one people, great in territory, great in resources, great in enterpize, great in credit, great in capital." In the Valley, this pro-development outlook meant that attempts to exploit the Canadian Rockies' mineral resources had already begun prior to the CPR's arrival. However, these prospecting and mining activities must also be seen against the background of the North American-wide goldrush mentality that ultimately extended from California in the 1840s to the Yukon in the 1890s.

As mentioned, prospectors who had been attracted to the region by the discovery of gold in the Kootenay River Valley on Wild Horse Creek in the 1860s first appeared in the Bow Valley in the 1870s. Some had come up from the goldfields in California to Walla Walla on the Columbia and then through Whiteman's Pass in their search for new placer fields rumoured to exist on the North Saskatchewan River. But to a degree they were drawn to the Bow Valley by the tale of the "Lost Lemon Mine," a story that had several versions and which would become the most sustaining lodestar in Rockies' history with respect to those in search of the elusive Eldorado. Essentially, the story had it that a group of prospectors left the Tobacco Plains in Montana somewhere between 1867 and 1870 planning to ultimately prospect the North Saskatchewan. Along the way, a certain Bob Lemon and one or two others (the story varies) left the main party and while travelling through the mountains between the Columbia Valley and main ranges accidentally discovered a huge gold find. Here the story took several different paths — from Lemon killing his partner(s) to the whole party other than Lemon being killed by Indians — the agreement of the various versions being that Lemon was the only survivor. Later he told his tale of the discovery of the mine to American trader Lafayette French at the infamous Fort Whoop-up whiskey post in southern Alberta, and the search for the elusive location spread from there. The lure of the mine was mentioned by numerous contemporaries, including one William McCardell, whose own prospecting activities would lead to the key discovery in the Banff-Bow Valley's history. In his memoirs, McCardell characterized the legend as follows:

A story that was to develop into a whispered legend, to be re-told over strange campfires, that was to send prospectors for a decade searching through the escarpment of the Rockies for a lost mine, an eldorado in the peaks. It became a silent lure sent out from the unknown valleys in the Rockies. Hopeful prospectors ranging through giant hills, spurred their dwindling hopes in search for gold by the thought that maybe they were on the trail of the "Lost Lemon Mine."[1]

There were never many prospectors in the Bow Valley in this period, but a few of those who appeared were to leave their mark. Perhaps the most significant proved to be Joe Healy (after whom Healy Creek is named) and his former Montana sheriff brother John Jerome Healy, Irish-born Americans who both had been connected with the establishment of Fort Whoop-up in the 1860s. The most noted of the whiskey forts, it had been inhabited by ruthless American free traders who swapped a laudanum, red ink and gun powder-laced concoction with the hapless remnants of the Blackfoot Nation for hides of the fast-disappearing buffalo. There, the Healy brothers had become acquainted with Lafayette French and were undoubtedly inculcated into the mysteries of the "Lost Lemon Mine" legend. Joe Healy, perhaps reacting to that story, claimed to have first visited the Bow Valley in 1863 and the Banff vicinity in 1874, travelling down the Spray River and therefore likely having come over Whiteman's Pass. He was accompanied by a small group of Montana prospectors, including Nicholas Sheran, "Red Dan" and Joe Corrand, and at the time discovered a small stream of hot water flowing into the Spray. On his own, he followed the stream to its source and thereby discovered the upper hot springs. He claimed to have also visited the cave and basin springs the following year, or perhaps the one after, and although he reported his discoveries to his brother John and a few others, never took any action to have them recognized. Healy seems to have been in the Valley fairly regularly at this time, and in 1881 a Stoney Indian, subsequently known as "Gold Seeker" (this was the same Stoney who later led Tom Wilson to Lake Louise), directed him to some copper outcroppings on what would become Copper Mountain, across the valley from Hector's Castle Mountain. When he showed samples around Fort Benton, Montana they elicited a great deal of interest, and in the summer of 1883, before the rails began penetrating up the Bow, the two Healys brought Jeff Tolbert, an acquaintance who had mining experience around Butte, Montana, to examine the find. He pronounced himself satisfied enough with the showings of copper and silver (later determined to be sulfide of lead) to raise some capital for development work.

By August, 1883 other prospectors began to drift in having heard the rumours of the discovery. The story of one of them, Joe Smith, originally from Montreal and destined to be the longest inhabitant of what became known as Silver City, was typical:

But it was in the summer of 1883 when Joseph Smith heard of a "strike" of silver in the mountains to the west. He left the construction gang which was then building the line of the C.P.R. at a point about 20 miles East of Medicine Hat, and struck out for this new Eldorado which he reached in the month of August of the same year. Andrew Sibbald and another man were on the ground ahead of him. Miners and prospectors now literally poured into the site, and they began to sink a shaft into the East end of Mount Castle. The mine shaft is situated about one mile due north of the present site of the C.P.R. water tank, descends into the mountain at an angle of 45 degrees and bore the proud name of "The Queen of the Hills."[2]

The mining promoters from Butte who had associated themselves with the Healy brothers and Tolbert began work on the so-called "Alberta Mine" on Copper Mountain about the same time. Shortly thereafter, the construction gangs of the CPR appeared on the scene and temporarily swelled the population to a reported three thousand, although most of them quickly moved on to the west. Nonetheless, hundreds of would-be mining magnates stayed on over the winter of 1883-84 and were joined by numerous laid-off railway workers turned prospectors and an even larger number of labourers cutting ties and bridge timbers for the next season's railway construction work. By October, 1883 it was reported that twelve houses had been constructed and many more were underway, with Joe Smith building a combination stopping house, store and pool hall. This structure, known as the "Montreal Pool Room," was joined by other commercial ventures such as hotels bearing euphonious names like Queen's Hotel, Castle Park Hotel, and the Miner's Home as well as saloons and restaurants. One of the most popular restaurants was run by two Irishmen, O'Brien and Connors, the former always claiming that the latter's true name was O'Connor. When his partner was away, O'Brien put up a new sign that read: "Restaurant — The house of GOOD eats! O'Brien, O'Connor, O'God Help Us!" This unique sign attracted a great deal of attention and soon the phrase was often being heard on the street, "Let's go down to the O'God Help Us Restaurant," ensuring it the best patronage in town.

Often the restaurants and saloons contained gambling dens run in the rear of the establishment. These, according to McCardell, attracted unsavoury "Tin Horn roughneck rounders:"

Silver City and Castle Mountain, ca. 1884

"Silver City" was getting the name of developing into a "Rip-Roaring Snorter," as American Montana capital was going to convert this place into another Anaconda. This being the only Canadian silver-mining venture in the Canadian Rockies, American capital and initiative was going to put life and vigor into this new and promising undertaking.

Among the numerous gamblers that drifted into this thriving community, were "Big George" Sutherland, "Gid" Milligan,"Dutch Pete", "Con" Whallen, "Three Fingered" Mike, "One-Eyed"Riley, "Black Jack" McIntyre. Besides these men, many others from the surrounding lumber company and tie camps would always "sit in." These professionals generally had some of the big contractors in their games, to be sporty and take a "stack." If these contractors sustained a loss, nothing further was heard about it, but sometimes they would make a killing.[3]

In charge of keeping a lid on this mass of human flotsam and jetsam were two members of the North West Mounted Police, the nine-year-old force that had originally been sent west to clean out the whiskey posts and was now charged with keeping law-and-order along the line of railway construction. Sergeant Bond was head of the detachment and used his "reputed suavity" to prevent resorting to "tooth and claw" tactics, but he was assisted by Constable "Dog Face" Brown, and "woe to the man that dared to question Brown's rights as part of the law enforcement with which he was endowed."

As fate would have it, all the inhabitants of Silver City, whatever their demeanour, were to have their dreams quickly dashed, as the discovery "didn't pan out." Observations on the situation varied from Healy admitting in the spring of 1884 that "there had not been sufficient ore uncovered to warrant his financial friends and backers to continue with the venture of creating a producing mine," to a less generous assessment that "two mining promoters of Butte, Montana, floated a company, sold stock, and collected all the money they could" and then "'salted' the mine and quietly departed leaving the bubble to burst in their absence."[4] Whatever the truth of the matter, the result was the same — by the fall of 1884 the town was all but deserted as the railhead pushed down the Kicking Horse and many of the buildings were packed up to follow it along with the gamblers, tinhorns and other n'eer-do-wells. Within a short time, Joe Smith, who never gave up on the idea of a motherlode hidden in the nearby peaks, became the only permanent inhabitant, and remained so for more than fifty years.

While Silver City may have been a bit on an anomaly as a typical American-style booming, there was already a more Canadian approach to realizing Macdonald's national policy beginning to be formulated. Its instruments were federal government agencies and departments, the Geological Survey of Canada, a branch of the Geological and Natural History Survey of Canada, and the Department of the Interior, responsible for the administration of lands in the North West Territories, which sponsored topographical and resource surveys in the mountain region beginning in the early eighties. Dr. George M. Dawson of the Geological Survey of Canada, Hector's true scientific successor in the Valley, began geological analyses of western Canada in 1881 and by 1884 had completed the first major assessment of the Rockies since the Palliser Expedition. Dawson concentrated on the Spray, Kananaskis, Cascade and Red Deer River Valleys, while his associate R. J.

McConnell focused on the Bow River Valley, both noting structures containing significant coal deposits. From their combined work (Dawson's report was published in 1885 and McConnell's in 1886) Dawson was able to produce a geological map in 1886 containing specific information on the Banff-Bow Valley region, spurring many more prospectors attempting to stake claims and make their fortunes. As a byproduct, both Dawson's and McConnell's reports provided important scientific information and opinions on such matters as forest fires, vegetation, wildlife and Indian names in the area.

Similarly, the Department of the Interior's concerns incorporated timber resources, and in 1883-84 Dominion Land Surveyor Louis B. Stewart (after whom Mt. Louis is named) was instructed to lay out a number of "timber limits" or "berths" (surveyed blocks of timber) along the Bow River and its tributaries from Morley to Castle Mountain. Stewart surveyed two limits west of Banff, identified as limits "D" and "C", two up the Spray Valley, identified as "E" and "F", one to the east of Canmore, identified as "A," one around Lac des Arcs, identified as the "Cochrane limit," and four up the Kananaskis Valley, identified as "G" through "J". The three along the Bow River he found to be largely burnt over, stating that "most of the timber of any value is confined to the immediate banks of the river along which it forms a belt varying in width from one to ten chains." However, while having experienced some fire as well, particularly in the Kananaskis, the timber on the Bow's tributaries was seen to be more valuable and worthy of commercial logging.[5]

Once these resources were identified in the annual reports of the relevant body, it did not take long for commercial exploitation to begin. The first coal deposit to receive attention proved to be the so-called "Cascade Coal Basin," discovered in 1883 to the east of present-day Banff at the confluence of the Cascade and Bow. In 1884 the Department of the Interior delimited the thirty-six square mile district, and within its boundaries withdrew all lands from sale or settlement. Coal mining regulations required that coal lands would be sold outright for $10 per acre, except in the

Cascade district where the resources were seen to have so much potential that the price was set at $20 per acre (later reduced to $12.50). By 1885, the Department of the Interior had begun selling the Cascade lands by tender and several groups began some small development activity. The largest of these, composed of Canadians William B. Scarth of Winnipeg, John Stewart of Fort Macleod, Archibald and McLeod Stewart of Ottawa, and a number of American investors, formed themselves in 1886 into the Canadian Anthracite Coal Company (C.A.C.) with head offices in Eau Claire, Wisconsin. The company bought the rights to 1,280 acres and began tunneling operations employing ninety men that year. A townsite to house the miners was established on the banks of the Cascade River and was named Anthracite, and shortly thereafter the company began to let lots for commercial development.

With mining activities at Anthracite commencing at exactly the same time as the new railway was becoming operational, the CPR provided an important market for the coal. In addition, it provided transportation for sales elsewhere, and before long the C.A.C. was test marketing its product in San Francisco and other west coast ports. But the coal from the Anthracite mines was extremely friable, breaking down into small fines when extracted, and the mine temporarily shut down in 1888 while the company's gaze turned eastward to the better quality coal that had been discovered near the railroad's divisional point at Canmore. First reported in 1884, it took until 1887 for the coal at what became known as No. 1 Mine on the south side of the river across from the railroad operations to be developed. The original entrepreneurs were a Welshman, Jack Weyburn, and an Irishman, Pat Dailey, who would later develop the Premier Gold Mine at Premier, B. C. Initially the coal was scowed across the river in summer and carried by sleigh in winter to the railroad, where it was hauled away in fifteen ton boxcars, and it proved to be of sufficient calorific value to attract other development. A Mr. Brinkerhoff, representing Minneapolis interests, had coal lands surveyed one mile west of the No. 1 Mine and in 1888 a second mine, known as the Cochrane Mine, was put in production. By 1891 the Brinkerhoff

The original No. 1 mine at Canmore

claim was being operated by the North West Coal and Lumber Syndicate, but their decision to build a coking facility overextended them and their interests passed to the H. W. McNeil Co., along with the original Anthracite Mine, to be operated on a ten year lease.

The McNeil interests employed up to 400 miners, the majority in the mines at Canmore, leading to a significant change in the community's development pattern. Originally, residential and commercial buildings in the town had hugged the railway line on the north side of the river near the divisional point round-house. Eating and sleeping accommodation were needed for layover crews and for those servicing the trains, leading to the construction of Bill Coffee's restaurant in 1883 and the Conroy family's "Mountain House" boarding house in 1884. These were joined in 1886 by other interests such as MacNulty Brothers' general store, S. C. Vick's watchmaking business, and E. L. Smith and Co. hardware and tinware. A row of boxcar houses soon extended along what was known as Section House Avenue (today's Railway Avenue) and they were joined by more permanent habitations, several of them constructed from logs of dismantled buildings at Silver City. One of these, owned by engineer Charles Carey, stood beside a spring-fed creek that took his name, Carey Creek, until the North West Mounted Police barracks were constructed nearby and the name was changed to Policeman's Creek. The barracks stood on what became known as Main Street which ran south from the original boxcar station, and it soon became the home of four hotels, including the still existing Canmore Hotel built by the Count de Rambouville of France in 1890. By 1889, Canmore's population already stood at 450 (compared to 167 in Anthracite) and their number was soon joined by those beginning to settle in the "new" mineside part of town south of the river. Here the first few miner's shacks had been built into the hillside in conjunction with the opening of the Cochrane Mine and similar shacks, a bunkhouse and a cookhouse were constructed near No. 1 Mine. In 1893 the first mineside hotel, the "Oskaloosa," was built, as was the subsequently famous company store, later known as the Rundle Mountain Trading Company (added to in 1904 when H. W. McNeil closed down its Anthracite operations and moved its store to join the Rundle Mountain store). By the early 1890s then, the two faces of Canmore — townside and mineside — were firmly in place.

Exploitation of the Banff-Bow Valley's timber resources, first noted by the Department of the Interior at the same time as its coal deposits were revealed, progressed at the same pace as mineral development, but not in such a noticeable fashion. A Crown Timber Office was opened in Calgary in July, 1883 and tenders were quickly received for the fifty square mile timber berths being surveyed on the Bow and its tributaries. In fact, on the Cochrane berth around Lac des Arcs cutting had actually begun in 1882 to supply the needs of the Cochrane Ranch, the first major cattle ranch in the North West Territories established by Senator Matthew Cochrane of Montreal in 1881. The ranch's manager, former N.W.M.P. officer Colonel James Walker, saw the potential for logging in the area and in 1883 resigned his position with the Cochrane Ranch to go into the lumber business himself. His sawmill was established at Kananaskis (near Padmore), the first such operation west of Winnipeg, and he actively logged the area west to Canmore. His commercial activities in this area joined those of another important early Bow Valley entrepreneur, a Mr. McCanleish, who was already operating a lime kiln near Kananaskis by 1884. This development, shortly afterwards taken over by Englishman Edwin Loder, was the forerunner to the major lime and cement businesses that would dominate the Gap area to the present day.[6]

An early log drive just above Bow Falls

While the first to attempt to exploit the Valley's timber resources belonged to Colonel Walker, his operations were relatively small compared to those which followed. In the early eighties, Kutusoff MacFee, an Ottawa lawyer with a keen eye for timber, hired expert timber interests in Eau Claire, Wisconsin to examine the forests being laid out in timber berths in L. B. Stewart's survey. Their reports were favourable and MacFee's company, the Eau Claire and Bow River Lumber Company, was chartered in 1883 and was first to line up at the door of the new Crown Timber Office in Calgary. Rights were initially obtained on two berths, although it was 1886 before company men had been sent out from Wisconsin to set up a mill along the Bow River in Calgary. Two logging camps were established, one near Walker's operation at Kananaskis and the other near Castle Mountain, breathing new life into the all-but deserted Silver City townsite. Timber was cut over the winter and floated down the Bow in huge spring log drives to the Calgary mill, where it served the rapidly increasing needs of the growing community and the surrounding agricultural settlers.

It was this same desire to find and exploit the resources of the Banff-Bow Valley, manifested in the development of the coal, timber and lime riches of the area, that led to the most important natural resource discovery in the Valley's history. The "discoverers," William "Billy" McCardell and Frank McCabe, would unwittingly become among the most famous prospectors in western Canada, even though their find would not be mineral in origin. Their "discovery" of the hot springs long known to first peoples at Banff, as contentious as it became, would lead to the development of an international tourism industry that would quickly become and remain the dominant economic force in the Valley. There were differing accounts of the discovery arising from the often typical influence that time has on the memory and point-of-view of those involved in major events. In this case, the time factor extended from McCardell's and McCabe's testimony before a commission of inquiry into the discovery and development of the springs held by William Pearce, Superintendent of Mines, at Banff in July, 1886 and McCardell's memoir, *Reminiscences of a Western Pioneer*, written some fifty years later. As was quite often the case in a memoir of this type, the writer tended to increase his own importance in the event and show his own involvement in the best possible light. However, despite these drawbacks, McCardell's story, published in a serialized form in Banff's *Crag and Canyon* newspaper in the 1930s, became one of the best sources on the activities taking place and the people frequenting the Banff-Bow Valley area at the time the railroad arrived.

Both McCardell and McCabe had been born in 1857, the former in Ontario and the latter in Nova Scotia, and both went west in the early eighties to work on the railroad. They likely first met in the spring of 1882 after commencing work on construction of the CPR mainline in Manitoba and spent the following winter together building a wire fence between Winnipeg and Emerson, Manitoba and getting out cordwood for a contractor. In the spring, McCabe left for St. Paul, Minnesota and made his way westward to San Francisco and ultimately British Columbia, while McCardell and his brother Tom went to work on the prairies for Simms and Armington, one of the major construction contractors building the line. According to testimony McCardell gave at the hot springs inquiry, he and his brother remained employed by Simms and Armington until about the end of September, 1883 when they again encountered McCabe in Calgary, freshly returned from the coast, and discussed what they should do. It was agreed that McCabe would try to obtain a section foreman's position in the mountains until winter closed down construction and the McCardells would work for him. This occurred, McCabe being taken on as section foreman at Padmore and the McCardells working with him until the line shut down in December, with the rest of the winter being spent in hunting, exploring and prospecting. It was while doing so in November, 1883 that fate led them up the Bow Valley on a hand car to the vicinity of today's Vermilion Lakes, McCardell's description of how they came to discover the springs being recorded as part of the proceedings of the inquiry:

We came across the River, we ran up with a hand car and we laid off here, and we spotted Sulphur Mountain several times, and we thought we would like to go to the bottom of it, and we made a ferry and crossed the river and we discovered a big pool by the Cave, . . . and we just went around looking about, and we carved our names on the bark of the trees with a knife; I had not an axe, but I don't know whether any of the other fellows had; we intended to come back again, and as soon as I got down to Canmore I took planks and axe and tools and came back up here and built the shack that is there now, but I think while I was away somebody took the roof off and put a new one on, and I put a door on it, but I had no window: I got the door from a camp across the river; I did not chink up the cracks; we got light in through the door; there was no chimney in it, but the smoke went through the roof; I was two or three days building the shack, and then I returned to Padmore, and the following winter I visited the cave occasionally.[7]

While McCardell's testimony did not address the reason for their visit to the area and their exploration of the lower slopes of Sulphur Mountain, McCabe's did:

Q. What about November?

A. We came up in November 1884 (1883) and we stopped here and we went across the River on a raft and found the Cave and other Hot Springs; we went across to the hot springs Mountain to see if there were any mineral in there.

Q. You were going across to the Hot springs Mountain to explore for mineral?

A. Yes; I crossed about opposite the pond where the Cave is; we came in and saw the pond and went around the pond and saw the water running down and the grass was very green and we smelt the sulphur, and we went up and saw the cave and then went home; we looked around there a long time, and it got late; we did not stop over night; there was no place to stop there and we came across here and stopped at the Rail Road overnight.[8]

McCardell and McCabe's prosaic description of their discovery given at the inquiry is not the exciting tale of wonder and revelation that has become part of Banff legend. That version came from McCardell's *Reminiscences* and his frequent re-telling of the tale of how he, his brother Tom and McCabe were deprived of the benefits of their discovery, for he would live much of the remainder of a long life in Banff and vicinity. According to it, the two McCardells and McCabe left the railroad construction gangs early in the summer of 1883 and proceeded to Calgary, where they decided to join a contractor named Riley on his trip up the Bow to estimate a grading bid for the work to the west. Their intention was strictly to see the country before the rails went through and to do some prospecting, as McCabe had some experience in that line from his native Nova Scotia and extensive travels in western North America. They accompanied Riley as far as Aylmer Park and there met the Healy party on their way to their claim at Castle Mountain. Inspired by their story of the Lost Lemon Mine and the supposed silver and copper discoveries in the region, "we constituted ourselves there and then a mineral exploration party."

After setting up their "wigwam" on the bank of what would become Forty Mile Creek, they began by prospecting up the Cascade River towards Lake Minnewanka. While doing so they encountered a camp of Stoney who told them of coal seams along the river, which they called "rock that burns," and drew some maps in the earth "that conveyed information concerning the nature of the country." After this, they headed westward to examine the Healy find, climbing up to investigate the Hole-in-the-Wall and stopping at the future site of Hillsdale, where they met Reverend John McDougall returning from the Windermere area with a group of Stoney. Following a visit to the Healy camp at the future site of Silver City, McCabe and the McCardells returned to their own camp and decided that their next course of action would be to explore the south side of the river. Employing a raft made on the spot, they crossed over and began climbing the lower slope of the mountain, noticing that the ground quickly became soggy and the water warm:

Soon we were climbing up the strange formation of which the bank was composed. Once on the top (of) the first bench we rushed around to try and locate the place the warm water came from. This did not take long. Out of a beautiful circular basin, jammed full of logs all the way in size from four to eight inches in diameter, some ten inches, seeped this warm water. Our enthusiastic interest at this discovery was beyond the description of words. Our joyousness and the invigorating thrill we experienced in thus locating this strange phenomenon, and hidden secret of the wilderness, knew no bounds. . . .

So we moved on up to another bench and to our utter astonishment we came upon a great cave 35 to 40 feet in depth. This was the greatest climax to a major discovery, that we had ever seen. Frank McCabe, Tom McCardell and myself just stood in silence looking at this mysterious grotto where warm clear water bubbled from its depths. . . .[9]

Deciding they must descend into the cave to investigate further, Tom McCardell was sent back across the river to the camp to fetch a rope while Billy cut down a forty-five foot lodgepole pine to get ready to put into the opening, cutting the branches to leave eighteen inch stubs to act as a sort of ladder. With the rope, the pine was lowered through the hole at the top of the cave and Billy, being the lightest of the three, was selected to go down first. The rope was tied around his waist and he began his descent into the inky blackness, initiating the thereafter oft-described and depicted penultimate moment in the Valley's history:

I shouted that I had reached the bottom alright, and that as soon as I had accustomed my sight to the darkness of the cavern, I would call to them at the top. This was the grandest sensation I had ever experienced in all my life. Taking the candle and matches from my pocket I struck a light, and again the flame affected my sight. But leaning up against the tree it was not very long until I could pretty well see, but could not see very far.

I scrambled around the edge of the water and I began now to witness one of the grandest spectacles, which I believed very few men had ever beheld. Beautiful stalactites hung in great clusters from the roof of the great amphitheater-like cavern. When I shouted up to Tom and Frank, it seemed as though I was speaking out of an immense drum, the sound rumbling and echoing in an erratic way. But the beautiful glistening stalactites that decorated this silent cave were like some fantastic dream from a tale of the "Arabian Nights." Glittering crystals, and stalactites bedecked that dome-like cavern.[10]

McCardell and his partners were soon taking their first swim in the cave's soothing waters and, in hindsight, he completed his description of the moment with the observation "little did I think at this time that prominent men from every part of the world would some day visit this famous cave and be delighted and invigorated with its healing and curative waters." Prominent indeed, for the story goes that none other than William Van Horne himself was soon to visit the springs and upon emerging from McCardell's cave was heard to say "these springs are worth a million dollars."

Because this moment has been portrayed as being so significant in the Valley's and the Park's history (it was the subject of a popular display in the Tussaud Wax Museum in Banff for several decades and is still depicted in a mural at the Cave and Basin Interpretive Centre), it is interesting to speculate on whether it ever occurred. The evidence from Pearce's inquiry would make it appear likely that it didn't and McCardell's *Reminiscences* must be viewed with some skepticism given the time that had passed and the circumstances that had led him to write it. As mentioned, the memoir was an attempt to state his case as the founder and original developer of the hot springs (in fact, in it he stated the date of the discovery as August 7, 1883 rather than November as he testified at the inquiry), since it was on that basis that Pearce ultimately awarded compensation among a number of claimants. However, in the final analysis it matters little whether his description of the discovery was a flight of fancy or fact, since it was what happened next that would set the stage for the Valley's future development.

Before long other railway workers were beginning to make their way to the springs for a refreshing bath in the warm mineral waters, Siding 29 section foreman David Keefe providing a boarding facility as part of his section house and building a better raft to ferry patrons across. Other "discoverers" and claimants, including Nova Scotia Member of Parliament D. B. Woodworth who duped McCabe into signing over his and the McCardells interests (such as they were) while the McCardells were away working on railway construction in B. C., began to appear like flies drawn to honey, eventually leading to the Pearce inquiry. Strangely, McCabe and the McCardells took very little action to substantiate their claim, probably not at first realizing the springs' value and being informed after writing to the Minister of the Interior concerning staking a mineral claim to them that such could only be done if they had the site surveyed. As the Dominion Land Surveyors responsible for mapping the area had by this time only reached Morley in their work, this was too expensive for them to undertake. Their first official claim was made early in 1885 when

McCabe heard that the upper hot springs, which they also claimed to have discovered after seeing steam rising from them on New Year's Day, 1884, were being claimed by one Theodore Siebring, who had built a cabin there.

The attention focused on the springs quickly brought them to public notice, and in June, 1885 J. M. Gordon, Dominion Lands Agent at Calgary, was instructed to inspect them. His report provided the Department with the first solid information and by that summer its officers were giving consideration to preventing private development from taking place. They were aided in their decision-making by the entreaties of Charles Drinkwater, secretary of the Canadian Pacific Railroad, who urged the Deputy Minister of the Interior, A. M. Burgess, to follow the example of the American government in taking control of the Arkansas hot springs to prevent private spoilation, and by several Members of Parliament who made a visit to the springs that summer. In October the new Minister of the Interior, Thomas White, visited the area and on the 16th of that month a critical aspect of the decision-making occurred when Prime Minister Macdonald sent a note to Burgess expressing the hope that "great care had been taken to reserve all the land in or near the Hot Springs at Banff." Although we cannot know with certainty, Sir John A. likely already had a new plank in his national policy firmly in view and on November 25, 1885 Order in Council No. 2197 reserved a ten square mile area around the springs. The enabling clause of this, the birth certificate of Canada's national parks, read:

His Excellency by and with the advice of Queen's Privy Council for Canada has been pleased to order, and it is hereby ordered, that whereas near the station of Banff on the Canadian Pacific Railway, in the Provisional District of Alberta, North West Territories, there have been discovered several hot mineral springs which promise to be of great sanitary advantage to the public, and in order that proper control of the lands surrounding these springs may be vested in the Crown, the said lands in the said territory including said springs and their immediate neighbourhood, be and they are hereby reserved from sale, settlement or squatting.

The government's ability to reserve the area so that "proper control of the lands surrounding the springs may be vested in the Crown" arose from its contention, as articulated by William Pearce, that there were no regulations under which title to the springs could be registered by discoverers because they constituted neither mineral nor agricultural lands. This interpretation proved extremely frustrating to those claiming discovery rights, particularly Member of Parliament Woodworth who had purchased an old hotel at Silver City to be moved to the springs, had received the right to run a ferry across the Bow from the Territorial Government, and had begun clearing a road from the river to provide better access. His letter to Prime Minister Macdonald concerning these matters seems to have been a catalyst for the calling of the public inquiry held under Pearce's authority in July, 1886. Apart from the testimony of McCardell and McCabe already referred to, Pearce heard from twelve other witnesses and claimants and as a result several interesting pieces of information came to light. Included was the fact that the first building to be erected in the vicinity of the springs was a small "shack," estimated to be worth $18.00, belonging to Willard B. Young, a prospector and trapper from Ohio, who had overwintered in 1875-76. Young had returned in 1878 to determine if his traps were still cached at the site and then again in 1885, when he found the location of his cabin over-run by other claimants. As well, the inquiry heard testimony concerning the discovery and early development of the upper or "hot" springs, including Healy's claim of discovery in 1874, McCardell and McCabe's visit New Year's Day, 1884 and a further claim made by sectionman Keefe who indicated that he had visited them in October, 1884 after building his ferry across the river. Keefe confirmed that after his visit, George Whitman had erected the first building at the upper spring and that subsequently others had been built by McCabe and Theodore Seibring, a former boarding house operator from Silver City.

Despite Pearce's position that no right of discovery of the various springs could be recognized, he did recommend that some compensation be paid, likely so that influential voices such as

"Improvements" carried out by the various claimants at the Cave and Basin springs before government development began

those of M. P. Woodworth and McCardell's and McCabe's lawyer James Lougheed be silenced and government development be allowed to proceed unimpeded. Some years later Pearce admitted that "none of the claims had any legal standing but after discussing the matter with the Minister of the Interior it was thought better to pay a small sum than exercise rigorously the law in this case." The awards included: $100 to David Keefe for making improvements and facilitating visitation with the provision of his ferry; $675 to McCardell and Frank McCabe in recognition of improvements and time spent in protecting their interests; and $1,000 to D. B. Woodworth as compensation for expenditures incurred as a result of supposedly acquiring the interests of McCardell and McCabe and those made for planned developments, such as the hotel and ferry service.[11] Although never admitted by Pearce, it seems on the basis of the awards made, given that they all sprang from actions or information emanating from McCardell and McCabe, that he believed they were the individuals most responsible for knowledge of and public attention to the springs leading to the reservation.

The events of the very short but extremely active period of the Banff-Bow Valley's history in the early eighties set an important tone that has dominated its story ever since. Exploitation and development in keeping with Sir John A.'s vision were the bywords, a tendency which historian R. Craig Brown has called "the doctrine of usefulness" in his contention that they were the foremost influences in the history of Canada's national parks.[12] Tourism would soon rise to become the most important economic force in the Valley, but mineral exploitation, particularly with respect to coal at Canmore and limestone at Exshaw, would continue to run a close second. And even the hot springs themselves, while not to be directly developed by private interests, were nonetheless to be utilized — in this case with the government itself taking the leading role. Tourism was to be strongly supported and promoted, and extractive and other industrial developments were to be allowed in the national park for many decades after its creation, with coal mining continuing right up until the 1950s in the Anthracite area. By that time the public perception of what was an appropriate activity in a national park setting had begun a slow but profound evolution.

Chapter Six
A Public Park and Pleasure Ground

The fact that the early park period in the Banff-Bow Valley coincided with its first tourism development led to an important tendency in its subsequent history. While the government was not prepared to let the CPR develop the hot springs directly, it was to become dependent on the railway to provide many of the ancillary attractions and services. And, for its part, the CPR was anxious to oblige in order to sustain the operation of the line in one of its most difficult and expensive sections. Indeed, Van Horne's rallying cry for the mountains would become "if we can't export the scenery, we'll import the tourists." Thus the government and the CPR, which became a major business and political force in the country, quickly found themselves pursuing mutual goals consistent with the "doctrine of usefulness" at a critical moment in park development and initial parks policy. This symbiotic relationship became the major force at work in the Valley's history for most of the next century, and vestiges of it remain present to this day. Of all the identifiable elements in creation of the area's heritage, it is perhaps the most sustaining.

Just as the early resource development of the Valley would be attached to the larger exploitation aspects of the national policy, so too early tourism was linked to greater forces at work. To appreciate this, an understanding of contemporary Victorian society is important. As early as the mid-19th century in Europe, the new middle class created by the Industrial Revolution had begun to take excursions to the countryside, resulting in the development of Thomas Cook's famous European continental tours in the 1860s. The same impetus which provided the money and leisure time to allow this new class to travel also created a milieu in which mankind could re-assess the world to be travelled in. Responding to the writings of Henry Thoreau, John Ruskin, and John Muir, a new aesthetic that idealized pre-industrial processes, rural life and the importance of nature emerged and swept over North America and Europe. The value of undisturbed nature for its own sake and the desire to study it firsthand and participate in its recreational opportunities became paramount in middle and upper class thinking. In the opinion of John Ruskin, the foremost British advocate of the movement, "mountains are the beginning and the end of natural landscape," and the Swiss Alps became the focus of much of continental travel. At the same time, one of the ways this new society could participate in nature, but without discomfort, was by "taking the waters," an activity that had been pursued by those of wealth in Europe at locations such as Bath, Baden-Baden and Aix-les-Bains for centuries. While the status of spas had diminished with increasing non-aristocratic accessibility, they were still popular among those seeking to establish their position in the social hierarchy. The fact that many European spas were located in alpine areas and the emerging equation of mountains with beauty meant that the Banff-Bow Valley, and particularly the area around the hot springs at Banff, possessed all the prerequisites for popularity. It was therefore not surprising in an atmosphere of belief that nature could help save Canadian society from the excesses of the materialism and faith in the curative properties of hot springs for body and mind, that the government would begin setting up the Banff hot springs as a "public park and pleasure ground."

The idea of creating parks in the mountains had first emerged from several individuals connected with the CPR. As early as the completion of his trip over the route of the new line in 1883, recounted in *England and Canada*, the visionary Sandford Fleming was waxing eloquent on the desirability of Canada setting up a system of national parks. In fact his ideas, put forward in the closing pages of his book, provided an uncanny vision of what would eventually transpire:

It is therefore suggested that the opportunity for establishing one or more national parks or domains should not be neglected. . . .

Such parks, with the marked salubrity of the climate, would attract visitors to frequent them. Rendered perfectly easy of access by the Railway, and with assurance that the life to be found there was to be marked by comfort at no extravagant cost, these resorts would, especially in the heat of summer, bring many within their boundaries on the score of health and recreation. Sportsmen and crowds of tourists would flock thither, some to hunt the grizzly, the cariboo or the bighorn, others to fish the splendid speckled trout to be found in the mountain streams; many with alpen-stock in hand to climb the glacier-covered heights, and all to enjoy the pure air and the charm of the scenery and the striking features of natural beauty nowhere else to be seen. Every year a limited expenditure in forming roads and bridle paths to the remote sections would render the localities more and more attractive. In no long time all the aid that art could furnish would be manifested in developing the landscape and in establishing retreats of quiet repose amid some of the grandest scenes of wild nature. Evidently such improvements being in the common interest, they should in some degree be borne by the Dominion.[1]

Fleming's theme was taken up by Van Horne himself. During one of his first visits to the mountains in 1883 he viewed the area around Lac des Arcs under ideal conditions of an early season snow and wrote to William Pearce that it should be considered for a park reserve. It was an unfortunate choice, since the more usual conditions of exposed mudflats and high winds swirling dust around made it an unlikely spot for a resort, and CPR workers for years afterwards jokingly referred to it as "Van Horne's Park." Van Horne did not pursue the suggestion, undoubtedly recognizing his error, but he kept the idea in mind, and when the matter came up again in 1886 he provided free transportation for a delegation of parliamentarians to travel over the new line and visit Banff and supported CPR secretary Charles Drinkwater in coming up with suggestions for legislation. Later, in 1886, when Minister of the Interior Thomas White asked him to comment on the idea of further park reserves at locations such as Lake Louise, Mount Stephen, the summit of the Selkirks, Three Valley Lakes and Shuswap Lakes, Van Horne queried CPR employees familiar with

Van Horne (front centre), pictured here with other CPR officials in 1894, took a direct interest in the establishment of the mountain parks

the areas for their ideas before responding. He indicated that they favoured Mount Stephen, Mount Sir Donald and Eagle Pass and added his own idea that "I think that the amphitheater at the Summit of the Selkirks [Rogers Pass] should be reserved as it is one of the most beautiful spots in the world." An Order-in-Council dated October 10, 1886 set the suggested areas aside as park reserves and although Eagle Pass was later dropped as being unsuitable for parks purposes, the other areas became the nucleus of Yoho and Glacier National Parks.

There is little doubt that both Fleming and Van Horne, as knowledgeable railwaymen, were putting forward ideas gained from the experience of the Northern Pacific Railway with Yellowstone Park in the United States. In that country the earlier and more intensive history of western railroad building had brought to public light a number of magnificent landscapes that both conservation-minded individuals and private railroad companies pressured the American government to preserve. The first of these park reserves was made in 1872 in Wyoming's Yellowstone region, where the hot springs, geysers, waterfalls and canyons combined with native bison to demand protection. The Northern Pacific Railway was one of the primary promoters of the idea of Yellowstone National Park and hoped to capitalize on that position when its line was later built near the park. Its charter prohibited direct involvement in business in the park, a restriction it got around by being a backer of local companies set up to serve the tourist trade once development got underway.

Van Horne did not envision any such restrictions in the Canadian parks situation, nor did he need to worry with the national policy in full sway. The federal government had been the handmaiden of the Canadian Pacific Railway — indeed it would not have existed without government subsidies during its construction — and direct cooperation was continuing during its operational phase in the land and settlement fields. In fact, there were those who felt that the whole development of the new park reserve at Banff should be left entirely in private hands with no government involvement whatsoever. The debate on this issue was held around the bill to establish Banff National Park put forward to the House of Commons by Minister of the Interior Thomas White in April, 1887, the government initiative to turn the first ten square mile reserve around the hot springs into a true park of 260 square miles extent and in the process provide the appropriations for its development. Members of Parliament Jones and Kirk argued during debate on the bill that "private enterprise always manages such undertakings much more economically and systematically than does the Government" and since only the Canadian Pacific Railway would benefit from the park reserve, it should therefore bear the full costs of development. Macdonald's response revealed that he felt the interests of Canada were equally at stake with those of the CPR and was not prepared to forego them, stating that "the Canadian Pacific Railway would be only too glad to take the land and make 1000 per cent out of it" and that "there is only one way of making that portion of the country what it ought to be, and that is by the scheme of the Government, undertaken with a full knowledge of their responsibility."[2] His view was that the park should be showplace for Canada and that it could also provide a financial asset, consistent with his policy:

I do not suppose in any portion of the world there can be found a spot, taken all together, which combines so many attractions and which promises in as great a degree not only large pecuniary advantage to the Dominion, but much prestige to the whole country by attracting the population, no only on this continent, but of Europe to this place. It has all the qualifications necessary to make it a place of great resort. . . There is beautiful scenery, there are the curative properties of the water, there is a genial climate, there is prairie sport and there is mountain sport; and I have no doubt that that will become a great watering-place and that there will be a large town on the south side of the Bow River where the Government have laid out a town plot. . . .[3]

In order to make it "a place of great resort," Macdonald realized some development needed to be done. He undoubtedly agreed with the government leader in the Senate who, in discussing the 1887 act noted that "in order to make a park of this tract of land, of course, it becomes necessary to improve it to a certain extent." This statement speaks volumes about the public perception of parks at the time. Despite its protection of a wilderness area, the Hot Springs Reservation was not thought of as a park and could only become one if "improvements," such as tourist amenities, roads and hotels, were carried out. The majority of tourists visiting a park would expect comfort and convenience during their stay, not the rough surroundings of some backwater. As Edmund Swinglehurst, author of a book on Thomas Cook put it when describing the Victorian English traveller: "They wanted and expected to find themselves treated in a manner suitable to an Englishman's station in the world, to be provided with a decent, comfortable room and board, deferential service, and the English newspaper at breakfast."[4] For his part, Macdonald hoped to attract a class of people who would build summer residences and provide the distinction he was looking for, taking steps to ensure that large villa lots were laid out on the south side of the Bow River to entice them: ". . . a portion of the park offers some beautiful sites for villas, and I believe in the plan the architect lays these out, to be leased to people of wealth, who will erect handsome buildings upon them. These buildings will have to be subject to the approval of the Government, to prevent any monstrosities being put there to destroy the general beauty of the park."[5]

The Governor-General's warrants of 1886 and 1887 for development to assist in realizing the task of making the reserve into a park accessible to tourists, amounting to $47,000, were the subject of much more debate than the substance of the act itself, illustrating that Macdonald's philosophy was widely accepted. Macdonald and his wife had taken a journey over the new line to the Pacific coast in July, 1886 and had stopped off briefly at Banff to look over the lay of the land. The Prime Minister noted that due to the numbers of those using the springs many had to be accommodated in a tent camp in their environs and therefore felt that the sooner a townsite with appropriate hotels and services was built, the better. To ensure the success of his villa plan, he had his wife, Lady Agnes Macdonald, acquire one of the best properties near the newly-constructed Banff Springs Hotel from Henry Abbott, Superintendent of the Pacific Division of the CPR, and had the rustic "Earnscliffe Cottage" built on it.[6]

To begin the process of development, proper surveys were needed. Dominion Land Surveyor George A. Stewart of Winnipeg had been assigned the task of surveying the original reservation early in 1886, arriving at Banff in February and establishing his headquarters in a tent near the railway siding. He soon began reporting to Ottawa that "a large tract of land lying outside the original reservation presented features of the greatest beauty, and was admirably adapted for a National Park," an observation that led to orders to extend the survey "to include all points of interest within reasonable bounds." Some of his work included extending the survey to the western end of Devil's Lake (Lake Minnewanka),

Sir John A. and Lady Macdonald travelled over the CPR line in 1886 and stopped at Banff to get an idea of its tourist development potential

perhaps the most historic location in the whole Valley and already becoming a favourite fishing spot, as well as down the Bow River past its confluence with the Spray. Eventually Stewart's survey encompassed an oblong block of land of some 26 by 10 miles and it became the proposed enlarged area for the park identified in the 1887 legislation. At the same time, a small settlement had begun to emerge on the north bank of the Bow River closer to the springs than the railway siding. Some of this area too was outside the original reservation lands and as several individuals and the CPR itself indicated that they were anxious to establish hotels, bathhouses and other businesses in this vicinity, Stewart's survey plan was extended to the laying out of a new townsite. In order to feature the view of Cascade Mountain on his main street, Stewart proposed to move the location of a temporary floating bridge he had erected at the bend in the river to a more permanent location to the east, a move that ensured millions of future photographs of Cascade Mountain framed by Banff Avenue. The scene, including the first building in the new townsite erected by the CPR's doctor, Robert G. Brett, was later recalled as he had seen it in June, 1886 by Dave White, a New Brunswick-born CPR section foreman at Sawback west of Banff at the time, but later one of the town's leading citizens:

The village, consisting only of a section house and small log store, nestled beside the newly-completed CPR line at approximately the site of the Buffalo Park. A buckboard trail meandered across country from the village to the present townsite, and the Bow was bridged only by a temporary arrangement of pontoons, but even at that early date the nucleus of our present Banff was to be seen in the excavation for the building of the original Sanitarium Hotel.[7]

The new townsite was originally known as "National Park," and initially the area's inhabitants were unsure as to which settlement, "old" or "new," would ultimately win the day. However, rapid development of the hot springs favoured the new and in June, 1888 a log station was constructed at the site of the present railway station and the name "Banff" went with it.

Responsibility for all development had fallen to Stewart, as he was the most senior government official on the ground. In recognition of his good work, he was appointed Superintendent on January 1, 1887, even though it would be several months before the park legislation was passed. Over the winter of 1885-86 he supervised the blasting of a tunnel into the cave spring to improve public access from the rough ladder going through the original opening used by McCardell and McCabe, indicating that the government would not be above improving on nature if it served the purposes of the tourist trade. By July, 1887, he had overseen the improvement of the trails to the Upper and Cave and Basin springs to the status of carriage roads capable of transporting large numbers of visitors, had improved Banff Avenue to a good standard and had provided a small log reservoir around the Upper Springs to impound water for distribution to the numerous bathhouses making application for its use. Meanwhile, the park bill had been read for the third time on May 6, 1887 and had gone to the Senate for approval, where a last minute decision to change the name of the park from "Banff" to "Rocky Mountains" was made. The Rocky Mountains Park Act received Royal assent on June 23, 1887 incorporating a dedication clause that firmly established its philosophy: "The said tract of land is hereby reserved and set apart as a public park and pleasure ground for the benefit, advantage and enjoyment of the people of Canada. . . ."

Stewart's survey of the townsite had resulted in the staking out of the ample villa lots south of the river that Macdonald saw attracting the wealthy as well as a combined commercial and residential district north of the river, laid out in the usual grid fashion and including Blocks A and B along Buffalo Street and Bow Avenue and Blocks 1 to 17 on either side of Banff Avenue bounded by Otter Street on the east and Moose Street on the north. These lots were taken up quickly, as by the end of 1887 some 180 had been applied for and there were six hotels, nine stores, two churches, a school and a post office already constructed. Stewart's own office had been moved from his tent at "Old Banff" to a log building on the 100 Block of Bear Street, which was to serve as the park's administrative headquarters until 1904. Matters of land conveyance were by this point taking up much of his time and had been confused by his actions in disposing of some lots by sale before it was clear what the government's land tenure system would be. Although only temporary receipts had been issued, it was a messy business to substitute leases for freehold and his stock with senior government officers suffered accordingly. Part of the reason for the confusion probably resulted from debate on the matter during the passage of the bill when the opposition had criticized the intention to give the Minister of the Interior authority to issue leases. They wanted a strict time limit to be fixed for any leases, preferably twenty-one years, but this was opposed by Macdonald. He felt that such restrictions would deter lessees from building substantial buildings and opening businesses and offered the view that if any terms at all were to be imposed there should be a right of renewal. Regulations which followed the passing of the act created lease terms of forty-two years with "perpetual renewal" clauses, an action that would have a major impact on land administration and Banff political matters far into the future. As for Stewart, at the end of 1887 he was finally provided with an assistant, E. A. Nash, former Dominion Land Agent at Battleford, to allow him to concentrate on other pressing matters.

Some of these concerned the Upper Hot Springs, where the government was more inclined to allow private businesses to provide the services, originally letting concessions to a number of operators at fees set by regulation. Two of them combined overnight accommodation with their bathing facilities — Whitman and McNulty and Dr. Brett, whose Grand View Villa included an oakum-chinked log pool as well as a pipe to carry hot water down to his Sanitarium Hotel. While some private development was to be allowed at the Upper Hot Springs, such was not the case at the Cave and Basin, and over the period of 1887-88 Stewart supervised the construction of the first major government facility at Banff — the upgrading of the pool and the building of necessary structures for those wishing to take the waters. This project was significant not only in that it provided clear evidence that the government regarded its role as providing amenities and attractions for tourists, but also in its architectural character. Work consisted of replacing the porous rock walls in both the cave and basin pools with masonry, including fitting them with pipes and valves to control the flow and level of water, and the erection of a bathhouse with men's and ladies' changerooms and a caretaker's residence. These buildings were designed in a "rustic" fashion, in this case constructed of local logs with a unique crossed-log and inlaid parqueted wall treatment, becoming the first public buildings to be constructed in what later became known as "the Banff style." Stewart described them as "in the Swiss style, of timber of the mountains," although they were essentially an adaptation of the already established local building tradition, the log cabin, in this case not serving their usual utilitarian residential function but rather a public use integrating European architectural images in an effort to promote tourism. This aesthetic would dominate national park design for a half-century and would be revived in more recent years to be reflected in contemporary Banff development.[8]

The rustic Cave and Basin buildings were the Canadian government's first park facility

Apart from his work on the hot springs, Stewart's attention was largely focused on the opening up of roads to provide access to the area's scenic attractions. These included the first road to Lake Minnewanka, a bridge over the Spray River and the construction of the famous Loop Drive on the river flats below the cliffs of Mount Rundle, the beginning of a road up the Spray Valley and the creation of the unique Corkscrew Drive which switchbacked its way over the shoulder of Tunnel Mountain. An extension of this, known as The King's Highway, provided Banff with a connection to the mining community of Anthracite. While Stewart was provided with sufficient funds to carry on the work of establishing this basic infrastructure to allow tourism development to take place, the tap did not stay open for very long. Within a few years, and in particular during the depression of the nineties, appropriations for new work and maintenance became rather penurious, and Stewart had to be extremely creative to keep matters on an even keel. In fact, this was to become a hallmark of the park's financial situation for generations to come — the federal government would never again open the public purse sufficiently to carry out all the work necessary to make Banff a first-rate resort, mainly relying on private enterprise to pick up the slack. The Canadian Pacific Railway, for one, was up to the challenge.

As indicated, Van Horne was keenly aware that the mountains were going to have to be treated differently than the adjoining prairies if they were to offset the tremendous costs of construction and maintenance that their geography entailed. The completion of the line in 1885 did not mean the cessation of expenditures, as much work remained to be done on ballasting the road, constructing sidings, stations and watertanks, upgrading bridges and in particular in the Mountain Section, building avalanche sheds to protect the line and the lives of passengers alike. In 1886 alone, more than half of the $6.2 million spent on upgrading was invested in the mountains between Calgary and the Pacific coast (including seventeen-and-a-half million board feet of sawn and hewn timbers) and by 1888 the section could boast fifty-three avalanche sheds and associated glance-works. Several steep grades were also a feature of the section, the most notable being the Big Hill near Field where the line descended the Kicking Horse at a grade of 4.4%, twice the usual maximum and requiring the building of escape tracks at key locations to stop runaway locomotives. It was mainly as a result of these grades and their operational difficulties that the CPR first became involved in the tourist business.

Van Horne prided himself that the CPR operated as high a calibre of passenger equipment as any North American road, including its ornate and distinctive dining cars which, it was claimed, "excel in elegance of design and furniture and quality of food and attendance anything hitherto offered to transcontinental travellers." Dining car meals were available at seventy-five cents during the first years of transcontinental service, putting them beyond the means of many passengers, and it became usual for privately-operated restaurants to spring up at divisional points where travellers could get a quick meal while the locomotive was being watered or fuelled. In the Mountain Section, the pulling of the heavy dining cars over the steep grades was uneconomical, and the company decided to build its own dining service rest-stops at key locations. Work on three such stops began in 1886 — Mount Stephen House at Field in the Kicking Horse Valley, Glacier House at the foot of the Illecillewaet Glacier near Rogers Pass, and Fraser Canyon House at North Bend — all designed by English architect Thomas Sorby with some assistance, it was said, from Van Horne himself. All of the buildings had a three-storey centre portion adjoined by one and two-storey wings, and were finished with clapboard and ornamental carving under the eaves and windows to give them a Swiss appearance. This adaptation of the Swiss aesthetic, utilized much as the federal government was doing at Banff, was to become part of the CPR's "Swiss" or "Canadian Alps" advertising campaign soon to be launched to good effect on the touring public. To accommodate those travelling the line who might like to stop off for a day or two at these glorious locations, each of the dining stops incorporated six or seven guest rooms, giving birth to the CPR hotel system.

These modest hotel initiatives paled in comparison with Van Horne's plans to reap the rewards of the hot springs at Banff for the company. There, on a promontory overlooking the Bow Valley with a view to the distant Fairholme Range, reportedly shown to him by Tom Wilson, he decided to build what he later called the "Finest Hotel on the North American Continent." While the previous railway dining-stops had been largely utilitarian affairs, the Banff Springs Hotel was to be just the opposite, meant to provide the best in accommodation and the epitome of service to the most discriminating traveller. New York architect Bruce Price, who had already designed the CPR's Windsor Station headquarters in Montreal, was commissioned to design a building marrying Van Horne's desire for luxury with the mountain surroundings, and chose for his inspiration the sixteenth-century chateaux of the Loire Valley, thereby establishing a second important architectural tradition in the Banff-Bow Valley. Price reportedly had "the entire resources of the Canadian Pacific Railway to draw upon" for his project, meaning that he had no real financial strictures and "could

Van Horne's Banff Springs Hotel was designed to provide the epitome of luxury in the wilderness for the discriminating Victorian tourist

build with certain materials in certain ways."

Work on the foundations began in the winter of 1886-87 and in the latter year General Superintendent William Whyte carried Price's completed plans from Montreal to Banff, stopping off in Winnipeg long enough to give a newspaper interview appearing under the title "The Great Hotel: A few facts About the Mammouth Building Being Erected at Banff:"

The hotel, which will be built by the company, the work being done under the supervision of their own officials, is to be a mammouth affair, and is to contain 250 beds. It is to be constructed entirely of timber, three stories in height with a dormer in the roof, and basement excavated in rock; it will be in two main wings, the front being the largest, and this will contain a rotunda, rising to the height of the building, and an eleva-

tor. The rear wing will be devoted mainly to the commissariat and domestic apartments. The hotel will have its own gas and water works, and also be supplied with electric lights and electric appliances.[9]

Despite the plan, when Van Horne arrived to view progress in the summer of 1887 he was horrified to find that it had been turned 180 degrees so that the kitchen would have the benefit of the magnificent view of the Bow Valley while the rotunda would face the more prosaic slopes of Sulphur Mountain. Employing his own not inconsiderable sketching talents, he immediately drew out a new rotunda pavilion to be attached to the kitchen, saving the view for the guests rather than the scullery maids. When completed, the edifice consisted of two frame wings, each four-storeys high with the top storey being contained within a dormered roof, and Van Horne's pavilion jutting out towards the river. Interior finishing and woodworking on the octagonal-shaped lobby overhung by ranks of balconies, dining rooms, parlours, smoking rooms and, for the gentlemen only, the billiard room and bar, were carried out over the winter of 1887-88. By early summer the Banff Springs was ready for its official opening, reportedly costing the huge sum of a quarter-of-a-million dollars and with rooms being offered for $3.50 and upwards a day. That summer, the hotel quickly became the showpiece of the fledgling town of Banff and so began the trend of the town growing up in the hotel's social and financial shadow.

Van Horne had ideas other than merely impressing the locals with his handiwork as the Banff Springs was to form the centrepiece of a promotional program that would bring the Rockies to the world and vice versa. Indeed, it was to become an important cog in the wheel of the CPR's grander vision of being the key player in the dream of an all-British route to the Orient. Company president George Stephen had from the beginning of his involvement with the CPR seen it linked with ocean steamship service to connect with Japan and Hong Kong. The company had become involved with steamship service on the Great Lakes as early as 1883 and in 1887 it chartered its first steamship, *Abyssinia*, to carry cargo and passengers from Hong Kong and Yokohama to

Vancouver, arriving at Port Moody just three weeks after the inaugural passenger train arrived from the East at the same point. This was just the first step towards the company developing its own steamship service as part of the all-British route with many interesting stops along the way, and it launched its international advertising campaign with Banff and the Bow Valley playing an important role in attracting the travelling public's interest.

Recruiting passengers in North America was the responsibility of the Passenger Traffic Department. It was headed by a passenger traffic manager assisted by a general passenger agent, both headquartered in Montreal, and a freight and passenger agent, positioned in Winnipeg. By 1889, the CPR also had twelve travelling passenger agents, half of them working with agents representing the company's interests in the United States. Passenger traffic business in Great Britain and on the Continent was initially handled by the CPR Emigration Department and later by the European traffic agent headquartered in London. Van Horne himself took a direct role in providing these agencies with promotional material to attract potential tourists, including the design and production of posters and the writing and illustrating of pamphlets and brochures. He understood that it would be the natural landscapes of Canada that would seize the attention of the travelling public and so made sure that the written material was well-illustrated with renditions of the country's greatest natural treasures. This desire placed the Banff-Bow Valley front and centre and, among other benefits, helped to spur the beginning of an artistic tradition in the country, often described as the "railway school" of art and artists. Details of this artistic tradition's influence on the Valley's cultural development can be found elsewhere in this work, but suffice it to say here that the artistic renderings of mountain scenery were exploited in major expositions and artistic exhibitions that were popular at the time and were reproduced with great fidelity as engravings in tourist literature.

Van Horne had begun working on a high-quality, tourist-oriented pamphlet in 1884 before the line was completed but did not have the illustrative material he wanted available from photographers and artists until 1887. The text of the pamphlet, *The Canadian Pacific, The New Highway to the East Across the Mountains, Prairies & Rivers of Canada*, was either prepared or directly edited by himself, and it began with a sport-and-scenery pitch which illustrates the role the mountains were to play:

May I not tempt you, kind reader, to leave England for a few short weeks and journey with me across that broad land, the beauties and glories of which have only now been brought within our reach? There will be no hardships to endure, no difficulties to overcome, and no dangers or annoyances whatever. You shall see mighty rivers, vast forests, boundless plains, stupendous mountains and wonders innumerable; and you shall see all in comfort, nay in luxury. If you are a jaded tourist, sick of Old World scenes and smells, you will find everything fresh and novel. If you are a sportsman, you will meet with unlimited opportunities and endless variety, and no one shall deny you your right to hunt or fish at your sweet will. If you are a mountain climber, you shall have cliffs and peaks and glaciers worthy of your alpenstock, and if you have lived in India, and tiger hunting has lost its zest, a Rocky Mountain grizzly bear may renew your interest in life.[10]

The pamphlet went on to describe the delights a traveller would find at various points on his rail journey across Canada, but assumed that their main intention was to see the mountains: "But you are impatient to see the mountains, and if you will permit me to choose, dear reader, we will start from Montreal by the main line of the railway, and in order that we may miss nothing we will return by the great lakes, and see Toronto and the Falls of Niagara then." Its illustrations also focused primarily on the wonders of the west and in particular the Rockies, with engravings made from photographs by the day's leading photographers, William Notman and Sons, whom he had sent west in the company's interests with a private photographic car in 1884. Engravings entitled "Mountains at Canmore," "Silver City and Castle Mountain," and "Kicking Horse Valley Looking East" were reproduced from some of the photographic images taken at this time.

The New Highway to the East was just the first of numerous broadsides pitching Canada and the mountains to tourists. Specialty companion pieces such as *Fishing and Shooting On The Canadian Pacific Railway* accompanied it (warning sportsmen that "the pursuit of what is generally dubbed by the craft 'big game' in the mountain wilds of Canada is no child's play") and Van Horne supplied photographs, etchings and other material to the privately-printed accounts of railway travel by well-connected individuals that were popular at the time. Similar materials were utilized for newspaper articles and for lengthy descriptions in the illustrated journals of the day, such as *The Illustrated London News*. The work of the day's noted artists, such as John Fraser, who was also sent west to gain material in the field, was likewise rendered into illustrative material and was displayed at the frequent international expositions of the times.

With the federal government building the infrastructure necessary to support the tourist trade and the CPR providing the carrot to attract tourists, the means for them to reach the mountains and the comforts and diversions they were seeking once they arrived, most of the elements needed for Banff and the Bow Valley to prosper were in place. Other requirements were provided by independent businessmen, some of whom also worked out beneficial arrangements with the CPR. Typical of them were Colonel James Walker of Calgary, Major John Stewart of Ottawa, and W. L Mathews, manager of the Banff Springs, who contracted as the CPR Transfer Company in 1893 to provide the necessary buggies, carriages and stages to convey guests between the station and hotel and to carry them over the growing web of sightseeing roads in Banff's vicinity. John Brewster, who came from Winnipeg in 1886 to join his brother who was working on building the Cave and Basin bathhouse, obtained the lease to a property at the corner of Moose Street and Banff Avenue (today's Traveller's Inn) and began a small dairy to provide milk to the Banff Springs and for domestic needs. Dr. Brett's brother-in-law, Raymond Montague Rooper, acquired a boat livery and rental service from J. J. Ryan, first run from the original floating bridge and then from a tent and rough dock at the near-by bend of the Bow, allowing CPR guests to view the beauties of the Bow from his small steamer, *The Mountain Belle.* Ryan went on with a partner, W. H. Disbrowe, to operate a steam launch and provide fish guiding services at Lake Minnewanka for the more adventuresome. Smaller independent businessmen also provided other tourist amenities and joined Dr. Brett in supplying more value-oriented accommodation in Banff's downtown area, including Leonard Fulmer's combined store and post office on the site of today's King Edward Hotel, the Hull and Trounce butcher shop at the corner of Buffalo Street and Banff Avenue, the Moulton Park Hotel located in today's central park area and the National Park Hotel on the site of today's Cascade Hotel. Law-and-order was provided by Inspector Constantine and Sergeant Fury of the North West Mounted Police from a log headquarters established out on what was referred to as Station Road (the 400 block of today's Banff Avenue) and school was first held in Superintendent Stewart's headquarters on Bear Street in 1887 and in a new building located on today's high school grounds beginning in 1888.

Given that the late-Victorian era was one where accounts of travel were highly popular, the reaction of the travelling public to the new "public park and pleasure ground" was well-documented. Impressions of the village itself came from several observers, including Englishman Stuart Cumberland who noted in his 1887 book *The Queen's Highway from Ocean to Ocean* that while it was comprised of "a few log huts" it had the potential to become an attractive community set in "a romantic glen." Countryman Henry Barneby concurred in his 1888 publication *The New Far West*, recounting that "there was more bustle going on in erecting houses than in any other place I had seen along the line," and that while as yet there were more tents than houses, "the preparations everywhere showed that in another year's time all this would be changed." The Banff Springs Hotel brought delight to tourists seeking the sybaritic pleasures of the wealthy, the well-travelled Londoner Mrs. E. H. Carbutt noting in her 1889 memoir *Five Months' Fine Weather in Canada, Western U. S. and Mexico* that "when this delicious place is better known, it will become the Switzerland of America." Canadian Charles Wood in 1890 marvelled at the vista from the hotel, finding it so moving that it "is beyond my power to describe," and at its price tag, reporting "the hotel cost an immense amount of money, some $200,000 I was told, and is certainly a model of perfection in every respect."

The hot springs were visited by virtually every tourist, and the improvements made by the government were commented on favourably by many. Most were also convinced of the healing powers that were heavily promoted to prospective users. An acerbic Englishman, Edward Roper, in his 1891 journal *By Track and Trail: A Journey Across Canada*, despite many criticisms of Banff, found that the government's claims about the springs were accurate, stating "that the curative effects of these hot springs are not mythical is clear. We talked to many patients up there, who were enthusiastic in praise of the good they had received from the use of the waters." Henry Barneby noted a sign at the Cave and Basin that became famous and was "such a natural and primitive one that no one could object to it. Some poor person who had sought a cure and found it here, had hung up his crutch with this inscription, 'The man who used this crutch is cured, and gone home'." Perhaps the overall joy that a visit to Banff could elicit was best described by an American tourist, W. H. H. Murray, in his 1888 account *Daylight Land* wherein he waxed poetic on its delights:

We never enjoyed a happier week than we spent at Banff. We rolled leisurely over the fine roads that the government had constructed, winking in and out along the bends of the Bow River, running along the base of the gigantic mountains and through the cool forests of the firs. We explored, with the curiosity and eagerness of boys, the secluded places, and followed the dim by-paths, not knowing or caring whither they led us, happy, whether they conducted us to some noble prospect or terminated suddenly at some dripping ledge. We searched for curious minerals in the sides of the mountains, translated the geological records of the cliffs, and collected polished pebbles from the bed of the foaming Spray. We slept to noonday under the pines, lulled to sleep by the Falls of the

Bow, and fished, not in vain, for its noted trout in the rapids. . . . We admired the ample design of the commodious house, — a veritable palace, with interior finish of native woods polished to a gleam; its wide stairways and galleries; the noble dining-room, with its lofty ceiling, which the Judge pronounced "fit to be a banquet-hall for the gods; . . .[11]

It is not known with certainty how many tourists arrived in Banff in the early park period, as the government kept only hotel statistics. The best available indicator would be the guests registered at the Banff Springs Hotel, who numbered 1,503 in its first operating season between June and October, 1888, and had grown to 3,389 in 1891, when the effects of a worldwide depression began to be felt. Initially 53% of these guests were from Canada, while 26% were from the United States, 19% were from Great Britain and 2% were from other countries. By 1891, however, the statistics for country of origin had changed dramatically as a result of improved rail connections between the United States and Canada, with 56% being American and 25% Canadian, a trend that was to remain in place for many years While the 1890s would be difficult for the tourist business everywhere, the twin requirements of infrastructure and services had been well established, mainly through the efforts of the federal government and the CPR, and the Valley was poised for a remarkable and sustained period of growth beginning in the new century.

Chapter Seven
This Way to the Stars

As the development of tourism got underway in the Banff-Bow Valley with the provision of attractions such as "taking the waters" at the Upper Hot Springs and Cave and Basin or facilities such as the Banff Springs Hotel, most visitors were seeking the "luxury in the wilderness" the CPR was promoting. However, very quickly another, more adventurous breed of tourist began to make their presence felt as the "Canadian Alps" were discovered by the growing international mountaineering fraternity that had become an emerging feature of the late-Victorian period. The fact that literally hundreds of unclimbed peaks lay within reach of the CPR line soon became known to adventurers who were already becoming satiated with the busy European Alps. These men, and a few women, would undertake the challenge of detailed exploration of the wilderness at a different altitude than those who had come before them. While early travellers such as Thompson, Rundle, Douglas and Hector had made a few climbs, mainly to get an impression of the landscape, these latter-day explorers were motivated by sport, scientific discovery and the exhilaration and social distinction that came from doing great things in high places — in particular first ascents. With the trumpeting of their feats in publications and in lectures to outdoor and scientific groups interested in exploration, the Canadian Rockies became an attraction to a broader public. And with them began the alpine tradition in the Valley that would become one of the most distinctive aspects of its heritage.

Actually, by the time the forerunners of these alpinists descended on the mountains along the railroad, many of the peaks they might have been interested in bagging had already been scaled. This was due to the same government policy that had led to the geological and timber surveys of the mountains in the early 1880s now being extended to topographical surveys. The Technical Branch of the Department of the Interior was charged with carrying out the government's Dominion Land Surveys (DLS) program in the North West Territories and along the Railway Belt that extended twenty miles on either side of the CPR line through British Columbia. Under the direction of Surveyor-General Edouard G. Deville, a handful of DLS surveyors were given the task of surveying the mountains between the Gap and the Pacific coast employing the same grid-based township system that had been used on the prairies. This led to the adoption of a new form of surveying in Canada using cameras as a tool, known as photo-topographical surveying or photogrammetry, which eliminated the almost impossible task of applying the normal flat land transit and theodolite method to rugged mountain terrain. The technique was perhaps best described by A. O. Wheeler, who utilized it during his long career as a DLS surveyor in the mountains:

The photographs are perspectives from which, by the inverse rules of perspective, the visible line or points defining the topographical features, therein seen, may be projected on a ground plan. It is necessary that the features to be mapped be seen in, at least, two views taken from some distance apart and of which the position and elevation above a given datum, generally sea-level, have been ascertained. A topographical map usually consists of contour lines, which represent the projection on the plan of imaginary lines following the inequalities of the surface at given intervals of altitude. A sufficient number of points are determined from the photographs to enable an accurate delineation, within the scale of the map, to be made upon the plan.[1]

The requirement to secure these photographs from camera stations on the summits of mountains whose altitude could be determined by triangulation meant that during the years from 1886 to 1892 several hundred peaks along the line were climbed, often under dangerous conditions, by men doing it all in a day's work.

The surveyors most closely associated with the Valley were W. S. Drewry and, in particular, James J. McArthur, who left his name attached to a number of geographic features including McArthur Pass, McArthur Creek and McArthur Lake near Lake O'Hara and Mount Aylmer, after his home at Aylmer, Quebec, on the shore of Lake Minnewanka. First commissioned as a DLS surveyor in 1879, in 1886 he was, according to Deville, "employed as topographer, and mapped the country on both sides of the railway from Canmore to Revelstoke." In the typical understated fashion of government reports, McArthur described his initial work in the Valley as follows:

I left Ottawa on the 3rd of May and began work at Canmore on the 13th. The first ascents were attended with considerable labor and discomfort, not to speak of danger, as there was still a great quantity of snow in the mountains, and snow slides were a frequent occurrence. The continual low temperature, strong winds and flurries of snow rendered sketching and reading an instrument rather difficult work at times. . . .

The first ascent was up the mountain on the north side of the valley and directly behind Canmore Station. The Bow River flows at the base of this mountain in a valley one to two miles wide, and on the opposite side appear the Rundle Mountains, which are snow-capped and very perpendicular. To the south there are three strongly defined peaks called the Three Sisters, and up the valley, about a dozen of miles or so, stands the Cascade Mountain. On this mountain I located one of my stations, and from here is to be had one of the finest and most extensive views in the Rocky Mountains, embracing the Bow River and the Cascade, Spray and Simpson Passes. . . .

Between Castle Mountain Station and the Slate Mountains I was not required to do any work and therefore moved to Laggan where I was instructed to fill in the topography of the country to the north of the railway. Owing to the character of the mountains on the south side of the valley and the great quantity of snow still resting on the rocky slopes, I was compelled to establish my stations on the Slate Mountains to the north. South from these stations are numbers of large mountains having glaciers, and to the north-west Mount Hector stands out alongside the pass to the North Suskatchewan.[2]

A. O. Wheeler, DLS, carrying out a photogrammetrical survey

The downplaying of the extent of his labours became typical of McArthur's subsequent reports. In describing his work in 1887 he stated that "we never occupied more than one day in making any one ascent this season, although this entailed an almost continual strain upon us during from twelve to eighteen hours. . . ." Similarly, in 1890 he summed up the season with "my work of this year covers more than 400 square miles . . . . I occupied 13 triangulations and 20 camera stations, which, with the setting of signals, involved the climbing of 38 mountains ranging from 7,000 to over 10,000 above the sea."

By the time any prospective alpinist might have been led to McArthur's reports, there were more mainstream descriptions available emanating from the first mountaineers to arrive in the Rockies and Selkirks in the late-eighties and early-nineties. The impetus for this traced its roots back to 1884 when a number of scientists and academics attending the meeting in Toronto of the British Association for the Advancement of Science took an excursion to the end-of-steel in the Kicking Horse Pass. One of those participating was the Reverend Henry Swanzy, and accompanied by Richard Barrington, an accomplished British climber, he carried on over the surveyed line in an arduous seventeen-day journey through the Selkirks and Gold Range before arriving at Kamloops and rejoining the railway. One of those to whom he related his adventure was his cousin, the Reverend William Spotswood Green, who was so entranced by the story that he convinced Swanzy to accompany him on a further exploration of the Rogers Pass area for six weeks in the summer of 1888. By that time the CPR's new hostelry, Glacier House, was conveniently located at the foot of the Illecillewaet Glacier in the very heart of the country the pair wished to examine, and it became the headquarters for their work. As was expected of all English gentlemen exploring in the colonies, this work was to include something useful, in this case a botanical and geological examination as well as a plane table survey for purposes of drawing a walking and climbing map of the Rogers Pass area. Their ascents in carrying out this task included Mounts Bonney and Abbott as well as several lesser peaks, and while not up to the standard of some of the work being carried out by the DLS surveyors, did provide the inspiration for Green's subsequent classic Victorian adventure account *Among the Selkirk Glaciers*, published in 1890. The influence of this publication on those wishing to emulate these feats was attested to by American mountaineer Walter Wilcox's report that upon stopping at Glacier House in 1891 he found a group of enthusiasts "who were accustomed to gather every evening around a blazing fire and read selections from Green's *Among The Selkirk Glaciers* just as our forefathers were wont to read a daily chapter from the Bible."[3]

Wilcox, at the time a prep student bound for Yale University, would soon add to that trend himself, as he was to become one of the most assiduous explorers of the alpine as well as a deft photographer and writer, publishing his seminal *Camping in the Canadian Rockies* in 1896. While the earliest mountaineering exploits took place in the Selkirks in the vicinity of Glacier House, he would find the area too confining because of the dense forests and lack of trails, which "soon made me transfer my affections to the Main Range, E. of the Columbia, where there were more open forests and even these made easier by Indian trails." His gaze would fall upon those interesting, glaciated peaks around Lake

Louise seen by McArthur from his vantage on the Slate Range in 1886, and since that time made more accessible by a trail to the lake and "a log hut on the lake shore" managed for the CPR by Willoughby Astley. Wilcox's examination of the area convinced him of its desirability for alpine pursuits on Mounts Temple, Lefroy and Victoria (at the time known as Mount Green), a feeling that was shared by another Yale student, Samuel E. S. Allen, who similarly visited it in 1891 on his way home from climbing in the Sierras of California. Allen spent the summer of 1892 in Switzerland, where he climbed the Matterhorn, but in 1893 he and Wilcox, obviously having met at Yale and discussed their shared discovery, decided to team up for an exploration of the Lake Louise area. They spent that summer camped on the shore of the lake, the original lodge having burned down, and though ill-equipped launched attempts to scale both Mounts Victoria and Temple. Two assaults on Victoria failed, but one of them led to an important discovery. While approaching its base, the climbers witnessed avalanches falling from the upper Victoria Glacier into a narrow col connecting Victoria with Mount Lefroy. Allen correctly surmised that this col was the key to successful ascents of both peaks and provided it with an ominous name — the Death Trap.

One further attempted climb of Temple was also mounted, the approach being by way of skirting around the southern shoulder of the mountain and camping out overnight at 7,000 feet beside what became known as Temple Lake. At four o'clock the next morning Wilcox and Allen pushed off in the gloom of the early dawn with the intention of traversing until they reached the southeast shoulder, which appeared to provide a route to the summit. But the way was anything but simple and led Wilcox to cogitate on the darker side of nature that climbing could sometimes bring into sharp relief:

By eleven o'clock we had reached an altitude of nearly 10,000 feet without meeting with any very great difficulty, but here we came suddenly to a vertical wall of rock about 400 feet high and actually leaning over in many places, a barrier that completely defeated us, as the wall extended beyond our view and offered no prospect of giving out. At the base of this cliff was a steep, narrow slope of loose, broken limestone, and then another precipice below. Along this dangerous pathway we continued for some distance, keeping close to the base of the cliff. The loose stones, set in motion by our feet, slid down and rolled over the precipice, where we could hear them grinding to powder on the cliffs below.

Never in my life have I been so much impressed with the stern and desolate side of nature. The air was bitter cold and had the frosty ozone odor of winter. A strong wind rushed constantly by us, and, as it swept up the gorges of the precipice above, and over the countless projections of the cliffs, made a noise like the hoarse murmur of wind in a ship's rigging, or the blast of some great furnace. To the south and east, range beyond range of bare, saw-edged mountains raised their cold, sharp summits up to a cloudy sky, where the strong wind drove threatening clouds in long trains of dark and lighter vapors. The intervening valleys, destitute of vegetation or any green thing, were filled with glaciers and vast heaps of moraine, and the slides of debris from the adjacent mountain side. All was desolate, gloomy, cold and monotonous in color. . . .

Overcome with the terror of this lonely place and the hopelessness of further attempts to reach the summit, where a snow-storm was now raging, we turned back.[4]

Inspired by this chilling view, Wilcox would name the defile they had been looking into Desolation Valley, but Allen would provide the more euphonious name of *Wenkchemna,* signifying the Stoney numeral "ten" for that number of great peaks it harboured, to which he also applied Indian numerals. In 1899 in much more agreeable conditions, Wilcox would pay a visit to the shores of the lake they had seen three thousand feet below from their aerie and would name it Moraine Lake on the assumption that the massive debris pile damming its outlet was formed by a glacial moraine.[5] The Valley of the Ten Peaks, as it would become known, was destined to become a Banff-Bow Valley tourist attraction ranking second only to Lake Louise itself.

Their lack of success in 1893 only whetted Wilcox's and Allen's appetites for what would become some serious mountaineering and exploration of the region in the years ahead. However, they were not the only mountaineers active in the Rockies by that time. Knowledge of the area opened up by the CPR had spread both quickly and widely and several other adventurers had heard the clarion call. Apart from the attraction provided by the superb alpine peaks of the Lake Louise region, there were two other beacons that would attract their attention. One was Mount Assiniboine, the peak that mirrored the epitome of mountain forms represented by the wedge-shaped Matterhorn, lying to the south of Banff, and the other was Mounts Brown and Hooker, the legendary sentinels of Athabasca Pass, lying far to the north of Lake Louise. Their mysteries and unconquered summits would soon account for many other mountaineering parties taking to the field out of Banff and Laggan.

Mount Assiniboine, although having seemingly been viewed by de Smet, was first positively reported on by Dawson, who saw it during his geological survey work and named it for the plains tribe of whom the Stoneys were a branch. McArthur and other topographic surveyors also viewed it and determined its exact location, and accounts at the time held that it was the highest mountain between the International Boundary and Mounts Hooker and Brown. Into this situation came Chicago paper manufacturer Robert L. Barrett in August, 1893 looking for a high peak upon which to test his mountaineering skills. L. O. Armstrong, CPR land commissioner, directed him to Tom Wilson, already recognized as the man having the most knowledge of the Rockies and the ability to get those of Barrett's ilk to the location of their climbs. Wilson, who had himself seen Assiniboine while with W. S. Drewry's topographic survey party near Simpson Pass in 1889, recommended it and by early September was guiding Barrett by that route to its foot. While trails were virtually non-existent on the other side of Simpson Pass, they managed to cut their way through and pioneer the route through to the Simpson River and up it to Assiniboine's foot. However, after a reconnaissance of the great peak from its heavily timbered ridges and an exploration of the beautiful lakes laying at its base, it was determined that the

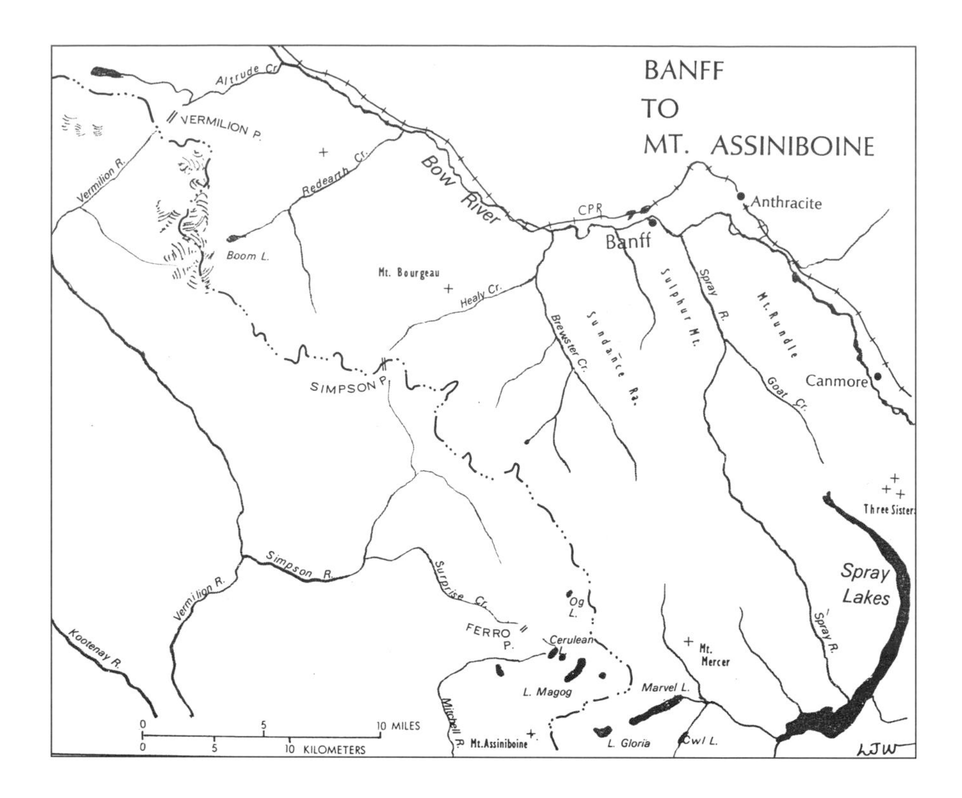

season was too late and the mountain in too bad a condition to launch an assault, and the party returned to Banff by way of the Simpson River and Vermilion Pass. Nonetheless, Barrett was impressed with what he saw, stating in a letter to Wilson written many years later from a camp in the Himalayas that "I don't think even old K2, the 28,000, looked to me as high and imposing as old Assiniboine when you and I finally won through to where we could have a good look at him."[6] When he reported on his unsuccessful but exciting outing on returning to Banff, a new lodestar was presented to the alpine world.

Meanwhile, an older one was attracting its share of attention. University of Toronto geology professor A. P. Coleman had begun visiting his brother's ranch at Morley in 1884 and had used it as a headquarters to explore the Columbia River in search of the famous giants of Athabasca Pass. Coleman stated his inspiration in his book *The Canadian Rockies, New and Old Trails* written a number of years later: "No one will wonder, therefore, that when I studied the atlas and saw Mount Brown and Hooker, the highest points in the Rockies, standing one on each side of Athabasca Pass, I longed to visit them." In 1884 and 1888 he had approached Boat Encampment by water, but in 1892 decided to try to reach Athabasca Pass overland from Morley. Together with his brother Lucius and L. Q. Stewart, a professor of surveying at Toronto, they succeeded in making an extended overland trip along the foothills and into the Main Ranges by way of Brazeau Lake, Poboktan Pass and eventually onto the headwaters of the Sunwapta and Athabasca. Hiking up a stream they thought might be the Whirlpool, they soon realized that they were on the wrong watercourse, but became the first to report on the rugged Fortress Lake area. This ended their exploration for the year, but in 1893 they were back and succeeded in finding the correct approach to the pass. However, when they reached its summit there was no sign of Douglas's great peaks. Members of the party ascended the one that Douglas had described as Mount Brown and found it to be only some 9,000 feet. Coleman could not hide his disappointment:

We looked in vain for the magnificent summits rising ten thousand feet above the pass, one on each side. Instead, we saw commonplace mountains with nothing distinguished in their appearance, undoubtedly lower than half a dozen peaks we had climbed as incidents along the way for the fun of things, or as lookout points to choose our route. . . .

We had reached our point after six weeks of toil and anxiety, after three summers of effort, and we did not even raise a cheer. Mount Brown and Mount Hooker were frauds, and we were disgusted at having being humbugged by them.[7]

While the reports of a trained geologist and a surveying instructor should have been sufficient evidence to deflate the legend, there were other mountaineers who would come to believe that Coleman was mistaken and the giants of Athabasca Pass would remain an object of their desire for further expeditions to the environs of the pass in the years ahead.

With three drawing cards bringing alpinists to the Valley to climb or begin their expeditions, the years around the turn-of-the-century were busy ones on the mountains. It would be the Lake Louise region that continued to receive the most attention and, indeed, soon even world-wide notoriety, due to Canada's first mountaineering fatality. Wilcox's and Allen's outings in the area continued in 1894 accompanied by several of their Yale classmates, and they were successful in the first ascent of Mount Temple. Upon their return to the chalet, they met Professor Charles E. Fay, a professor of modern languages at Tuft's College in Massachusetts who had made his first of what would be over a quarter-century of visits to the mountains in 1890. Fay was unable to accept an invitation to join them in further climbs, but immediately began to lay plans for a visit by Boston's Appalachian Mountain Club, of which he was a leading member, to the region the following summer. The majority of the club members who came in 1895 were women, but among them were also some of America's leading climbers. Philip Stanley Abbot, a railway company lawyer who had accomplished many notable climbs during his college years at Harvard including ascents in Alaska, Mexico and the Swiss Alps, was perhaps the most celebrated. Along with Fay and Charles S. Thompson, the best mountaineers in the group, he intended on doing some serious climbing. A preliminary expedition was mounted northwards to Mount Hector, whose ascent they found rather easy, and was followed by sojourns at Field, where they climbed Mount Stephen, and at Glacier, where Mounts Abbott and Castor fell to their ice axes. But their main goal was the first ascent of Mount Lefroy at Lake Louise, and in this case success eluded them due to poor weather, making Abbot even more determined to capture its summit the following year.

On August 3, 1896 a team composed of Abbot, Fay, Thompson and a fourth Appalachian Club member, Professor George T. Little, set out by boat for the far end of the lake about 6:15 a.m. At 6:45 they began the actual climb, reaching the bottom of the Death Trap col at 8:40 and roping up for the most dangerous part of the ascent, where avalanches from the Victoria Glacier regularly funneled down. In forty minutes they scrambled up the 900 feet to the top of the col, from which Abbot scanned the western side of Lefroy and seeing a promising route joyfully exclaimed "the peak is ours." All agreed, and the labourious task of cutting steps in the ice or warily climbing unstable rock slopes began, occupying them for the next four-and-a-half hours until they reached a seventy-five foot bastion near the summit which called for a decision. All possible routes around it appeared dangerous and time-consuming, which given the lateness of the hour might force the party to bivouac on the mountain. This moment, perhaps one of the most important in the history of Canadian mountaineering, was graphically described by Fay in a memorial to Abbot:

But now Mr. Abbot, who had moved forward along the rock wall to the limit of the rope, cheerfully announced an alternative. His view beyond the angle in the bastion revealed a vertical cleft up which it was possible to climb by such holds as offered themselves. Bidding Thompson and me to unrope and keep under cover from falling stones, he clambered some thirty feet up the rift, secured a good anchorage, and called upon Professor Little to follow. This the latter proceeded to do, but while standing at the bottom of the cleft preparing to climb, he received a tingling blow from a small stone dislodged by the rope. A moment later a larger one falling upon the rope half-severed it, so as to require a knot. As danger from this source seemed likely to continue, our leader had Little also free himself from the rope and come up to where he stood. From here a shelf led around to the left, along which Abbot now proceeded a few yards and discovered a gully leading upward, unseen from the point first attained, and this also he began to ascend. To Mr. Little's question, whether it might not be better to try turn the bastion on the shelf itself, he replied: "I think not. I have a good lead here."

These were the last words he ever uttered. A moment later Little, whose attention was for the moment diverted to another portion of the crag, was conscious that something had fallen swiftly past him and knew only too well what it must be. Thompson and I, standing at the base of the cliff, saw our dear friend falling backward and head-foremost, saw him strike the upper margin of the ice slope within fifteen feet of us, turn completely over and instantly begin rolling down its steep incline. . . .[8]

It took three hours for the shaken climbers to reach Abbot's limp body some nine hundred feet below, and to their amazement they found he was still breathing. But as they attempted to carry him down, it became evident he had succumbed, and as night was now coming on they prepared to spend the next dreadful hours guarding his remains. Early in the morning they made their way to the chalet in pouring rain and reported the accident, but the weather had turned so poor that it took a hastily-assembled recovery party of Manager Astley, Tom Wilson, Fay, Little and some railway workers until August 8th to bear Abbot's body to the chalet.

For all its pathos, the story of Abbot's death had an important effect on Canadian Rockies mountaineering. In writing of it, Professor Fay concluded "it occurs at the very dawn of a new era of genuine alpine climbing, for the extension of which among our young countrymen Abbot was so earnest an advocate" and went on to argue that with respect to climbing that "we maintain that the gain therefrom for the general and the individual life in an age of growing carefulness for ease and luxury must be held to outweigh the deplorable losses, and that this casualty should not call a halt in American alpinism."[9] Apparently many agreed, for rather than discouraging alpinists who heard of it — and there were many as the newspapers and journals spread the story far and wide — it seemed to have exactly the opposite effect. Mountaineering interest in Mount Lefroy and the Rockies was redoubled, and new climbers, particularly from overseas, would be attracted to the Valley as a result. The following year an Anglo-American party was put together to climb the peak on the anniversary of the accident, a result of an invitation by Abbot's father to his son's friend Harold B. Dixon of the Alpine Club (London) to participate. Dixon also extended the invitation to two of his clubmates, J. Norman Collie, a climber with a growing reputation for his work in the Alps and the Himalayas, and George P. Baker.

Dixon arrived from England with Peter Sarbach, a Swiss guide

Mount Lefroy first ascent party, August 7, 1897 including Charles Fay (second left), H. B. Dixon (seated), J. N. Collie (third right), Charles S. Thompson (second right) and Swiss guide Peter Sarbach (right)

with whom he and Abbot had climbed in the Alps, and met with the Appalachian Club representatives, including Fay, Arthur Michael, Herschel C. Parker, Rev. Charles L. Noyes, and J. R. Vanderlip, at Glacier House for a week of warming up and planning the ascent of Lefroy. The route was discussed in great detail and when Collie arrived the entourage moved on to Field to meet Charles Thompson and then to Lake Louise to launch their attempt. It went off without a hitch, the beginning being made very early at 2:40 a.m., the top of the Death Trap, now renamed Abbot Pass, being made in five hours, and then from there three separate roped parties proceeding to the summit by 11:00 a.m. Two days later Collie, Fay, Michael and Sarbach made the first ascent of Mount Green and renamed it Mount Victoria. On August

7th, the group was joined by George Baker and set off to the north with a plan of tracking down Mount Balfour, a large peak they had seen from the top of Lefroy. Making their way by packtrain to Bow Lake, they approached the mountain over the Wapta Icefield and ascended what they took to be the peak, discovering on reaching the summit of what they subsequently named Mount Gordon that Balfour still lay some distance away. While unsuccessful, this ascent allowed the party to see two fine peaks to the northward which they named Mounts Mummery and Mount Forbes, spurring further explorations by Collie and Baker and, despite Coleman's debunking, getting them thinking about the highest of all mountains reputed to lie in that direction, Hooker and Brown. However, their search for the giants would lead in 1898 to a discovery of far more importance — the Columbia Icefield.

Another offshoot of the Abbot tragedy that would play an important part in the Valley's future was the influence it had on the introduction of Swiss guides to the mountains along the CPR line. Peter Sarbach's sojourn with Collie and company in 1897 showed the value of trained mountain guides in the Rockies, and by that time CPR management was already beginning to receive suggestions for their use from others. One, a Doctor J. H. Stallard who taught at the Medical School of the University of California, wrote to the CPR's passenger traffic manager, David McNicoll, and noted that "a great defect of the district is the almost complete absence of qualified guides," and went on to state "I would rather trust a Swiss guide on a mountain he had never seen than any man I saw in the Rockies who had been there half his life." This situation, he believed, had been partly to blame for Abbot's death and admonished that "if the party had been conducted by a competent Swiss guide, the death of Mr. Abbot would not have occurred. . ."[9] It took some time for the company to react, but after witnessing Sarbach's exploits in 1897 a letter was sent to the CPR office in London requesting it to examine the possibility of employing some Swiss guides. Through a contact with an Englishman named Clarke living in Interlaken, Switzerland, the office was able to arrange for the hiring of two of the area's foremost guides,

Edouard Feuz and Christian Häsler, in the fall of 1898. Their trip to Canada in the spring of 1899, accompanied by Clarke's son Charles, himself an certified guide, was a publicity dream, fitting in with the CPR's growing "Swiss" campaign. The guides were paraded around Trafalger Square in London dressed in their distinctive climbing costumes and upon arriving in Montreal staged a climb in a gravel pit for the press. Clarke was stationed at the Banff Springs Hotel while Feuz and Häsler were placed at Glacier House for the first season, and it appears that a good deal of their time was spent in similar promotional activities that year. Charles Fay, arriving at Glacier House on August 3, 1899, noted that the two Swiss were delighted to see a real mountaineer and have the opportunity to show off the skills they had been hired for:

I believe I may assert with no immodesty that my advent was a source of unmixed pleasure to at least two of the varied company gathered on the platform to witness the event of the evening, the arrival of "No. 1" — as the west-bound overland train is commonly designated. I refer to the two unique-looking, bronze-faced men, who, religious in the performance of their duty, paced the platform during these important half hours in hob-nailed shoes, pipe in mouth, and otherwise attired as the regulation Swiss guide. No pair of twin brothers were more nearly duplicates in raiment; no two guides ever more effectively supplemented the one the other in excellences than did Christian Hasler and Edouard Feuz of Interlaken. Glad they were, for they were longing for more enterprising labors than these promenades, and the hardly bolder ones that constituted the chief of their functions, the guiding of tourists to the foot of the Illecillewaet Glacier, with the possible roping up for short trips on the ice-foot itself.[10]

In order to get in shape for a planned ascent of Mount Abbott when his climbing companion Herschel Parker arrived, Fay hired Häsler for a warm-up climb on Eagle Peak, which had defeated he and Parker previously. The climb went better with the assistance of a guide and Fay later wrote that "on this occasion our trip was a success in all respects. It proved to me that Hasler was a first-class guide." While there were only a few customers of Fay's ilk

The first CPR Swiss guides, Edouard Feuz (left) and Christian Häsler, in 1899

that year, the guides did achieve some notable climbs, including the first ascent of Mount Dawson with Fay and Parker and the second ascent of Mount Sir Donald, and were to become much more active and valuable in pushing forward climbing in the years ahead.

The real value of the Swiss guides lay in the fact that the mountaineering was much safer with their involvement. Previous to their arrival, the only people doing climbing in the Rockies and Selkirks were the experienced members of climbing clubs, but with their appearance any visitor of an adventurous mien and in reasonable condition could be competently instructed in the delights of the sport. These Swiss guides also added something to the region's culture, as articulated by Bob Sandford in his mountaineering history *The Canadian Alps*:

I*n 1899, the first Swiss guides came to the Canadian West. With them they brought significant evolutions in mountaineering technique garnered from long experience in the Alps. But, perhaps more importantly, they brought an attitude about mountains and a disposition towards climbing that would gradually change the way many Canadians would think about their own summits. The Swiss had a reverence for the alpine that would gradually permeate the fabric of Canadian culture. Through the Swiss guides, Canadians would gradually learn the real* *value of the overwhelming heritage of peaks that nature left behind for hikers and climbers to enjoy. It was the Swiss guides who made manifest the meaning of having so many mountains.*[11]

While the first generation of guides were, with a few exceptions, stationed at Glacier House or Mount Stephen House, a second generation would follow and in 1912 would see the focus of their operations moved to the Lake Louise Chalet. This added their influence to sustaining its already considerable reputation as a climbing centre, one that remains intact to the present day.

The CPR was also involved in other mountaineering activities which brought attention to the Rockies as a field worthy of international attention. One that became the hallmark of the 1901 season was an invitation to the much-touted Edward Whymper, the 1865 conqueror of Switzerland's Matterhorn, to explore the mountains with their assistance. Such was Whymper's fame that other mountaineering parties were discouraged from taking the field so that attention could be focused on his activities and conveyed to the world through the dispatches he intended to supply leading newspapers. As it turned out, his visit proved to be somewhat of a fiasco due to his advancing years, irascible nature and, it was claimed by some, fondness for the bottle, but it did make for some good public relations hay. However, another decision the company would soon make to support a mountaineering endeavour would have even more important consequences for the history of alpinism in the Valley, and indeed all of Canada, for it would lead to the formation of a national mountaineering club.

In 1892, surveyors J. J. McArthur and W. S. Drewry had been pulled off their topographic surveys in the Rockies and Selkirks and sent north to work on the delineation of the Alaska-Yukon boundary. Although their efforts had produced a topographical map comprising several sheets and covering an area of some sixty square miles along the railway reaching almost to the Continental Divide, it needed to be extended through the remainder of the Rockies and into the Selkirks, since as one surveyor succinctly put it "travellers in a new territory ask for maps." In 1901 Deville chose Arthur Oliver Wheeler to take up the work, thereby initiating a chain of events that would lead to the real awakening of Canadians to the importance of their alpine heritage and the joys of ascending and introducing to the mountains an individual who would have a major impact on the future history of the Valley.

The Irish-born Wheeler had apprenticed as a Dominion Land Surveyor on Indian reserves and railway townsites in western Canada in the years around 1885, and after serving in the Surveyor's Intelligence Corps during the Riel Rebellion of that year, he went into private practice. By 1893 he was back with the DLS and, although assigned mostly to irrigation surveys, was an enthusiastic devotee of Deville's photogrammetry work. This led to a survey of coal lands in the Crowsnest Pass area in 1900 and his assignment to the completion of the topographic work along the main line in the Rockies in 1901, until Whymper's visit led to the government's decision to "leave the field open and in no way hamper his operations." Accordingly, he was re-assigned to the Selkirks, his instructions directing him "to make a topographical survey of the Selkirk mountains adjacent to the line of the Canadian Pacific railway, paying most attention to that portion in the vicinity of the summit, visited by tourists and mountain climbers during the summer months."[12] Unfamiliar with mountaineering technique, Mrs. Young, manageress of Glacier House, provided him with no less than six Swiss guides on Mount Overlook, his first climb. But before long he became a very adept climber, a skill he very much needed for what turned out to be a remarkable two-year exploration of the range in his work. During this period, as well as accomplishing his own mountaineering record, he either met or heard about all of the great climbing names to whom Glacier House and the Selkirks were a mecca.

Wheeler's own explorations and collection of the stories of these peoples' adventures became grist for the mill of his monumental work *The Selkirk Range*, published by the Department of the Interior in 1905. It was the first Canadian book on mountaineering and spurred interest in Canadian climbing. Wheeler himself began questioning why there was no Canadian alpine club, as almost all those he met were connected with one climbing organization or another. In 1902 Professor Fay led the movement that created the American Alpine Club, becoming its first president, and suggested to Wheeler that he might like to assist in the formation of a Canadian section of the club to support national mountaineering efforts. Wheeler thought otherwise and tried to get support for a distinctly Canadian club, something which initially proved difficult since he "met with skepticism and indifference." That is until he was on the verge of giving up and following Fay's concept, publishing the idea in a series of letters in Canadian newspapers. This elicited a response from an editorial writer in the Winnipeg *Free Press*, identified only as "M.T.," who in reviewing Wheeler's just-published book tore a strip off him for being so unpatriotic in promoting the idea of a Canadian section in an American club. The writer believed "we owe it to our own young nationhood in simple self-respect, to begin an organized system of mountaineering on an independent basis." Sensing an ally, Wheeler wrote back and suggested that if the *Free Press* would open its pages and support such an idea, he would agree to work along more "patriotic and imperial lines." To his amazement he found out that "M.T." was actually a woman. Elizabeth Parker was an active Winnipeg supporter of social causes and a daily newspaper columnist, and, although not a climber herself, was a lover of the mountains from having spent eighteen months living in Banff to recuperate her health in the hot springs. Mrs. Parker gained the support of the newspaper's editor, J. W. Dafoe, and began writing a series of articles promoting the formation of a Canadian alpine club. Others soon joined the cause, including the Reverend J. C. Herdman of Calgary who began submitting a series of similar letters to the Calgary *Herald*, and soon there was support coming from a number of sources. But support in spirit was one thing, while the kind to actually get a club up and running was another, and here the CPR played a vital role.

Wheeler was invited to address a meeting of CPR executives at Mount Stephen House in February, 1906, including Second Vice-President William Whyte, and later described the results:

As I closed my statement, he [Whyte] asked abruptly, "What do you want?" I replied, I want twenty passes to Winnipeg and return from any part of the Railway to bring delegates there to found an Alpine Club for Canada similar to the European and other big alpine clubs of the world representing mountain ranges such as the Canadian Cordillera. He looked astounded, then incredulous, then scornful, as much to say "What confounded cheek." Then he roared, "Twenty passes to Winnipeg from any part of the Railway!" and turning to Mr McPherson [Western Passenger Traffic Manager], he said in a most sarcastic tone, "What do you think of that, McPherson?" Mr. McPherson replied, "I think it would be a first class idea, Mr. Whyte." "All right!" Mr. Whyte replied with a broad smile, "Fix it up with him." And that little episode was the climax that enabled a meeting of delegates at Winnipeg to found an alpine club for Canada.[13]

The Winnipeg meetings, held on March 27-28, 1906, were attended by such noted mountaineers as A. P. Coleman, who took the chair, Rev. J. C. Herdman, A. O. Wheeler, Stanley H. Mitchell and a good sprinkling of Rocky Mountain outfitters and guides, CPR officials, newspapermen, gentlemen of the cloth, as well as Mrs. Parker and her daughter Jean. It passed the club's founding constitution and also appointed its first executive. Wheeler was elected president and the objectives of what was to be called the Alpine Club of Canada were stated as: 1) the promotion of scientific study and the exploration of Canadian alpine and glacial regions; 2) the cultivation of Art in relation to mountain scenery; 3) the education of Canadians to an appreciation of their mountain heritage; 4) the encouragement of mountain craft and the opening of new regions as a national playground; 5) the preservation of the natural beauties of the mountain places and of the fauna and flora in their habitat; and 6) the interchange of ideas with other Alpine organizations. In the promotion of these objectives it was determined that the club would hold an annual mountaineering camp where new members could attain their graduating climb and all in attendance could enjoy alpine pursuits and camaraderie. Although not dealt with specifically, it was understood that

Delegates to the founding meeting of the Alpine Club of Canada at Winnipeg in March, 1906 including A. O. Wheeler (front, third left), Mrs. Elizabeth Parker, Jean Parker (behind), Rev. J. C. Herdman (front, fourth right), A. P. Coleman (front, third right) and Bill Brewster (front right)

women were to be allowed admittance as Active Members on the same basis as men, and by the next year fully one-quarter of the club's members were of the fair sex. The meeting also determined that it should attempt to publish an annual journal as soon as possible, and decided on its motto, *Sic itur ad astra,* a quote from Virgil's *Aeneid,* meaning "this way to the stars."

Yoho Pass near Emerald Lake was selected as the site for the club's first camp the following summer and it proved a tremendous success, with the CPR volunteering the services of Swiss guides as well as camp equipment and a cook, four outfitters offering their horses and outfits free of charge, and grants to defray costs coming from both the federal and the Alberta governments. Participation was limited to a hundred and many graduating climbs were made on lesser peaks while at the same time some

The Alpine Club of Canada's clubhouse near Banff's Middle Springs became the Valley's headquarters for alpine pursuits

significant ascents were made by the more experienced. Club camps thereafter became an important component of mountaineering activities along the railway, with their location being moved between the Rockies and Selkirks on a rotating basis. Equally significant was the decision to emulate other major climbing clubs and publish an annual journal, the *Canadian Alpine Journal*, documenting the club's activities and proving a forum for well-written articles on mountain exploration, geology, botany, toponymy and a host of other alpine subjects that would greatly increase the country's knowledge of its mountains. However, specific to the Banff-Bow Valley, the club was to make its most lasting impression beginning in 1909 when the decision was made to headquarter it at Banff. A magnificent clubhouse was constructed on the Upper Hot Springs road in the vicinity of the Middle Springs, and thereafter it became Wheeler's summer headquarters and the social and operational centre for those attending the annual camps or carrying out independent climbing expeditions in the Rockies. From this point onward, the growing climbing community, increasing mountaineering activities, and an emerging respect for the mountain environment would become integral parts of the Valley's alpine complexion.

Chapter Eight
Trail Language

While it was those interested in scaling the heights of the Rockies that made the greatest impact on the further discovery and exploration of the Banff-Bow Valley's wilderness, they were not alone. In the period after the line's completion, the Banff area was heavily promoted by the CPR as an attraction to those wishing to hunt big game or to angle for its excellent trout. Similarly, the inquisitive nature of the late-Victorian and early-Edwardian period meant that there were many tourists who were gifted amateur scientists wishing to visit the mountains to indulge in botany, glacier study, geology or private surveying and mapping. Taken together, this group had one thing in common — they needed outfits, horses and guides to allow them to enjoy their pleasures. It was the appearance of these tourist-explorers in the Valley that therefore sustained guiding and outfitting, one of its most respected professions. The desire of these visitors to see "the back of beyond" and the fact that they were usually of means provided the elements that allowed the mountain cowboy if not always to thrive, to at least be able to survive and follow his passion for revealing the secrets of the mountains from the back of a horse. Men of strong character and totally competent backcountry travellers, they would provide a good deal of the grist for the legends and tall tales of the region.

Trail guiding is perhaps the most deeply-rooted of any tradition in the Valley. As described, the practice of guiding extended back to the appearance of the first fur traders and missionaries, where native peoples with knowledge of the mountains and their passes, such as Peechee and Nimrod, provided those services to white Europeans. With the paucity of fur traders frequenting the area they were not much in demand until the completion of the

CPR changed the situation. Even while the railway was being built, mention of the Stoney as hunting guides was made by Reverend Grant, and for a short time they were looked upon as the most knowledgeable sources of information and providers of guiding expertise by those early travellers anxious to leave the vicinity of the railway. A. P. Coleman used Stoney guides in 1892 in his attempt to reach Athabasca Pass from his brother's ranch at Morley. Jimmy Jacob and Mark Two-young-men were reputed to be familiar with two-thirds of the route to the Athabasca (in fact Coleman titled the chapter in his book on this trip "Trails of the Mountain Stonies") and Two-young-men was noted for his work with horses. But Coleman reported that even though "the Stonies had explored more of the mountains than any white men, it was hard to get any definite information from them." North of the Kootenay Plains he found that they were not familiar with the trails and passes, and on more than one occasion had to do the guiding himself or threaten dire consequences should they "mutiny" and try to return to Morley. The next year, he decided to dispense with their services as "they had been of little use except on their own familiar ground," and hired Frank Sibbald, a young Morley rancher, to help with the horses and packing instead.[1]

Coleman's experience with Stoney guides pointed out the difficulties that they faced in becoming an important element in the subsequent era of tourist-exploration of the Rockies. The Stoney's pattern of use of the mountains, based on individual bands' or families' traditional hunting territories, resulted in a situation noted by Coleman in his statement that "each family had its own hunting-grounds, however, so that few were familiar with any wide stretch of the mountains." Their other weakness stemmed from the inability to outfit prospective tourists, having only enough horses for their own use and not being in a position to put together a supply of pack saddles, camping equipment and other paraphernalia that would become the stock-in-trade of a successful outfitter. In these circumstances, the tradition of guiding in the Valley, and indeed the whole of the Canadian Rockies, would pass to white men who had gained sufficient knowledge of the mountains to provide the information the tourist-explorers were looking for and could also supply the outfit to get them where they wanted to go. Initially, at least, that mantle rested squarely on the shoulders of Tom Wilson.[2]

Upon completing his work assisting Major Rogers on the CPR survey at the close of the 1883 season, Wilson had continued to be a player in the story of the mountains. Over the next few years his activities included prospecting at Silver City and in the Yoho Valley, working at Colonel Walker's sawmill near Padmore, participating in the Riel Rebellion as a member of the famous Steele's Scouts, and then joining some of his survey compatriots on one of the excursion trains headed for Craigellachie to witness the completion of the CPR. On the raw morning of November 7, 1885 he disembarked and joined a group of onlookers associated with the building of the line while Donald Smith drove home the last spike, his stetsoned head just barely visible peering over the crowd of onlookers in that most famous Canadian photograph. Seemingly having already experienced enough western Canadian history to last a lifetime, Tom was soon to take a an even more direct role in contributing to the Valley's story. In October, 1885 he had married Minnie McDougall, a cousin of the Reverend John and David McDougall, and in the spring of 1886 the Wilsons had homesteaded near Morley and began raising horses and cattle. But Tom's travels occasionally took him to the site of his old survey camp at Aylmer Park, where he found the bustling town of Banff springing up across the river from the Cave and Basin. Always on the lookout to improve his prospects, he spoke with officials of the CPR for whom he had done some trail work around Lake Louise in the years after 1883. They were amenable to employing his knowledge of the area for further development work, and in the summer of 1887 he blazed a new trail into the lake in preparation for the construction of a rough log shelter, the same one used by Wilcox and Allen during their brief sojourns of 1891. However, their next request of him was to be even more consequential — the need for a guide to accompany a party interested in hunting big game in the mountains — for it would launch his career in the guiding and outfitting business. Using three saddle and two pack horses brought from his Morley homestead, in September, 1887 he took the party of two English sportsmen to the area between the Kootenay Plains and the headwaters of the North Saskatchewan and, at their insistence, returned to the railroad through Howse Pass, which he had personally explored for Major Rogers in 1882.

The success of this trip brought Wilson's abilities and usefulness into focus for the CPR authorities, who were attempting to organize services and amenities for the tourists who began arriving at its grand new hostelry, the Banff Springs Hotel, when it opened in 1888. As mentioned, the CPR Transfer Company had gained the right to run a livery business in the vicinity of the hotel for those wishing to take short carriage or horse-back sightseeing rides in the neighbourhood of the village, but it was not interested in providing services for the more hardy wishing to get off the beaten track. Before long, Wilson was granted the right to advertise himself as "Guide to the CPR" and had obtained a lease on a property at the corner of Banff Avenue and Buffalo Street on which he built a corral and outfitting headquarters. At the same time, he acquired more pack horses from the Stoney at Morley and accumulated pack saddles, pack boxes, cooking utensils and camping gear in order to prepare himself for the needs of his customers. Soon numerous tourist-explorers appeared at Banff requesting his services, and one of them, Walter Wilcox, provided a fascinating picture of the scene around his corrals:

During the summer season 'Wilson's' is frequently the scene of no little excitement when some party is getting ready to leave. Then you may see ten or fifteen wicked-eyed ponies, some in a corral and the rest tied to trees ready for packing. If the horses are making their first trip of the season there will be considerable bucking and kicking before all is ready. Several men are seen bustling about, sorting and weighing the packs, and making order out of the pile of blankets, tents, and bags of flour or bacon. The cayuses are saddled and cinched up one by one with many a protesting bite and kick. The celebrated 'diamond hitch' is used in fastening the packs, and the struggling men look picturesque in their old clothes and

A Wilson packtrain preparing to leave Banff, 1899

sombreros as they tighten the ropes, bravely on gentle horses, but rather gingerly when it comes to a bucking bronco.

A crowd of businessmen of Banff, who usually take about 365 holidays every year, stands around to offer advice and watch the sport. Then the picturesque train of horses with their wild looking drivers files out through the village streets under a fusillade of snap-shot cameras and the wondering gaze of new arrivals from the east.[3]

Many of those seeking Wilson's services were, like Wilcox, part of the growing movement of alpinists wishing to come to grips with the area's unconquered peaks. As pointed out, he had already gained familiarity with these pursuits by packing for some of the the DLS surveyors during their topographic work, and had even accompanied W. S. Drewry on his ascents of Mount Lougheed and Storm Mountain in 1889. His outfitting and guiding of R. L. Barrett to the foot of Mount Assiniboine in 1893 and subsequent work with the Applachian Mountain Club expedition to Mount Hector in 1895 firmly established his reputation as the one whose services serious mountaineers should seek. Wilson initially tried to take care of their needs himself, occasionally assisted by George Fear, his partner in a heads and hides business at Banff, but soon their demands coupled with those of surveyors, hunters and fishermen were more than he could handle. He therefore began to hire competent men to assist him, and in so doing helped populate the Valley with its henceforth most famous characters.

Although ranching was already beginning to become a major industry in the foothills adjacent to the Valley, employing tough and competent cow men, the mountain cowboys that Wilson hired needed to have distinctly different skills than their ranch counterparts. Ranch cowboys essentially watched over, rounded up and herded beef cattle through familiar prairie and foothill territory in all seasons, while mountain cowboys guided clients, built trails, fought downed timber, penetrated high passes and forded pack trains across rampaging rivers in what was largely unknown country during the short summer and fall seasons of the Rockies. The trials and tribulations of the mountain trail were perhaps best summed up in the words of one early tourist-explorer who recalled being constantly assailed by "muskeg, burnt timber and bad language." In these circumstances, Wilson, above all, had to find men who could at least get along with the often highly-educated and wealthy dudes from the east, something in which he was not always successful for there are numerous accounts where a guide or packer "locked horns" with a member of his party. His men also had to exhibit leadership, a sense of direction and good judgment in order to avoid the thousand-and-one pitfalls that could befall a pack train travelling through the uncharted wilderness, or to extract the party from any dangerous predicaments, or "jackpots," it did get into. Knowledge of and the ability to handle horses of all temperaments was a shared trait of the ranch and mountain cowboy, but the length of time away from the home corral, the rugged country traversed and the perils of moving large numbers of horses through difficult conditions put an increased emphasis on the latter's skills. The guide had to know the peculiarities of each horse in his string in order to predict how it would react in all situations; he had to assess each one's strengths and weaknesses in order to coax it through a typical day's march of five or six hours; he had to understand how to correctly pack each horse to prevent it from getting a sore back or lame; and he had to judge what was proper feed to allow each member of the string to stay up to strength in all types of weather and terrain. In short, he had to appreciate each animal as an individual and be able to respond to its personality and needs.

Fortunately for Wilson, there were a number of such men appearing in the mountains at this time who either already had some of these skills or showed themselves adept at picking them up. In the early 1890s, the precursors of what would be a flood of immigrants from the British Isles were trickling into western Canada, and they were joined by a few Americans and eastern Canadians who were also free-spirited and adventurous. Some were inevitably attracted to the rough-and-ready atmosphere of pioneer Banff and hoped to live out their fantasy as latter-day explorers, leading them to Tom's door.

Among their ranks were several noteworthy British expatriots who would adopt the mountains as their permanent home: Jim Tabuteau, a young Irish immigrant who became Wilson's first real guide; Bill Peyto, a wanderer originally from Welling, Kent who had prospected, trapped and worked on the railway for a few years before hiring on about 1893; Ralph Edwards, likewise from Kent, who guided some of the most important parties setting out from Banff in the nineties; and Jimmy Simpson, a rascally lad from Lincolnshire who had been sent to Canada with sufficient funds to start him in farming and keep him away from the home fire. They were joined on Tom's crew by a number of Americans who already had some wilderness or livestock experience: Fred Stephens, a Michigan-born logger, trapper and hunter who drifted into Banff about 1896 after finding the north-western U. S. becoming too populated; Fred and Jack Ballard, likewise from Michigan, where it was said they had been born with axes in their hands; and Tom Lusk, a Texas cowboy, slightly longer in the tooth, of whom it was whispered that he had escaped across the Canadian border driving someone else's steers with a Texas sheriff in hot pursuit. And, like Tom himself, there were also a few Ontario lads seeking a new beginning in the west: Bob Campbell hailing from close to Wilson's home at Barrie, who came to Banff as a schoolteacher but quickly became Tom's partner; and Jack Otto, a trapper and logger from Haliburton, who with his two brothers, Bruce and Closson, would later become one of the pioneer outfitters in the Jasper region. Each of these men brought their own level of skill to the outfit, ranging from the very green, such as Simpson, to the highly experienced, such as Peyto, Stephens and Lusk.

Simpson later recalled arriving in Banff and, wanting to emulate his idol Bill Peyto, had to learn something about riding:

My next exploit in colonization was "topping off a horse." I had never ridden a horse other than a wooden one when six years old, but I was now in the west and it had to be done or lose face. The horse was tied in a clump of poplars down below the school house and quite a few spectators were on hand. I wondered why the man holding the horse had it gripped by the nostrils with his left hand and by its left ear with his right. I know now. I climbed into the saddle like a sailor climbing up the hind leg of a camel and heard someone yell, "let him go!" He meant the horse — and he went. So did I. A leaning poplar tree took me on the chest, under the chin, and I was in a bunch of scrub brush, head down. Other than a skinned cheek, and a limp I was all right, but they did not get that horse for three days, five miles east and minus the bridle.[4]

At the other end of the spectrum when he joined the outfit was Fred Stephens, who quickly gained a reputation as the most skilled axeman to ever appear in the Valley and one who understood horses perfectly and spared no effort in their welfare. While out on a trip from Banff to the Athabasca River, one of his clients, newspaperman Stanley Washburn, was witness to the way in which Stephens justified delays in the interests of his livestock:

"Now old Sorrel," remarked Fred, as we sat around the pack cover at dinner. "He's sure got skinnier'n h— these last few days, and I don't think the old devil's got the ginger under his hide to cut the mustard, when it comes to swimmin' this young flood which you fellers see abilin' past. The little Bay now, he's some peaked too since he fell down the

mountain and skinned his knees. He ain't a bad horse, the Bay ain't, and I don't want to see him get his'n in this rampagin' river. And then there's the old White — he's just barely been draggin' his hinders over the trail this week, and besides, Nick's saddle horse has been gettin' down in the dumps worse and worse every day for a month. Now, fellers, if we was to tackle the job this minute, a lot o' them critturs would just naturally turn up their toes to the surface and drift off down the river to the Arctic Ocean.[5]

Simpson and all those in Wilson's employ would eventually achieve a high degree of competency with horses, packing, guiding and trail cooking, each of them earning excellent reputations during the period they worked with him.

In the years leading up to the new century, these guides would succeed in assisting their tourist-explorer clients to fill in the remaining unknown spaces in the Canadian Rockies away from the railroad. As they did so, Wilson's outfitting business became more formalized and expanded to meet the demand. In 1888 most of his customers had been Banff Springs Hotel guests taking fishing, hunting and sightseeing trips lasting about a week, but by the late-1890s he was outfitting major mountaineering, exploration and hunting trips lasting up to two months. As the time on the trail increased and as many of these customers were influential, they were soon gaining the CPR's permission to ride on the freight trains running between Banff, Laggan and Field or staying at the company's Lake Louise Chalet or Mount Stephen House at Field, meeting the pack train en route. This led to Tom to expand his operations, stationing guides, horses and outfits at these locations in the summer to meet the changing needs, and inevitably resulting in a more business-like relationship with the railway company.

Wilson was always noted for his public relations abilities and as an accomplished story-teller, eventually being employed by the CPR fully in these capacities. In his early years, he assisted the company by providing them with interesting material for newspaper articles, by securing specimens of native animals often requested of the CPR by scientific institutions, and by personally caring for VIP clients who visited Banff and the Rockies. He also came up with an idea to entertain stranded CPR guests when floods washed out the line in June, 1894, in so doing unwittingly initiating the last chapter of the Stoney's direct relationship with the Banff area. His solution to the boredom and disgruntlement of the captive guests was to ride to Morley and recruit some Indians to come to Banff to perform in a number of native competitions and athletic events for prizes put up by the company. The Stoney responded by riding up to Banff and camping near the foot of Cascade Mountain before parading up to the Banff Springs Hotel in full regalia to make the patrons aware of their presence. They then proceeded back to their camp and staged horse races, bucking and roping contests, teepee pitching and bow and arrow demonstrations, much to the visitors' delight. In fact the idea worked so well that the event, henceforth known as Banff Indian Days, was duplicated and became an annual highlight of the tourism season after 1907. For the next sixty-odd years the tradition carried on, undoubtedly enjoyed by thousands of visitors and looked forward to as a source of funds and a diversion from their hum-drum life on the reserve by the Stoney, but, in the end, relegating their status in the Valley to little more than tourist attractions in the area they had once dominated.

In any event, Wilson's status with the CPR grew accordingly and when the company decided in 1902 it wanted securely contracted outfitting and livery services at its disposal, he was given his choice of locations. Believing the future of the business lay in the "long trail," rather than short day trips in the vicinity of Banff, he chose to contract at Laggan and Field and leave Banff to others. Banff school-teacher Bob Campbell had already purchased a small share of his business and now became a full partner in Wilson and Campbell, handling a good many of the trail parties at Field and Emerald Lake while Tom looked after those at Laggan and Lake Louise. This left a wide-open field at Banff, and for a few years some of those who had initially worked for Tom decided to go out on their own as outfitters. One of them was Bill Peyto, who was already well on the way to earning a reputation as the foremost mountain man ever to set foot in the Rockies. His piercing blue eyes and rugged appearance, described by Wilcox as "wild and picturesque," were backed-up with a proficiency at handling all the hazardous and unknown situations encountered in the mountain wilderness. His prowess as a prospector and trapper would equal that as a guide, leading to some legendary stories, such as the one related by Banff pioneer Pat Brewster revolving around his capture of a lynx for Norman Sanson, the curator of the Banff Zoo:

Bill Peyto taking a lynx to the zoo

Somewhere out in his prospecting country he had obtained a lynx. He had brought it down alive to his cabin on Healy Creek and the next day decided to bring it to Banff. He devised a means of carrying the beast by tying the animal on his back — the head and claws toward the rear. . . . .The head of the lynx and its legs were, of course, free; also it was facing away from Bill so he could not do any harm. He walked down the street and arrived at the popular old Alberta Bar at about eight-thirty in the evening, just when the place was at its liveliest. Bill entered the bar, headed for the first free space and hollered for a drink. A minute of so passed before the other patrons realized just what was going on and just what it was they were looking at. Shortly, he had the entire bar to himself.[6]

Peyto's reputation as a guide was earned for his ability to get those interested in reaching the sirens of the mountains, Mount Assiniboine and Mounts Hooker and Brown, to their vicinity as quickly and efficiently as possible despite the obstacles of the trail. In 1895, Barrett returned to Banff to renew his quest for Assiniboine and teamed up with Wilcox, also anxious to come to grips with the famous peak. Wilson assigned Ralph Edwards to the party as guide and Peyto as packer, but soon after crossing Healy Creek Edwards had to return for a lost axe and Peyto took over the guiding chores. Despite his unfamiliarity with the area, he was able to lead the party through snow-choked Simpson Pass, employing his own mount as a pack-horse when one of the string broke its leg, and delivered them to the foot of Assiniboine in good order. The party remained two weeks in its vicinity, Bill assisting them with accomplishing the first circumnavigation of the mountain involving a forty-six hour hike covering fifty-one miles of the roughest country imaginable, but revealing no easy route to its summit. It would not be the last time Peyto led a party to the foot of "the Matterhorn of the Rockies," but in the meantime his attention was taken up with helping Collie, Stutfield and Baker in their quest for the big peaks north of Lake Louise. It was he who acted as guide for the expedition in search of Mount Balfour after the successful ascent of Mount Lefroy in 1897, and for the trip of Collie and Baker later that summer to the Mount Forbes area.

During this trip, Collie was forced to re-assess his opinion of Bill and the value of trail guides in general. While making their way up the Bow north of Laggan, Peyto stopped early in the afternoon because of the hot weather and the swarms of mosquitoes antagonizing the horses. Collie felt such an early stop was unnecessary and told the guide so, leading to Bill patiently explaining to him that he had no idea how far a pack horse could travel in a day or what problems pushing them too hard early in a trip could cause. Collie acquiesced, but was resentful at, in effect, being told off, a sentiment which changed as the trip unfolded:

That Peyto was right was abundantly proved in the sequel; for, owing to the excessively hot weather, we soon had more than one pony with a sore back and ill. This remedied itself, however, for later the weather got cooler and the packs lighter. Moreover, it was no vain boast of Peyto's that he was there to look after the horses; many a time after arriving in camp after a long day's journey, when something to eat and drink was one's first thought, Peyto could be seen driving the sore-backed ponies down to the stream where he carefully washed them and smeared the raw places with bacon-grease to keep off the flies.[7]

Collie's growing respect for his guide led Wilson to re-assign Peyto to his expedition of 1898, when the professor returned to lay to rest once and for all the mystery of Hooker and Brown. This trip proved even more arduous than the previous ones, and at one point on the North Fork of the North Saskatchewan Peyto was all but prepared to give up until Collie suggested a drink of whiskey, which immediately revived his guide's spirits. Although the expedition failed to reach Athabasca Pass, a major peak Collie named Mount Athabasca was discovered near the headwaters of the Sunwapta River, and when he and Herman Woolley ascended it they became the first climbers to lay eyes on a far more significant geographic feature — the Columbia Icefield, the true hydrographic apex of the North American continent.

Peyto left Banff in 1900 to fight in the Boer War, where he distinguished himself drawing enemy fire by parading around the South African veldt holding up an umbrella, and upon returning as a local hero in 1901 started his own outfitting business. He got his enterprise off to an excellent start that fall by guiding the Reverend James Outram to Mount Assiniboine in record time, where he accomplished the first ascent. The next year he built on this success by outfitting the reverend gentleman for a trip to the area between the North Saskatchewan and the Columbia Icefield, where he added the first ascents of Mounts Columbia and Lyell to his belt. One of the guides on this latter trip, Jimmy Simpson, had left Wilson's employ by 1902 and had gone to work for Peyto, leading to his own decision to go into the outfitting business. In 1904 he initially went into partnership with George Taylor, a

Yorkshireman who had been chief packer for A. O. Wheeler's topographic survey in the Selkirks, and later with Suffolk-born, Boer War veteran Syd Baker, beginning a career as an outfitter and tourist operator that would span the next seventy years.[8]

Although Peyto, Simpson and others left Wilson and went their own way in the years after the turn-of-the-century, it would be some new faces in the business who would ultimately dominate the field. In so doing, the Brewster brothers, Bill and Jim, would begin a family business tradition in the Bow Valley that would be second in importance only to the CPR itself and would flourish to the present day. The patriarch of the Brewster family, John Brewster, hailed from Kingston, Ontario and had been drawn west in the early 1880s by the abundant opportunities being created by the construction of the CPR and the reports of his brothers, already in the region. After a few years spent in Winnipeg as a blacksmith and boilermaker, he was convinced to come to Banff in 1886 by his brother William, a carpenter who was working on the construction of the bathhouses at the Cave and Basin. As related, he set up the town's first dairy right on Banff Avenue, and with the Banff Springs Hotel being his main customer, soon flourished. On March 17, 1888 (St. Patrick's Day), he brought out his wife Bella and growing family of four boys from Winnipeg to the pioneer townsite, setting in motion a remarkable series of events.[9]

The two eldest boys, Bill and Jim, spent most of their spare time out hunting, fishing and exploring in the mountains, educated as to the trails, the ways of the wilderness and the habits of the animals by a wise and knowledgeable Stoney, William Twin. William had received some education from the Reverend John McDougall and his prowess in the mountains had been recognized by the CPR, which had hired him to do some of the early trail clearing and guiding in conjunction with the log chalet they were building at Lake Louise. Wilcox, who met him at work when he visited the lake in 1894, found him to be the epitome of the idealized "noble savage" common in the literature of the age, describing him as coming "nearer to a realization of the ideal Indian features such as one sees on coins, or in allegorical figures, than almost any savage I have ever seen." John Brewster first hired him about 1888 to help take off a hay crop in a small field between the first and second Vermilion Lakes, and thereafter he became a close family friend and appeared often at the dairy. He taught Bill and Jim the rudiments of Cree and Stoney as well as demonstrating to them how to properly handle horses in the mountains, becoming a prime example of how first peoples passed on knowledge to white men that was thereafter used in the development of the Valley. Utilizing the skills taught by William, the boys began escorting fishing parties at the request of Manager Mathews of the Banff Springs Hotel in the summer of 1892, at the tender ages of twelve and ten respectively. They continued to perform such activities when not in school or working for their father at the dairy, and eventually Jim Brewster received a position similar to William's working for the CPR at the Lake Louise Chalet. Destined to become one of Banff's most colourful and famous individuals as well as its most prominent and influential businessman, it is interesting to note how his abilities and potential as a fifteen-year-old guide were assessed by two early American alpinists, Charles E. Fay and Rest F. Curtis, who employed him in the first traverse of Abbot Pass to Lake O'Hara in 1897:

Would make a capital guide with proper training. A little too fresh just now and fond of telling big stories. We learned within two days, to our amazement, that he had saved Curtis's life on the way to the Pass! C's feet went from under him on a steep snow slope and he slipped fully a yard. No crevasses near.[10]

The Brewster boys formalized their entry into outfitting and guiding in 1900 when they began advertising themselves as "W & J Brewster, Guides and Packers," and initially received most of their business from a packing contract for the Jubilee coal mining property near the headwaters of the Cascade River. But in 1902 they got the break they needed to compete successfully with Wilson when the CPR asked them to represent the company at the annual Sportsmen's Show at Madison Square Gardens. Accompanied by William Twin, the boys departed for New York bearing game specimens, a tepee, and camping and outfitting equipment, with the idea of re-creating a sportsman's camp in the mountain wilds. Their display proved tremendously popular and introduced them to numerous prospective clients, two of whom would play a key role in their future success. Princeton University students Fred Hussey, scion of a successful Pittsburgh steel manufacturing company, and Philip Moore, a future heir to Old Crow Whiskey Distilleries money, befriended Bill and Jim and decided to try convince their parents to make a hunting trip in the Rockies a reward for achieving graduation. They succeeded, and that fall were guided on a hunt by Jim which proved the highlight of their young lives. Completely taken with Banff and the Rockies (and

The Brewster family, pictured here about 1898, would become one of the most influential in the Valley's history -- left to right; Jim, Fred, Bill, Jack (front), John, Pat, George (front), Pearl (front), Bella

Moore with their guide's young sister Pearl, whom he would marry in 1907), Hussey and Moore indicated that they would like to invest in the Brewster business, and the opportunity was not long in coming. In 1905 the CPR finally decided to formally award the outfitting and livery concession at the Banff Springs Hotel and chose W & J Brewster as the successful contender. This concession gave Bill and Jim a powerful instrument upon which to build their business, and Hussey and Moore were ready with the capital to allow them to do so. That year a new company, Brewster Brothers, was formalized with the Americans as silent partners, and it quickly added to its stock-in-trade of horses, pack outfits and livery vehicles as well as extending its interests to include a Banff Avenue livery stable, a general merchandise store and an opera house.

The numerous guiding and outfitting interests vying for clients in the century's first decade established Banff and Laggan as major outfitting centres and helped to define their early character. A variety of livery stables on Banff Avenue were complemented by outfitting headquarters on the town's periphery, such as Peyto's and Simpson's corrals and pack shacks between Bear Street and the Bow River, and the comings and goings of pack trains were an everyday occurrence. However, if anything, there was a surfeit of outfitters, and the future story of the profession was one of a gradual consolidation into a few key hands. Tom Wilson himself was the first to make his exit, selling his remaining interest in the business to his partner Bob Campbell in 1904 and using the funds to help stock a horse ranch he was establishing near the mouth of White Rabbit Creek on the Kootenay Plains. Some of those who had initially worked for him and had then gone out on their own also left the Banff scene, among them being Fred Stephens, who headed for the Yellowhead Pass area around 1905. He was later joined by Jack Otto and his two brothers and by Fred and Jack Brewster, younger brothers of Bill and Jim, all intent on establishing outfitting businesses at Jasper on the route of the new Grand Trunk Pacific Railway. Back in the south, Brewster Brothers took their first steps towards gradually monopolizing the tourist transportation business at the CPR hotels along the line through the mountains. In 1908 they acquired the outfitting and livery concessions at Lake Louise and Field, succeeding Bob Campbell whose agreement had expired, and in 1915 bought out Syd Baker at Glacier House. Bill Peyto also succumbed, abandoning the outfitter's profession for the solitary life of a prospector and trapper after his wife's untimely death in 1906, and later going on to become one of the park's first and most competent wardens. The only one of the Wilson old-guard who was to successfully resist the onset of the Brewsters' incredible success was Jimmy Simpson.

Later in life, Jimmy was often asked how he got started in the outfitting business and typically replied, "I cabled our English lawyers that I had passed my twenty-first birthday ten minutes ago to get the legacy coming to me on that date from some relative I never knew, who in a moment of weakness left it thus, over to Canada immediately, if not sooner." With it he bought horses and saddlery from Frank Ricks of Morley and "started into packtrains and have done it ever since." In reality, the story wasn't quite so simple, as he would experience ups and downs along the way, but perseverance proved to be his by-word. One of his early clients was Mrs. Mary de la Beach-Nichol, daughter of Britain's Chancellor of the Exchequer, who scoured the Rockies in a weather-beaten black gown and Panama hat carrying an ear trumpet, looking to add to her world-renowned butterfly collection, with Jimmy in hot pursuit with the butterfly net and collecting box. Another was her nephew, John Blandy-Jenkins, known as the "Millionaire Kid," who Jimmy described as "being constantly on one's mind and the main concern was when he was going to get off." Around June, 1910 he received a telegram from Mrs. Beach-Nichol telling him to prepare for Blandy-Jenkins's four month hunting trip, and before he could reply that all hunting was closed at that season, the "Kid" arrived with "a chauffeur, two jockeys, and two trunks full of bowie knives and guns."

Jimmy Simpson tightening the diamond

Despite such unusual clients, Jimmy also had his share of normal ones, being particularly successful in attracting wealthy big game hunters to pursue the trophy bighorn sheep that frequented the area north of the North Saskatchewan River, especially in the Brazeau River basin. One of his clients reported that Jimmy "would rather hunt bighorns than occupy a seat in the heavenly choir," and several others noted his uncanny ability to sense the presence of game in a certain locale. These instincts stood him in good stead on November 2, 1920 when he took the then world's record bighorn ram, measuring 49 1/2 inches around the curl. The following year, 1921, he successfully negotiated with the Parks Branch for a lease on a four-acre parcel of land at one of his favourite camping spots on the shore of Bow Lake and quickly set to work to build a subsequently famous, six-sided log building he eventually named the "Ram Pasture." It provided not only a wilderness outfitting headquarters but also proved to be the forerunner of a larger operation, Num-Ti-Jah Lodge, which would secure his career in the tourism business and become one of the most distinctive landmarks on the future Banff-Jasper Highway (Columbia Icefields Parkway).

While out on the Alexandra River with the "butterfly lady" in 1907, Jimmy encountered a party led by a fellow English guide, Billy Warren, who had also worked for Wilson. His client was a plucky Philadelphia Quaker named Mary Schäffer, and her story would attract an abiding interest second to none from future generations of backcountry travellers in the Rockies.

Mary Sharples had been brought up within the strict confines of Quaker life, studying art and botany, but had always exhibited an adventurous mien and a strong interest in native peoples. As a young woman she travelled to the western United States and then in 1889 took a trip over the new CPR line to the Selkirks. At Glacier House, she visited her friend Mary Vaux and her two brothers, George and William, who were engaged in photographing and measuring the Illecillewaet Glacier as their contribution to the area's natural science. They introduced her to Dr. Charles Schäffer, a Philadelphia medical doctor and amateur botanist, spawning a romance that soon resulted in her becoming the charming, albeit considerably older, doctor's wife. Together they would spend their summers throughout the 1890s gathering botanical specimens in the Rockies and Selkirks in preparation for the writing a book on the subject. Unfortunately, Dr. Schäffer passed away in 1903, and after a period of grieving Mary decided to complete his unfinished work. This led her to Tom Wilson's door in 1904, and he assigned her to the care of Billy Warren, a native of Harlow, Essex who, like many of his confreres, had served in the Boer War before coming to Canada. After experiencing the wilderness trails of the Rockies under his guidance, Mrs. Schäffer's assessment of him was flattering indeed, offering "there are older ones [guides], there are better hunters, perhaps, with wider experience in forest lore, more knowledge of the country, but for kindness, good nature (such a necessary adjunct), good judgment under unexpected stress, he had no superior."

Assisted by fellow botanist Stewardson Brown, she completed the book in 1905 and it was published as *Alpine Flora of the Canadian Rocky Mountains* in 1907, illustrated with plates from her beautiful watercolour illustrations. With her friend Mollie Adams, Mary then discussed explorations further from the railway than her botanical expeditions and, despite the fact that such exploits were not thought proper for women, they found that their "cups splashed over." With Warren as guide, assisted by Sid Unwin and Reggie Holmes, the two intrepid ladies spent the summers of 1907-08 exploring for a mysterious lake described to them by Sampson Beaver, a Stoney chief of the Wesley band, known as *Chaba Imne* and supposed to exist between the Brazeau and Athabasca Rivers. Their "discovery" of what was henceforth known as Maligne Lake made for a stirring tale in Mrs. Schäffer's subsequent book, *Old Indian Trails of the Canadian Rockies*, which appeared in 1911, the year she made a second trip to the lake in order to assist in its surveying for the Canadian government. Shortly thereafter, in 1915, in a fairytale-like ending to her mountain travels, *Yahe-Weha*, (Mountain Woman) as the Stoney named her, married her guide Billy Warren and settled down in Banff, becoming one of its most interesting and active citizens. The spark to women's involvement on the trail and in other alpine pursuits she provided would have a lasting effect on the traditions of the area and is still emulated to the present day.[11]

The heyday of the tourist-explorer and the pioneer guides and outfitters in the Banff-Bow Valley essentially began to wane with the appearance of the Alpine Club of Canada. It was apparent to A. O. Wheeler in contemplating the logistics for the annual climbing camp that it would require "a corps of reliable guides and outfitters, who shall be available in connection with the work of the club." Consequently, Tom Wilson, Syd Baker, Bill Brewster, Bob Campbell and Tom Martin were among "the twenty" who attended the Winnipeg founding meeting. Several of these outfitters provided their services and equipment to the first camp free-of-charge, recognizing the value of such an organization to the future of their businesses. And, indeed, this proved to be the case, as future camps necessitated several of them to work together to provide all the required services. In 1908, Wheeler announced the need for an official club outfitter so that it could be assured that the wherewithal to provide for the growing popularity of the annual camps would be available. The Otto brothers were the successful candidates, being appointed "Official Outfitters to the Alpine Club of Canada" in 1909 with Jimmy Simpson assisting as "Equerry." That year's camp in the Yoho Valley was followed by a six-day horseback expedition to explore the valley in which thirty-three club members took part, ensuring a good pay-day for the Ottos and Simpson.

The beginning of the institutionalization of outfitting and guiding, apparent in the Alpine Club situation, became even more evident in the years after the First World War when the appearance of automobiles and the first roads in the parks, some of them penetrating to areas formerly only accessible by horseback, began to change the face of tourism. This period saw the growing popularity of conducted trail ride parties, groups organized by individuals or businesses and taken on extended outings in the mountains. Caroline Hinman, Secretary of the Board of Education in Summit, New Jersey, pioneered the concept. Having herself taken a conducted trip to Europe in 1914, she decided to offer a modified version in the wilderness on horseback after visiting and becoming enamoured with the mountains at an Alpine Club camp. Her "Off The Beaten Track" tours, consisting of wealthy, teen-aged American girls, began under Jimmy Simpson's supervision in 1917 with a three week outing to Mount Assiniboine, Sawback Lake and the Ptarmigan Valley. The first trip proved so popular that it inaugurated several decades of similar journeys throughout the Rockies, mostly outfitted by Jim Boyce of Banff, and earned the conductress the name of "Timberline Kate." Other entrepreneurs modified the concept to suit different circumstances, one being outfitter Jack Brewster of Jasper who, in 1924, began offering a six week trip known as "The Glacier Trail" which used twelve camps, including one at the foot of the Columbia Icefield, during a trail ride from Jasper to Lake Louise and return..

The version of the concept that had the most impact on the Valley was organized by Wheeler himself and was called the "Banff to Mount Assiniboine Walking and Riding Tour." Operating with Ralph Rink, a former Brewster guide, as his outfitter, Wheeler established a headquarters and corrals on a lease he obtained at the Middle Springs, next door to the Alpine Club clubhouse. The tour was to be circular, starting out from Banff and going to Mount Assiniboine, where he had obtained a campsite on a lease from the club at Magog Lake, by way of the Spray Valley and Bryant Creek and then returning via Sunshine and Healy Creek. Smaller camps were established at the former Eau Claire Lumber camp seven miles up the Spray from Banff, at Goat Pass near lower Spray Lake and on the open meadows near the head of Sunshine Creek, the distance between camps varying from seven to sixteen miles. Wheeler's close association with the Alpine Club and the *de facto* creation of his own outfitting operation through the agency of Rink was seen as unfair competition by the other Banff outfitters, who were afraid it was simply a cover for providing longer trail trips, leading to complaints to the government and becoming a factor in the creation of the Rocky Mountain Outfitters' (later Guides') Association in 1922. Its objective was "to have one official body who will be empowered to negotiate with the dominion and provincial governments in all matters pertaining to the outfitting business throughout the Rocky Mountains, such as the inter-provincial recognition of guides' licenses, betterment of trails in the park, game and fishing regulations etc."[12] The creation of this body, the complaints his operation received and the perception that he was using the Alpine Club as a springboard for his own business made matters difficult for Wheeler and the Mount Assiniboine tour disappeared by the end of the twenties.

It is not surprising that even the CPR would become more directly involved in trail riding as these new tendencies took hold. Emulating the successful model of the Alpine Club's annual camps, CPR General Publicity Agent John Murray Gibbon suggested the idea of an "order of trail riders" in 1923 and, after gaining support from some influential people active in the mountains, threw the whole weight of the CPR behind the concept. Although the Trail Riders of the Canadian Rockies had objectives similar to those of the Alpine Club, such as the study of bird and animal life and the promotion of Canada's national parks, its main one was the encouragement of horseback travel in the Canadian Rockies by means of holding an annual ride and camp, or "pow-wow" as it was called. Badges of various grades were offered to those riding fifty, one hundred, five hundred, one thousand, two thousand and twenty-five hundred miles of mountain trails, giving participation an air of distinction. Outfitting services were placed in the hands of the new Outfitters' Association, and because the Trail Riders became very popular many postwar trailmen, such as Bill Potts, Walter Nixon, Pat Brewster and Soapy Smith, did very well from them. After the first years' ride in the Yoho Valley in 1924, the response was so strong that the organization had to start offering both three and five day rides with "squadrons" starting off from different points and rendezvousing at the "pow-wow" site, usually in close proximity to one of the CPR's bungalow camps.

By the end of the decade, the Trail Riders could boast a membership of some 1,500, and their executive was full of historic figures who had played a role in the success of the activity, including James Outram, Carl Rungius, Mary Schäffer Warren and Mary Vaux Walcott. The fact that veteran trailmen, such as Jimmy Simpson and Bill and Jim Brewster, joined them in official posts with the Trail Riders provided clear evidence that the pioneer era of outfitting and guiding was drawing to a close, but also that the profession's importance to the Valley's future was not in doubt.

Chapter Nine
The Eye of the Beholder

Changes taking place in late-Victorian and early-Edwardian society that gave rise to the interests of tourists, be they the usual sedentary hot springs type or the more active tourist-explorer variety, were to be reflected in the Banff-Bow Valley in another way. The growing appreciation of nature evident in the philosophy of writers such as Thoreau, Ruskin and Muir and a heightened consciousness of landscape was being brought to bear by the deepening public interest in scientific thought and investigation. Combined with the expanding ability of many in society to have time to contemplate matters such as the divine plan or concepts of beauty, it became an age of growing aesthetic appreciation. Mountains, of course, lent themselves to such interpretation, and it would be a type of visitor who would see them with a more sensitive and artistic eye that would contribute enormously to the broader public's admiration of them. The mountains of the Bow Valley would inspire generations of artists and photographers to attempt to capture their aesthetic vision and in the process create an artistic legacy that encapsulated the essence of the area's cultural identity.

Indeed, from the earliest days of the fur trade, the Rocky Mountains had inspired those who gazed upon them. Early travellers' records are replete with references to days of dreary travel across the prairies when each member of the fur brigade anxiously longed for their first glimpse of the fabled peaks. When they hove into view, it was usual for a hearty cheer to be raised. Observers such as Thompson, Rundle, Hector and others went to great lengths in their journals to describe the scene and the feelings it elicited in them. This uplifting reaction was one typical throughout the world for those coming into contact with mountains and had long been the subject of artistic impression in European art, such as that of its famous mountain painter J. M. W. Turner.

Several fur trade era travellers attempted to capture this same feeling by sketching the mountains as adjuncts to their journals. David Thompson recorded on October 12, 1800 near the head of the Red Deer River that he "went up a high Knowl & took a rough Sketch of the Appearance of the Mountains." Similarly, Reverend Rundle recorded on November 13, 1844 that he "took rough sketch of Devil's Head Mountain." The year following Rundle's effort, 1845, proved to be a bumper one for artists in the Rockies, considering the few white voyagers frequenting them. As mentioned, Captain H. J. Warre of the Royal Engineers sketched his way across the country during his reconnaissance trip to the Oregon Territory for Sir George Simpson, producing the first recognizable artistic conceptions of the Valley between July 23rd and July 26th before passing southwestward though Whiteman's Pass. A few months later, Toronto artist Paul Kane, the first professional artist in the west, set out with the Columbia brigade armed with a commission for twelve paintings from no less a luminary than Sir George himself. Inspired by American artist George Catlin, who had painted native life in the American west in the 1830s, Kane sketched buffalo and the natives of the prairies as he proceeded westward. He began portraying the mountains as his party approached the Athabasca Valley in late October, 1845, and early November found him accompanying the brigade in an arduous crossing of Athabasca Pass, Kane making the first sketches of this historic location as well. He would spend the next year sketching and painting in the Oregon Territory before returning across the pass in late 1846, but by April, 1847 was at Rocky Mountain House performing some of his most important work. Two portraits of Stoney chiefs he carried out at that time became notable accomplishments, both as works of art, being styled very much in the European romantic tradition, and as ethnographic records.

Kane exhibited some of the work from the trip in Toronto in November, 1848, the exhibition being one of the first one-man shows held in Canada. It took him eleven years to complete the paintings inspired by his journey, and was followed by work on the very successful account of his travels in his book *Wanderings of an Artist among the Indians of North America* published in 1859. By the time he passed from the Canadian art scene in the 1860s, artists were beginning to search for a national focus. However, it would not be until the 1870s that it was noted that Canadian art was following in the great European art tradition of depicting nature at its most sublime, a critic stating in 1877 that "that Canadian scenery has its own characteristics, and that the chief merit of our best artists is that they produce these with striking fidelity. . . ." This focus on realism continued to develop as the North American tradition of pragmatism and reason, its belief in nature as a divine creation and its preference for recognizable scenes took stronger hold. These forces soon began to coalesce with the growing interest of the Canadian public in the northwest and the mountains brought about by the completion of the railway, growing Canadian nationalism, and the needs of the CPR for illustrative material for its burgeoning international advertising campaign. This would lead to the creation of what may be called "the railway school," Canada's first national art movement.

Paul Kane's highly romanticized portrait of the Stoney chief **Mah-Min**, *1848*

With the extension of the rails westward it was the "artists of the lens" who would be first to take advantage of the new mode of transportation to access the Valley's great landscapes. At the time, photography was going through a period of rapid development after the appearance of the daguerreotype less than fifty years previously. The wet-collodion process, invented in 1851, had allowed for the production of multiple prints from a glass-plate negative, and in the 1870s it began to be replaced with the new gelatin dry-plate process, making field photography even more practical. The Montreal firm of William Notman had been the first successful commercial photographers in Canada and in 1871 had sent out two photographers, Benjamin Baltzly and John Hammond, to accompany and record a Geological Survey of Canada team on the first CPR surveys. William Notman made good use of the material from this expedition, and therefore was anxious to have his son, William McFarlane Notman, visit the west on the new CPR line as quickly as possible. He was able to arrange for a darkroom-equipped private car and it set out for the end of steel from Calgary in July, 1884. The younger Notman produced some important views, particularly of Mount Stephen and the Kicking Horse Pass as well as the first images of the new settlements along the line, such as Canmore and Silver City. The next summer, Alexander Henderson, like Notman an established Montreal photographer, went west "to take photographs of scenery for the Company," according to Van Horne, who provided him with free travel and accommodation and subsequently bought a number of his negatives. A third photographer, Professor Otto B. Buell, a touring lantern-slide lecturer, also visited the mountains with the company's sponsorship in 1885. He met Van Horne at Calgary during his return from the last spike ceremony and presented him with an album of his views. Van Horne commented that they were "a more faithful portrayal of our magnificent scenery than anything I have yet seen."[1]

The work of Notman, Henderson and Buell provided the general manager with the highly naturalistic views of the mountains he desired, mainly to be used as the source for half-tone engravings for publication in popular journals and in the first international guide book he envisioned producing. But they would also ultimately play an important role in the work of John Fraser, the first artist commissioned by the CPR. Fraser had emigrated to Canada from England in 1860 and had initially worked for Notman hand-tinting photographs before becoming his partner in a new venture, Notman and Fraser, in Toronto. He quickly organized the most important art group in the country, the Ontario Society of Artists, and became its first vice-president. As we have seen, Van Horne had taken a very personal interest in crafting the proposed guide book, *The New Highway To The East Across The Mountains, Prairies & Rivers of Canada,* wanting to get it out before the line became operational in 1886 and desiring it to be the most up-to-date design as possible. This led him to an interest in the idea of complementing the photo-engravings with similar engravings done from works of art when the idea was put to him by Fraser in October, 1885. Fraser, following up on an earlier conversation, wrote and indicated he could do the illustration work "with photos you have and arrange for work in the field in the summer." Van Horne favoured the idea and put in Fraser's hands some of the aforementioned photographic views from which to work. This was followed up by an even more important proposition made by the general manager in a letter to Fraser dated January 6, 1886. George Stephen was at the time considering the CPR's contribution to the Colonial and Indian Exhibition to be held in London that year, a preview of Queen Victoria's Golden Jubilee scheduled for 1887, and Van Horne's letter hinted at the solution:

Mr. Stephen, our President, is anxious that some large watercolour views of our mountain scenery should be exhibited at the Colonial Exhibition, which is to be held in London next May. We have a quantity of photographic views here, new ones, which I presume would have to be depended on for material, as nothing could be done otherwise at this season of the year and Mr. Stephen will undertake to buy the pictures himself, if no better sale is made before the Exhibition closes.[2]

Fraser jumped at the opportunity and hastened to Montreal to affirm the offer and collect the photographs Van Horne had mentioned, apparently taken by Alexander Henderson. By March the artist had completed three works, the major one being a depiction of Mount Stephen, and they subsequently found primacy of place in the London exhibition. Here they were viewed by literally thousands of Britons, who for the first time were able to get some idea that the scenic wonders of the new line through the Rockies was about to open up. The commission completed, Fraser returned to the work on the pictures to be used in *The New Highway To The East*, and because its production was delayed was actually able to visit the Bow Valley and the Rockies to assist in his depiction during the summer of 1887. Van Horne found the completed pieces not grand enough to support the rhetoric being employed in *The New Highway* and, being an amateur artist and connoisseur of art himself, held no compunction in instructing Fraser to make specific changes to have the mountains appear more majestic. Apparently the artistic conception of the mountains was to only be that which was acceptable to William C. Van Horne and the CPR![3]

Fraser's work would only be the tip of the iceberg in the CPR's subsequent use of artists to convey the mountains' scenic splendours. While the company rarely commissioned artists directly, Van Horne seems to have been willing to provide free passes for travel so long as he had the opportunity "not only of judging his [the artist's or writer's] work, but also the channel through which it will reach the public."[4] Frequently passes were granted to artist on the recommendation of fellow artists who had previously received a pass, or on the approval of a well-known personage interceding on their behalf. This was the case with Lucius O'Brien, president of the Royal Canadian Academy, whose friendship with Sir Charles Tupper, Canadian High Commissioner in London, led to a successful request by Tupper to Van Horne for travel privileges for O'Brien in 1886. Van Horne was so pleased with the results of O'Brien's work that summer that he granted a similar pass the following year as well as passes O'Brien requested for fellow RCA members Thomas Mower Martin, F. M. Bell-Smith, Forshaw Day and Marmaduke Matthews. In return, the railway often received complimentary paintings for extending its courte-

F. M. Bell-Smith painting at Kicking Horse Pass, 1887

sies and sometimes Van Horne, Stephen or another official bought a painting, although the company itself rarely did.

In July, 1887 Frederic M. Bell-Smith, henceforth one of the most prolific railway artists, made his first journey west on a complimentary pass. He later recalled that he was not initially too impressed with the Rockies as the peaks were all hidden in clouds when he disembarked at Banff. But while sketching along the Bow, the clouds lifted "and Cascade Mountain with its crags and gullies white with fresh snow appeared as I have never again seen it, and my sketch provoked the remark from Mr. L. R. O'Brien, president of the Royal Canadian Academy of Arts, that it was the first time he had seen 'Cascade' look interesting."[5] The summer apparently proved to be a profitable and exciting one for the artist, according to a report the Winnipeg *Free Press* made during his journey back to Toronto:

Mr. F. M. Bell-Smith of the Royal Canadian Academy of artists has just returned from a two month's sketching tour in the Rockies. He has brought back with him studies enough to make work for him for two or three years. Tourists who passed through the mountains while he was there have given him orders for $3,000 worth of pictures to be elaborated from the sketches which they saw. . . . On the present excursion he was accompanied by Mr. O'Brien, president of the Academy and Mr. Notman, the photographer of Montreal. They worked hard, and had only one adventure which fell the lot of Mr. Bell-Smith. He was sitting sketching one day when a large bear passed within a hundred feet of him. It made no attempt to molest him, however, but slowly trotted off into some bushes. He did not give it an opportunity to reflect upon the capital meal left untasted, but lit out for home.[6]

Despite his scare, Bell-Smith was not deterred and would return to the Rockies and Selkirks to paint for a further fifteen summers in his long and illustrious career.

The stylistic roots of most of the railway artists resided in the tradition of English Romantic landscape artists and in the ideals of writer John Ruskin, who felt that art should have a social and moral purpose. The more authentic the depiction of nature and the higher the quality of the work, the more uplifted and closer to God the viewer would be. They consequently strove for an accurate portrayal of nature and paid particular attention to the changes wrought by light and weather effects, goals that help to account for the concurrent popularity of landscape photography. Their works also often introduced a human element — a train, a tourist on horseback, boaters — which both helped to illustrate CPR tourists enjoying themselves in this new mountain playground as well as the power and majesty of nature dwarfing man and his creations.

Coincidental with the appearance of these Canadian railway artists in the Valley was the visit of the first of a number of prominent American artists, thereafter equally important cultural influences. Bell-Smith later recalled his early days at Lake Louise in 1889 "in company with Mr. Albert Bierstadt, of New York, an artist very celebrated in his day." Celebrated indeed, for the German-born Bierstadt, who had been brought to the United States as a child but later returned to study in Dusseldorf, had achieved an enormous reputation for his huge landscapes of the American west, particularly in California and Colorado, during the period of rapid expansion and railway construction in the 1860s and 70s. Bierstadt was noted for using a technique of oil on paper which gave a texture to his paintings particularly well-suited to showing the effects of light sweeping across the landscape, an influence that would play a role in how Canadian railway artists, in particular Lucius O'Brien, would later paint Canada's west. Bierstadt's influence on Canadian painters had already been felt by the time he arrived in the mountains, since he had courted two successive Governors-General of Canada, Lord Dufferin and the Marquis of Lorne, in the 1870s and early-80s and had accomplished several important views of such landmarks as the Parliament Buildings in Ottawa and the Citadel in Quebec with their support.

Given his reputation and influence, it is not surprising that Van Horne should react favourably to a request from Bierstadt in June, 1887 for information concerning a proposed tour of the west, making him the unprecedented offer of free transportation and accommodation for both himself and his proposed entourage of his wife, his maid and a group of friends visiting from Europe. Circumstances intervened to prevent Bierstadt from accepting the offer that year, but it remained open and at the end of July, 1889 he departed from Montreal for the mountains. As Bell-Smith's reminiscence recalled, they joined forces when they met at Glacier House and decided to camp and sketch around Lake Louise during the month of September. They separated in early October, with Bierstadt returning to Glacier House and then making a quick trip to Alaska by steamer before returning to the mountains in early November. By mid-November he was back in New York working on some of the paintings inspired by his visit, the main ones being his magnificent *Lake Louise* and the huge *Mount Sir Donald*, but also including smaller pieces such as *View of the Rocky Mountains*, *Bow River Valley*, *Canadian Rockies*, and *Sunrise from Glacier Station*.

In May, 1890, George Stephen visited Bierstadt in his New York studio and made arrangements for *Lake Louise* and *Mount Sir Donald* to be exhibited for a forthcoming Montreal visit of Princess Louise, wife of the Marquis of Lorne and the lady for whom the lake had been named. In gratitude for his "repeated invitations to travel the C. P. R. line" and for arranging the Montreal exhibition, Bierstadt presented George Stephen with *Sunrise from Glacier Station* as a gift. It was shipped to Stephen's palatial Montreal residence, which was later to become the popular Mount Stephen Club, and hung there in public view until the early 1990s. Unfortunately, it was one of the few Bierstadt paintings to remain in the country, as most found their way into American hands. However, his lasting influence on Canadian painters such as O'Brien and Bell-Smith would also form an important part of his artistic legacy.[7]

There were other prominent artists who made appearances equally as brief as Bierstadt's in the Rockies that added to the American patrimony. One who would eventually gain a reputation equal to his own was the foremost recorder of disappearing western American life, Frederic Remington. Working as a magazine illustrator at the time, he visited the Canadian Rockies in 1887 and 1890 to find landscape material to provide background for his depictions of frontier life. He apparently heavily relied on photographic views in his work, and one of the few surviving Remington landscapes, entitled *Banff*, shows a view of the Valley from the Upper Hot Springs bearing a remarkable resemblance to a Notman photograph. Cleveland Rockwell, an artist, mapmaker and topographer known for his defense maps produced for the Union Army during the American Civil War, was another American artist who briefly frequented the area. Rockwell was Chief of the U. S. Geodesic Survey of the Northwest stationed in Portland in the 1880s and 90s, a period during which he painted extensively in the British Columbia Rockies. In 1904 he captured several scenes around Banff, a notable one being a panorama-like, highly romantic view of the Banff Springs Hotel. A third prominent American was John Singer Sargent, the foremost American portrait artist of his day, who in 1916 was inspired by a postcard view of Twin Falls in the Yoho Valley and a commission to paint it, to spend the summer camping and painting in the Yoho and around Lake O'Hara. Perhaps two of the most accomplished landscapes ever produced in the mountains were the result — *Yoho Falls* which resides in Boston's Isabella Stewart Gardner Museum and *Lake O'Hara* which is at Harvard's Fogg Art Museum.

But it would be another German-American painter who would have the most important influence on the aesthetic vision of the Valley, one who would spend a lifetime interpreting its natural and scenic splendours in ways never accomplished before or since. Carl Rungius came from a different artistic tradition than did his countryman Bierstadt, following in the footsteps of such great European natural history painters as Edward Landseer and Richard Friese. After training at the Berlin *Kunstschule* (Art School) and later the *Kunstakademie* (Academy of Art), during which time he became interested in sketching animals at the Berlin Zoo, he was taken under the wing of a professor of animal drawing and painting at the *Kunstakademie* and by 1890 was exhibiting in the Greater Berlin International Art Exhibition. Then, in 1894, by a stroke of good fortune his uncle Dr. Clemens Fulda in New York invited him to come to America to hunt moose. The hunt took place in Maine, and although it was unsuccessful it unleashed a desire in young Rungius to explore and paint the great animals and wildernesses of North America. He returned to Germany for one last year and then emigrated to the United States to begin a career as an illustrator for the many sporting magazines and books then popular in the country. Although he had little money, he spent a portion of each summer and autumn until 1901 in Wyoming, painting elk and pronghorn antelope.

Rungius made his first visit to western Canada in 1904, accompanying Dr. William Temple Hornaday, the director of the New York Zoological Society, in his investigations of the species of sheep inhabiting the Yukon Territory. The trip not only introduced him to Hornaday, whose connections in the growing hunter-conservation movement in the United States would subsequently provide him with many wealthy clients, but also resulted in a painting that would have major consequences for the heritage of the Banff-Bow Valley. In 1910, Banff outfitter Jimmy Simpson, by this time himself a collector of wildlife art, saw a reproduction of a Rungius painting of Dall sheep in the Society's *Bulletin* and wrote to the artist care of the Society, stating that he admired his ability to capture sheep in paint and inviting him to come to the Canadian Rockies where, he said, the landscape and big game were awaiting an artist of Rungius's skill. Rungius at first threw the letter in the trash, but at his wife's insistence re-read it and decided to take Simpson up on his offer. It was the beginning of a story that would see two of the area's most important traditions — outfitting and guiding and wilderness art — intersect, for after their first successful hunting and painting trip, Simpson and Rungius would for many years make a "packhorses for paintings" deal. Jimmy would supply the outfit and one of his men to act as packer for the annual sketching expedition and Carl would pay him in paintings later worked up in his New York studio.

By 1922 Simpson had found two lots on Cave Avenue to allow Rungius to build a Banff studio, subsequently referred to by the artist as "The Paintbox." It provided him with the leisure to work up paintings in their surroundings, spending longer periods over different seasons in the mountains' changing atmospheres and affording him the opportunity to observe elk, moose, deer and bear easily. But while it allowed him to earn the reputation of "the Rembrandt of the moose," as one writer put it, there were also other benefits, as it added to his ability to master pure landscape. In 1913 he exhibited his first landscape, a painting of Mount Athabasca, at the National Academy of Design and by 1925 his skills in the genre had won him the Academy's prestigious Carnegie Prize for his magnificent *Lake McArthur*. In short, "The Paintbox" allowed him to become the consummate wilderness artist. An assessment of this transformation from an accomplished wildlife artist to a complete painter is provided in Jon Whyte's and E. J. Hart's *Carl Rungius, Painter of the Western Wilderness*:

Carl Rungius's success as a big game painter came from knowledge gained through hunting and the study of large animal anatomy

The nature of light in the Rockies induced him to see the world as he had never seen it before. His Yukon summer of 1904 introduced him to northern light, the oblique, sharp light that reveals distance, form and mass. In the harsh relief of the Canadian Rockies, the perceptions of a northern artist that had been incipient in the Yukon became a truth he could not deny. . . . The northern Rockies became his deliverance.[8]

Rungius was not the only American wilderness artist whose residence in Banff added to the town's growing cultural character as well as its artistic legacy. Belmore Browne, a native of Staten Island, New York, had studied at the New York School of Art and the Academie Julien in Paris before establishing a life-long reputation as an explorer and painter of Alaska's Mount McKinley region. First visiting Alaska in 1889 with his father, a timber merchant in Tacoma, Washington, in 1901 he spent the first of two seasons as a hunter, expedition artist and specimen collector in northern Alaska, working for the American Museum of Natural History. He honed his mountaineering skills in the Olympic Mountains of Washington State and the Cascade Range of British Columbia, leading the first ascent of Mount Olympus in 1908, and, like Rungius, made his living largely as an illustrator for the many fishing, hunting and exploration magazines of the day. While travelling in the Canadian Rockies he met Professor Herschel Parker of Columbia University, one of the prominent American tourist-explorers climbing in the area, and together they planned a 1910 expedition to climb Mount McKinley. They were unsuccessful and would return in 1912 in an attempt that would take them to within 450 feet of the summit of the highest peak in North America, leading to Browne's work on establishing McKinley (Denali) National Park and the 1913 publication of his landmark book on Alaska, *The Conquest of Mount McKinley*. After 1915 he worked largely as a landscape and figure painter, making mountains his specialty and inevitably leading him back to the Canadian Rockies.

Browne married in 1913 and soon had a young family, tempering his desire to live in Alaska with a less remote location. He had passed through the Rockies at least once on his way north and was an acquaintance of Rungius's, both being members of New York's Salmagundi Art Club and the Camp Fire Club of America, leading his gaze to fall upon Banff. In the summer of 1921, he acquired a home on Spray Avenue, which he named "Illahee Lodge" (now Elkhorn Lodge), and brought his wife and family out for a summer filled with pack trips and painting expeditions. These family adventures, interspersed with teaching assignments at the Santa Barbara Art School, would continue to 1940 and would make Browne part of the growing artistic milieu in Banff, allowing him to fine-tune his skills as a landscape painter and become an accomplished interpreter of big game as well. By the mid-twenties these trips often took the Browne family to Jimmy Simpson's camp at Bow Lake, and, as in the case of Rungius, he acquired a fine representative sample of the artist's work. In 1941 Browne wrote an article for *The American Alpine Journal* in which he reflected on the challenges that painting the mountain wilderness presented to the artist and how the inability to achieve perfection was compensated for by the wonderful life of the trail:

You will feel the same mental exaltation in reaching such a spot that you would feel in being the first to gain a difficult summit, and on these painting trips you will have adventures aplenty, for in packing horses beyond the blazed trail you will lead the life of the early pioneers.

For the past twenty summers I have taken my family into the mountains surrounding Banff. On each trip we have tried to reach places we have not seen before, but vast stretches of untried country still beckon us on.

So grasp your paintbrush firmly, courageous reader, for, while its strange whims may lead you to the belief that you have clutched a witches' broomstick, it will carry you to visions you will never glimpse otherwise.[9]

The early twenties also saw a re-affirmation of Canadian artistic influence in the Rockies, a standing that had gradually dwindled as the first wave of "the railroad school" declined after the turn-of-the-century. However, some of the early painters, such as Bell-Smith, had continued to come west and were joined by a few second-generation railway artists, although these were now more often commercial illustrators working directly for the CPR on its advertising program. Among them were John Hammond, a Montreal artist who had first worked as a Notman photographic assistant on the 1871 CPR-Geological Survey Expedition, and George Horne Russell, one of the newer members of the RCA noted for his eastern seascapes who regularly performed commissions featuring miniscule trains passing through the majestic landscape. Photographers, too, continued to have their place. Independent photographers such as A. B. Thom, Boorne and May, Bailey Brothers and R. H. Trueman gradually established themselves in the centres of population between Winnipeg and Vancouver and made much of their living in the 1890s and early

Byron Harmon's goal was to photograph every peak in the Rockies and Selkirks

years of the new century selling postcards, prints and viewbooks of photographs taken "along the line." In Banff itself, Byron Harmon, an itinerant photographer from Tacoma, Washington, appeared in 1903 and soon established himself in business, stating as his objective the photographing of every peak in the Selkirks and Rockies. His success at becoming the official photographer of the Alpine Club of Canada shortly after its creation in 1906 allowed him the opportunity to make good on his ambition, and his views and postcards were subsequently sold to millions of visitors to the Banff from a family-run business on Banff Avenue. The work of these photographers and others of their profession, much of it eventually being produced in hand-painted or machine-coloured form, would provide the most widely distributed and often the most vividly recalled visual records of the Valley.

Meanwhile, in eastern Canada, the long-standing search for a distinctive national school of Canadian art began to bear fruit in the early twenties with the formation of the "Group of Seven." Artists A. Y. Jackson, J. E. H. MacDonald, Franz Johnston, F. H. Varley, Arthur Lismer, Lawren Harris and Franklin Carmichael had deliberately set out to express in their art the rising spirit of

Canadian nationalism through the creation of a distinctive style reflecting the Canadian character as expressed through the depiction of its rugged landscape. Reminiscent of Scandinavian painting and the Fauvist, Symbolist and Post-Impressionist movements of Europe, their work relied on flat, patterned splashes of vibrant colour rather than the rather dark, tonal landscapes popular in England and Europe at the time. At first interpreting the most rugged landscapes available close to their Toronto base, such as Georgian Bay, Algoma and Algonquin Park, it was inevitable that their collective gaze would eventually fall upon the mountains. It was in 1924 that the Group, travelling the country in search of the true images of Canada, began to actively paint the Rockies and over the next six years Jackson, Harris, Lismer, Varley and MacDonald all worked in the Valley.

Two of the Group, MacDonald and Harris, were particularly entranced by the opportunities the mountains provided for their work. MacDonald returned to the Rockies for seven years, becoming especially fond of the Lake O'Hara region, until ill-health forced him to stop after 1930. As a painter who also practiced the art of the word in his poetry, he believed that art and poetry were complementary and that both were at their best when done with restraint and when rendered into understandable rhythms and patterns. His trips were conducted in the late summer and early fall when the larches were at their height, providing the patterns and strong colours he was looking for. His diaries are replete with thoughts on his philosophy and with comments on how the high alpine areas he loved to paint provided all that the artist could want: "In these great places all the functions of Nature are on a big scale and the material workings of the frost and wind and rain are clear to us."[10]

Fellow Group member Lawren Harris was also powerfully moved by the mountains, but for him they became more of a mystical experience than a poetic expression, a jumping off point between the earthly world and the divine. He too spent part of almost every summer after 1925 in the Rockies, travelling more widely to powerfully inspiring locations such as Jasper's Tonquin and Maligne Valleys as well as to the obligatory spots around Moraine Lake and Lake Louise in the Bow Valley. The sketches accomplished on these trips were worked up in the studio into austerely simplified abstract images that represented the spiritual simplicity that Harris felt was exemplified by the Canadian landscape: "We are on the fringes of the Great North . . . [whose] source of spiritual flow will ever shed clarity into the growing race of America, and, we Canadians being closest to this source, seem destined to produce an art somewhat different than our southern fellows — an art more spacious, of greater living quiet, perhaps of a more certain conviction of eternal values. . . ."[11] By 1929 Harris had become the only Valley artist of the historic period to make the leap to abstraction, leaving behind the confines of representational "nature as art" that is clearly its aesthetic legacy.

All of the artistic influences swirling around Banff in the early twenties had an impact on the Valley's first native-born artist. Peter White (later Whyte) was born in Banff in 1905, the son of Dave White, the pioneer CPR sectionman who had first laid eyes on Banff in 1886, and Annie Curren. Annie was the daughter of coal scout John Curren of Anthracite, himself a naive painter who had produced the first artistic interpretations of such local features as the original log building at the Cave and Basin and the rough shelter at Lake Louise. Peter White grew up benefiting from all of the recreational activities available to a lad in Banff, such as skiing, ski jumping, snowshoeing, horseback riding and hiking, making him an accomplished outdoorsman by his teens. Aware that artists such as Rungius and Browne were working in the area, he decided he wanted to emulate them and initially enrolled in a mail-order cartooning course before participating in school courses in art taught by Norah Drummond-Davies and Browne.

Drummond-Davies was one of Banff's most unique characters during the decade after the First World War, inhabiting a small cabin at the foot of Stoney Squaw Mountain surrounded by eleven dogs and numerous cats and making her living as an illustrator for British postcard-maker Raphael Tuck. But she also did some large paintings, particularly of wildlife, many of them twice the size of her diminutive five feet that required her to attach her paintbrush to a broomhandle to reach the upper sections. These paintings found their way into the hands of local hoteliers and businessmen and were displayed on the walls of hotel dining rooms and movie theatres, actually introducing many tourists to their first mountain art. While she was a great assistance to the young artist in his drawing, it was Browne, in particular, who was a formative influence on him. White began to take private lessons from him and commented that "he has a clear vision and a philosophy on life which I am always ready to listen to."

Living in a tourist town, White found summer employment with the Brewster Transport Company and was often assigned to chauffeur the numerous stars and other movie people working in the area. They convinced him to study art in California, and in the winter of 1924-25 he attended the Otis Art Institute in Los Angeles. About the same time he was asked by the manager of Lake O'Hara Lodge to accompany J. E. H. MacDonald on some of his painting hikes, as he was worried about running into bears, a marvellous opportunity for a neophyte artist to see a master at work. Then in 1925, he was assigned to provide a similar service to the New England landscape painter Aldro T. Hibbard, who modestly described himself as "a strict observer of Nature's facts" but was actually one of Vermont's finest artists. They painted around O'Hara together and Hibbard, impressed by his guide's latent abilities, convinced him arrangements could be made to attend his *alma mater*, the Museum School of the Boston Museum of Fine Arts.

White took Hibbard up on his offer, enrolling in the Museum School that fall. There he met Catharine Robb, a half-day student who was testing her own desire to become an artist, and in 1927 they fell in love. Catharine was a native of near-by Concord and had profited from the influence of her maternal grandfather Edward Sylvester Morse, a noted collector of Japanese ceramics and the first director of the Peabody Museum in Salem, Massachusetts, and her mother, a designer and producer of needlepoint patterns. Their artistic training was a formal one but

Catharine Whyte, Adeline Link, J. E. H. MacDonald and Peter Whyte at Lake O'Hara, 1930

Catharine was enamoured by Peter's descriptions of the freedom of painting the mountains, drawing the two closer together and eventually resulting in their marriage in 1930. In the winter of 1930-31 their log studio-home was built along the Bow River in Banff and they began a long and productive practice of spending as much time in the field as possible, executing small sketches of the landscape that were so similar one-to-another that in many it is difficult to determine who was the artist. Their home also contained a studio to enable them to work these field pieces up into larger canvases, but they rarely did, instead using it to paint portraits of their numerous Stoney friends and native life as well as some of Banff's old-timers, like Tom Wilson. As Jon Whyte has described in the exhibition catalogue *Mountain Glory, The Art of Peter and Catharine Whyte* they made no great leaps forward in their work but they did impart the human dimension and spirit of the

Valley in their portraiture, native life and ski paintings and also successfully captured the atmosphere and light of the mountains in their field sketches:

In Pete's paintings, gloomy, tragic, foreboding, hostile peaks hover over shadowed slopes. He responds to the mountains with emotions something like a climber's, ambiguously loving and fearing them. Catharine loves the sky and weather's brief moments. Since light and shadow intrigue her, she pursues effect more than form. Peter's compositional rigor — MacDonald's lesson — is so firm we seek to no avail the light which creates such strong relief, whereas we have no doubt what light rakes Catharine's scenes. Natural forces animate her sketches: sunlight, wind, storm, the dazzle of sunlight on water, the changing seasons, the flame of aspens in autumn.[12]

The Whyte's home was not only the headquarters for their own frequent sketching trips into the surrounding mountains, but also a place to which those interested in art or seeking their own special spot to sketch would gravitate to for tea, information and an opportunity to talk with kindred spirits. And with their establishment as, in effect, "artists-in-residence" in Banff, combined with the seasonal studio-residences of Rungius and Browne, the Valley had reached an important juncture in the evolution of its aesthetic tradition. Yet, this was only one of two important occurrences at the time that would have far-reaching consequences for its future artistic heritage. A second had to do with the creation of Alberta's first formal art school, an offshoot of which would lead to Banff's own contribution to artistic education and development.

In 1926 Lars Haukaness, an itinerant Norwegian landscape painter trained in the fundamentals of Impressionism who had been painting in the Lake Louise-Skoki area for several years, moved to Calgary. His large, heavily painted impressionistic canvases of the mountain landscape caused quite a stir in local artistic circles, particularly when they were shown at a class he taught at the Calgary Art Club that year. The notoriety led to an invitation in 1927 to begin teaching a painting course at the Provincial

Institute of Technology and Art (or the "Tech" as it became known). His ambition quickly turned to making these classes into the basis for a provincial art school, a goal cut short by his untimely death in 1929 from heart failure while returning from his sketching camp at Ptarmigan Lake. Haukaness's replacement at Tech was an English watercolour artist who had initially been introduced to the west and the mountains by the now well-established practice of the CPR to use artists in producing colour illustrations for its advertising material. Alfred C. Leighton had first come to the attention of the CPR's London office in 1924 when he was hired as an illustrator for its cruise campaign, and in 1925 he was sent to Canada to paint the mountains with fellow company artist Leonard Richmond. Much taken with the experience, Leighton was able to convince the railway to have him return in 1927 and join Gibbon's Trail Riders of the Canadian Rockies, giving him his first access to the high alpine meadows and rocky summits he became famous for painting. That same year he held his first exhibition in Canada, an incongruous mixing of his Kent and Sussex windmills with his mountain landscapes. The show travelled to Vancouver, Winnipeg, Calgary and Banff, bringing him to the attention of Dr. W. G. Carpenter, director of the Institute, and resulting in the invitation in 1929 to head its art school.

Leighton would quickly become successful in developing the Institute's painting program and, combined with his belief that sketching formed the basis for all good painting, led him to invite some of his most promising pupils to join him for a three-week summer sketching camp headquartered at a ranch established by the Brewster family at Kananaskis. This annual camp would become the genesis for the creation of the Banff School of Fine Arts later in the decade, and combined with the reception of artists of all ilk in the Whyte's studio-home, marked the beginning of Banff's subsequent fame as an artist's colony. Two remarkable institutions which continue to celebrate the Valley's aesthetic tradition and to dominate its cultural landscape to the present day, the Banff Centre and the Whyte Museum of the Canadian Rockies, would be the ultimate result of these influences.

Chapter Ten
Sanctuaries of the Original and the Wild

The marrying of a growing aesthetic appreciation of the Banff-Bow Valley's landscapes and natural life with its tradition of outfitting and guiding, evident in the "packhorses for paintings" arrangement of Simpson and Rungius, became apparent in another guise after the turn-of-the-century. A developing understanding of the need to protect the very elements of that mountain wilderness led to those who had learned its ways working as guides and packers being recruited for a new and unique line of work. How this came about had its roots in the increasing reassessment of the value of the Valley's resources separate from that implicit in Macdonald's national policy.

Initially the economic imperative that had dominated the opening of the park under the policy had almost totally excluded any strongly-held preservation or conservation philosophy, which was much more common in the American park system. This was recognized by no less an authority than James Bernard Harkin, Commissioner of Dominion Parks, who in 1924 made a telling admission about the parks' creation and evolution:

At the outset the main impulse was to set these areas aside; to mark them as public possessions. What specific purposes the parks could serve, what ideals should mould them, what policy should be adopted for development — these objectives were only dimly understood. The policy has had to be gradually evolved. Switzerland years before had demonstrated that mountain areas of supreme beauty were a distinct commercial asset and from the outset this aspect was kept in view. While those associated with the work have long since ceased to regard the commercial side as the most important consideration they have never disregarded the part it plays.[1]

Harkin's statement hinted at the fact that another, more important consideration — one that he himself was a powerful spokesman for — was coming to the forefront by this time. In fact, it was during the short term of office of Howard Douglas, his predecessor as Parks Commissioner, and his own twenty-five year service in that position that the first glimmerings of a conservation and preservation ethic, a conviction that would later become a fundamental principle of Bow Valley life, first saw the light of day.

If one wished to argue that some aspect of the conservation ideal had been recognized early in park history, they would have to go no further than the Rocky Mountains Park Act itself. Clause 4 of the bill spoke of the "preservation and protection of game and fish [and] wild birds generally," although there is no doubt that this clause was meant to be subservient to those promoting tourism and allowing resource extraction. While the source of this clause in the Act is unclear, it likely originated in the influence on the creation of the park brought to bear by the setting up of Yellowstone Park in 1872 by the United States government, where the inspiration was purely conservationist in orientation. It is also possible that part of the inspiration came from observation of the depredations on fish and game in the mountains resulting from railroad construction and post-construction resource exploitation. In any event, its inclusion was remarkable in the Canadian circumstances of a generally-held belief in the myth of superabundance of wildlife and the seemingly endless supply of forest, mineral, and water resources in the yet untapped North West Territories.

To better grasp the situation in the area slated to become the park, Minister of the Interior Thomas White in 1886 appointed former Commissioner of Fisheries of Canada W. F. Whitcher to "conduct an investigation into the park's flora and fauna and make recommendations concerning the husbanding of these resources for the benefit of the tourist." Whitcher carried out a desultory examination and in a communication to White on the last day of 1886 he reported:

Large game and fish, once various and plentiful in this mountainous region, are now scattered and comparatively scarce.

Skin-hunters, dynamiters and netters, with Indians, wolves and foxes, have committed sad havoc. The rapid settlement now progressing in that vicinity will add other elements of destruction. Therefore . . . the necessity for promptness and efficiency becomes a vital urgency in the adoption of any scheme for saving and increasing what is left. How to avert irreparable disaster to the remnant of game and fish, to restore partial exhaustion, to restock the mountain uplands, valleys and plains, and to replenish the waters is worthy of immediate and serious consideration.[2]

To prevent the "sad havoc" of fish and game destruction, Whitcher proposed that police officers and forest rangers having experience with wild animals and mountains be placed at Banff to "secure the park against injury and destruction." Lest he be regarded too much as a conservation visionary, it should be noted that he also regarded hunting in the park as an acceptable activity for "immediate sport and domestic use," believing that it would be easier to convince people of the reasonableness of wildlife preservation if some limited taking of game were allowed. As well, he was a believer that mankind could assist in the balancing of nature by weeding out "noxious" or "bad" animals and birds (wolves, coyotes, foxes, lynx, skunks, weasels, wildcats, porcupines, badgers and all raptors) that preyed on "good" animals (mainly ungulates such as deer, moose and elk). And, of course, this was all to be done to achieve the primary end for the park — "plenteousness of wildlife would be a source of profit and pleasure to Canadians interested in its development as a free popular resort for health and recreation. . . ." Still, the significance of the investigation and its findings should not be overlooked, and indeed some of the ideas that Whitcher put forward would eventually be adopted.

Superintendent Stewart' s attention was largely taken up with development and lease work, but he was able to act on one of Whitcher's suggestions. In 1888 he wrote the Minister seeking assistance in the difficult task of retaining order and good govern-

Superintendent George Stewart (second right), almost single-handedly carried out the early development of Rocky Mountains Park

ment in the park, asking for a "game guardian" with the powers of a constable to be stationed at Lake Minnewanka to protect game and to attend to "the prevention of fires, and the enforcement of the Rules and Regulations of the Park, particularly those relating to liquor," the latter a result of the frequent bootleg activities being carried out in the vicinity. In 1889 his request was answered with the appointment of John Connor as forest ranger responsible for the prevention of forest fires and enforcement of regulations against hunting, he essentially being the first member of what would later become the park warden service, another fundamental element in the Valley's life. The hunting regulations that Connor was to enforce, proclaimed in 1890, were far tougher than those forseen by Whitcher, as visitors to the park were prohibited from carrying weapons and from killing or injuring any wild animals and birds, with the exception wolves, bears, coyotes, cougars, wolverines, lynx, hawks and eagles. Despite these restrictions, Connor complained of "people carrying rifles around, and banging them off whenever they like" with the consequence of "rifle bullets flying across from one road to another."[3]

Unfortunately, Connor died in 1890 and Stewart was too distracted elsewhere to press for a replacement (he complained that he had to be an engineer, surveyor, architect, land agent, forest ranger, justice of the peace and accountant during his administration). Instead, he was forced to fight a rearguard action to protect himself, as an official with such broad powers as he was bound to create enemies. Disagreements with the local police detachment concerning the enforcement of liquor regulations were interspersed with having to defend himself against charges of mismanagement of lease matters and led to a variety of critics. When the Conservatives were ousted by the Liberals in the general election of 1896, the writing was on the wall in an age of blatant political patronage and an investigation into his administration, not surprisingly, found that "harmony and satisfaction could not be looked for." He was therefore dismissed, despite all his good work in almost single-handedly getting the park and the town up and running. The competition for his job soon heated up with two contenders — Major John Walker, who as mentioned was an influential businessman with interests in Banff and the Bow Valley, and Calgary coal merchant Howard Douglas, who was nominated by the Calgary Liberal Association and supported by A. L. Sifton, brother of the new Minister of the Interior, Clifford Sifton. Douglas won the nod, and despite the fact of his being a political appointment it was one that would have great benefit for Rocky Mountains Park and the protection of its natural resources.

Like his predecessor Stewart, Douglas was often seized by matters of development in the park, but he had the advantage of coming into office under a somewhat more enlightened government at a time when the depression of the early nineties was lifting and Rocky Mountains Park was beginning to experience a tourism boom. Soon after taking office he came to the conclusion that visitors to the park were not only interested in soaking in the hot springs and viewing the scenery, but also enjoyed the opportunity to see wildlife. To assist them, Douglas was able to convince his superiors to have an animal paddock built in 1898 in the vicinity of today's Indian Grounds, the first denizens being three buffalo that were donated by Toronto lawyer T. G. Blackstock. As plains bison were all but extinct by this time, the acquisition was a real coup and focused much public attention on the initiative. In 1899 Donald Smith (now Lord Strathcona) was convinced to donate his herd of thirteen head from his ranch at Silver Heights, and by 1906 the "Buffalo Paddock" herd, as it was being called, had increased to fifty-one by natural reproduction. While buffalo were the main attraction, other species were also housed at the paddock, several of them, such as mule deer, elk, mountain sheep and moose, being native species found in the wild in the park, but not, it seems, in great enough numbers that it could be assured tourists would see them. Douglas felt these animals would provide breeding stock for the re-population of their species in the park, and, indeed, within a few years he could point to some healthy increases. However, concepts of preservation at the time were only minimally evolved and he began introducing non-native species, such as angora goats and persian sheep, at the paddock. An even more immediate vehicle for tourists to view animals was created with the opening in 1907 of the Banff Zoo, eventually containing everything from polar bears to peacocks, adjacent to the Park Museum in the town's central park. Nevertheless, Douglas is perhaps best remembered for his success in achieving a great coup in the preservation field in 1907 though his involvement in bringing to Canada the largest remaining bison herd in North America, the Pablo-Allard herd of Montana numbering some 350 animals, which were to form the basis for later national park herds.[4]

Additional concern for game protection was shown by Douglas in his efforts to have the boundaries of the park expanded to protect wildlife from hunters, in particular natives. Stewart had also attempted to promote this, but did not have his superiors' ear to the same extent as Douglas, and reports debunking the myth of superabundance were beginning to reach federal officials by the latter's time. Other voices joined in supporting Douglas's position, including the influential A. E. Cross, member of the Legislative Assembly of the North West Territories, who argued that there was a need to have "an extent of country large enough for game to breed in and to have a National Park that the Dominion could be proud of." Also, William Pearce used his influence to lobby the Minister on the matter, stating that it was his understanding that Stoney and Kootenay Indians were responsible for wildlife destruction and that if it continued unabated many game animals would become extinct.[5] Douglas constantly brought the matter up in his annual reports to the Minister, arguing that Rocky Mountains Park was only one-tenth the size of Yellowstone and postulating that expanding its boundaries would also encourage its success as a centre for mountain exploration by tourists. The voices in favour were recognized in 1902 when the 1887 Act was amended to expand the existing 260 square mile parcel to an amazing 4,900 square miles. This took the boundary right to the headwaters of the Bow River, including incorporating the sources of most of its mountain tributaries, and downstream to the Front Ranges absorbing the coal mines at Canmore, the lime operations at the Gap and the timber berths in the Kananaskis.

Douglas's success in the movement to have the park enlarged indirectly led to what was perhaps his most far-reaching achievement — the creation of an effective warden service to protect the park's natural and game resources. In 1899, the federal government, in a recognition of the need to husband the forest wealth of the Rocky Mountain area, created a separate Forestry Branch whose responsibilities included protection of timber in the Park, following it up in 1906 with the passage of the Dominion Forest Reserves Act. The same year the first Canadian Forestry Convention, emulating similar initiatives in the United States, examined the growing understanding of the effects of forest conservation on water resources and irrigation. Both Stewart and Douglas had been charged with forest protection as part of their duties, but with the exception of Connors's brief service and the short-lived appointment of Bill Brewster as a forest ranger to patrol the railway line in 1901, there was no permanent source of manpower available to perform the task. Fire protection by default fell to the small police force, assisted by railway employees and volunteer local citizens, a situation which in 1889 would likely have resulted in the destruction of the Banff townsite when a serious fire broke out in the Vermilion Lakes hay marshes were it not for a fortuitous shift in the wind direction.

Douglas pointed out the need for more manpower to administer the huge new area under his control, and in 1907 was given permission to hire a new game guardian — none other than Philip Moore, silent partner with Jim and Bill Brewster in their burgeoning outfitting operations and rapidly becoming an accomplished outdoorsman himself. However, as the Brewsters were strong Liberal supporters, the appointment probably had as much to do with politics as ability, and, in any event, was as shortlived as his brother-in-law Bill's had been. Douglas understood that one man could do little in such a vast extent of territory, but felt that the appointment would help to cool the ardour of some of the more inveterate poachers while he continued to lobby for more assistance. By early 1909 he had been promoted to the new position of Commissioner of Parks, although still under the aegis of the Dominion Forestry Branch, and was calling for the hiring of a "chief game guardian" at Banff with two assistants, each of whom would be supplied with two horses and would be stationed at "outlying points."[6] These men would enforce fire regulations and keep an eye on potential poaching by monitoring guides and outfitters and those travelling through the park to hunt outside its boundaries. New regulations passed in June, 1909 for the first time specifically allowed for such a force and effectively became the "constitution" of the warden service. Section 75 read:

Game guardians may be appointed by the Minister of the Interior; and such Guardians shall have authority to enforce the laws and regulations in force within the Parks. Each game guardian shall be furnished with a badge of office which shall be displayed by him on every occasion when he is exercising the authority of his office.[7]

Chosen to head the new service was Howard Sibbald, a man who has been described as "an energetic and practical outdoorsman who would guide the Warden Service during its first quarter century." Sibbald was the son of Andrew Sibbald, the first school teacher at the McDougall Mission, and as a ten-year-old boy in 1875 had accompanied his parents on a 105 day wagon trip from their home at Barrie, Ontario to Morley. Raised on the reserve among the Stoney, he had learned their traditions and wilderness ways from childhood and could ride and hunt with the best of them. For several years he had worked at the Leeson and Scott ranch near Morley, and immediately prior to his appointment at Banff had been employed by the government as Indian Agent at Gleichen. He was soon impressing all with his abilities, and appointed to assist him in 1909 were Bob Robertson and Jock Hogarth of Banff, also competent mountain men familiar with backcountry conditions and travel. Their qualifications and duties have been well described by the official historian of the warden service, Bob Burns, in his report *Guardians Of The Wild: A History Of The Wardens Of Canada's National Parks*:

Howard Sibbald, the first chief game guardian of Rocky Mountains Park

In practice the new game guardians were to be chosen, following political considerations, from those who were familiar with life and survival in the mountains. This meant in most cases the choice of men who had served as outfitters, guides and packers in the Rockies. The delicate issue here was to pick individuals who had not in the past been too blatant in their violation of existing poaching and weapons regulations. . . .

Superintendents were directed that additions to the Warden Service "shall be strong, sober, industrious, used to operating in the woods, able to organize and manage a crew of fire fighters, and shall have education enough to report intelligently to the Department." The regulations also envisioned the work to be carried out by the guardians and referred specifically to "trails to be patrolled, old roads and trails to be cleared and repaired, new roads and trails to be made, (identification of) equipment needed, rangers cabins and other buildings to be constructed, signal towers to be erected, telephone lines to be built, and other work to be done.[8]

By the time the "game and fire guardian" service was created, the backcountry had begun to be opened up with the horse trails forged by the early guides and packers, themselves following traditional native paths and game trails, and by shorter trails in the neighbourhood of the railway and hotels cleared by CPR contractors. But simultaneous with the creation of the service, the government also began the task of creating new "bridle trails" to remote areas to spur greater wilderness travel and provide access for fire protection purposes. These were usually contracted out to local bidders such as Joe Boyce, who built the first six-foot-wide trail under this scheme extending nineteen miles from Banff to the summit of Simpson Pass in 1909. The next year tenders were called for fifty miles of trails, including one fourteen miles long on the north side of Lake Minnewanka and one twenty-four miles long joining Banff with the Spray Lakes. By 1914 Sibbald's successor P. C. Barnard-Hervey could state in his annual report that the trail system in Rocky Mountains Park extended over 600 miles.

Combined with the clearing of these new trails for access, the building of shelter cabins was to become a key part of the warden system and lifestyle. The idea behind the cabins was to give the men more freedom of movement in their wilderness patrols by not having to carry tents and camping equipment and to provide a safe location to store necessary equipment, such as that used for fighting fires. They were constructed by the guardians themselves from logs found on location, finished with wood roofs, shingles, shiplap floors, heavy doors and two windows, all hauled in by

Warden Ulysses LaCasse at RMP No. 3 "Windy" in 1917

packhorse. The basic design was one room of approximately fourteen by sixteen feet inside measurements, with walls six-and-a-half feet high, and equipped with a bunk, a collapsible stove and a table. By the spring of 1912, five such cabins had been erected, including one near Spray Lakes, one on the Kananaskis River and another forty miles north of Banff up the Cascade Valley on the Panther River, all eventually numbered consecutively "R.M.P. No. 1," "R.M.P. No. 2," "R.M.P. No. 3" etc.[9]

These and all subsequent warden houses and cabins built throughout the front and backcountry of the park would become an important feature of its history and character. In 1913 Sibbald decided to implement a new patrol system based on seven districts, and several of the cabins thereafter became a headquarters, with the district warden, often accompanied by his family, living in closest contact with nature and learning the characteristics and attributes of his area like the back of his hand. Such close association would lead to greater understanding, knowledge and appreciation of the park and its wildlife. The other non-headquarters or "patrol cabins" were to be left open to the public when not in use and each had a notice attached to it:

This cabin is for the use of the fire and game warden. In his absence it may be used by campers, but must be left clean. Any person who takes from this cabin any tool or utensil, except for the purpose of fighting a forest fire, is liable to a fine of $100.[10]

No abuses of this privilege were reported in the early years of the service's activities and this "open-door" policy allowed many backcountry travellers shelter from bad weather and may have even saved a few from freezing in cold winter conditions. The latter-day practice of locking the cabins became one of the most often recalled changes to the way the parks were operated by those remembering "the good old days."

The establishment of the guardian system immediately had the effects that had been hoped for. In an April, 1911 report to the Minister of the Interior, Douglas, writing from his office in Edmonton where he had been transferred to more closely oversee the establishment of the new Jasper Park, proudly stated:

Since the inauguration, in 1909, of a system of game and fire protection, by the appointment of permanent game and fire wardens, whose duty it is to patrol the park, the game in the park has greatly increased and the animals are coming closer to the village of Banff and the paths of tourists, and are less timid. As a matter of fact, it is not uncommon occurrence to see deer on the lawns of the residences of Banff. . . . This has been largely due to the exclusion of dogs from the park and the enforcement of the regulation prohibiting the carrying of any, but sealed, fire-arms within the confines of the park. The fact that these game wardens are constantly patrolling the park has resulted in the almost total abolition of the poaching. . . .

There is no doubt that the patrolling daily of the park by the fire guardians, and the enforcement of the regulations regarding camping parties, has been largely responsible for the small amount of damage by fire reported, and is sufficient proof of the wisdom of having permanent men on the ground. In many cases, when out on patrol, they have been able to discover and extinguish small fires before they had made much headway, and have thus been enabled to preserve much of the natural beauty of the park.[11]

The fact that Douglas and Sibbald were serious about enforcing game regulations was well-illustrated in 1912 when Sibbald and two deputy guardians apprehended former game and fire guardian Phil Moore and his brother-in-law Jim Brewster, two of Banff's foremost citizens, for killing mountain sheep in the park.

These results likely played an important role in the appointment of additional guardians in Rocky Mountains Park as well as in Yoho and Glacier Parks and the new Jasper Park. By the summer of 1912 Sibbald had twelve men at his disposal in Rocky Mountains Park and was even able to convince Ottawa to keep a number of them on muster over the following winter, as hitherto they had mostly been seasonal or temporary appointments. As mentioned, it was expected that most of the men would come from outfitting and guiding backgrounds, since that would best prepare them for their work with horses, firearms and wilderness patrol. An examination of the roster at Banff at the time shows that this practice was well-engrained. Of the twelve men in service, at least seven of them, including Jack Warren, Andrew "Scotty" Wright, William Fyfe, Howard Caine, Jack Bevan, Ben Woodworth jr., and the inveterate Bill Peyto, were known to have been actively involved in guiding and packing before signing on.

Bill Peyto was by far the most experienced and would soon become the exemplar which subsequent recruits would try to emulate. For many years his district was based on the Healy Creek drainage and he became famous as a holy terror in his ability to move through it like a phantom and appear to unsuspecting parties at the most inopportune times. A young Banff resident well recalled an occasion when he decided to get in a little early fishing on Healy Creek the day before the season opened and had no sooner made his first cast than the willows parted to reveal Peyto's steel-grey eyes accompanied by a gruff admonishment to put the line away for another day. Peyto was also a crack shot, serving in both the Boer War and World War I, and he easily bested all other wardens in his count of coyotes and mountain lions taken in the continuing prosecution of the predator control policy. In 1914 he was joined in the service by his brother Walter, who for most of his career was the "town warden," charged with keeping an eye on the activities of coal miners, controlling dogs, keeping coyotes out of local chicken coops and making sure tourists and bears didn't get tangled up too often. Between them, the Peyto brothers played an important role in establishing the *esprit de corps* for which the service soon became famous.

By the time the warden service was becoming well-established in the pre-war period, it was reporting to Harkin as the new Commissioner of Dominion Parks. In 1911 parks were removed from the Forestry Branch and a new Dominion Parks Branch was created with Harkin as its head, while Douglas remained on for another year as Chief Superintendent, the most senior field officer. In assessing Douglas's contribution, conservation writer Janet Foster had high praise for what he accomplished in her book *Working for Wildlife*:

Douglas's policies had been both successful and influential. Among civil servants, he was the first to become concerned about wildlife at a time when the concept of wildlife preservation was evolving. He understood that economic arguments alone would justify increased parks appropriations and greater wildlife protective measures, and he persuaded the government to embark on a course of park and wildlife protection by demonstrating that the result would be increased tourist revenues. Rocky Mountains Park was his shining example. . . .

By the time Douglas left office in 1912, wildlife preservation had become a policy in dominion parks. Rocky Mountains and all other parks were, at last, true wildlife refuges as well as public playgrounds. Largely because of the groundwork laid by Douglas during his fifteen years of administration, the new Parks Branch that was created in 1911 was in a far better position to deal effectively and efficiently with the question of wildlife protection in Canada.[12]

Harkin's background as a newspaperman between 1893 and 1901 and then as parliamentary secretary to two successive Ministers of the Interior, Clifford Sifton and Frank Oliver, prepared him well to build on Douglas's work. Like his predecessor, he was the right man for the times and was able to push forward the idea of preservation in the park system and on the wider Canadian scene with great dexterity. Taking a cue from Douglas, his most successful strategy for doing so lay in the side-by-side promotion of tourism and preservation and he seconded it by making the case that parks were good not only for the economy and for the mental and physical health of Canadians but, indeed, even for fostering their national pride and identity. His work would bring him into contact with Rocky Mountains Park frequently, as the most popular reserve in his growing system, and he would play a significant role in everything from the development of the Valley's infrastructure of roads and services to affecting its local politics.

In the conservation field, Harkin's influence encompassed success in matters extending from increasing the warden service's manpower to finding the funds to improve its facilities and equipment. The latter included the creation of a warden telephone system, first suggested in 1912, linking backcountry cabins and providing the means to warn of forest fires. By March, 1915 he could report that the first of two such lines, thereafter a major factor in both warden communications and maintenance requirements, had been completed the twenty-eight miles to Canmore and from the cabin at the east end of Lake Minnewanka to the wharf area. At the same time, he noted that there were now fourteen warden cabins in commission, including five built in the previous year. Similarly, in another effort to ensure the control of fire, he secured permission to respond to a request by Sibbald in 1914 for gasoline-powered water pumps with attached canvas hoses to beef up the simple tools of shovels, picks and mattocks being employed in the battle against the all too prevalent blazes. While the pumps were

Walter Peyto (left) and Howard Sibbald testing one of the first fire-fighting pumps

to be portable, in reality the first models were too heavy and cumbersome to be used except from roads or the railway, and consequently the following year Sibbald took delivery of a fire truck, one of the first vehicles in Banff. It was described as "a complete fire-fighting outfit, consisting of a Ford automobile with a suitable box body, a marine gas engine connected to a rotary pump capable of delivering a 40-foot stream through 300 to 1000 feet of 1 1/2 inch hose, and a portable gasoline engine, together with the necessary accessories."[13] Harkin estimated the apparatus could do the work of eighty men, but getting men who had grown up with horses and had never been behind the wheel to successfully navigate it proved to be a challenge. Bob Burns described the story that grew up around this situation:

Legend has it that the superintendent employed the following procedure to train new drivers, using the "Indian Days" fairgrounds east of the town. There the apprentice driver was given basic instructions and turned loose to hone his skills. This process came to be considered a source of local entertainment and invariably drew a crowd of avid spectators who could watch the proceedings from the comfort of the makeshift grandstand. The superintendent returned to his office in town and kept open his east facing office window. When the cheering from the grandstand died down, the superintendent knew the crowd had lost interest and that yet another warden had mastered the mysteries of operating a motor vehicle.[14]

Fish and game protection also flourished under Harkin's supportive regime, appropriations being secured in 1913 for the construction of a fish hatchery at Banff (across from today's Glen Crescent), something that had long been called for in order to restock the streams and lakes that had been so decimated during the railroad construction and early park periods. Furthermore, that year he succeeded in having the government appoint a fisheries inspector for Rocky Mountains Park and predicted that "dynamiting and trapping in the lakes and streams will now come definitely to an end." He believed, along with several prominent American conservationists such as William T. Hornaday, Director of the New York Zoological Society and author of *Our Vanishing Wild Life*, that North America was rapidly becoming a gameless continent and that unless drastic actions were taken many species would follow the passenger pigeon to extinction. Therefore, he thought it likely that parks would be the only place where "native flora and fauna will be found in a natural state," and constantly put forward the successes of his department in this regard. His report of March 31, 1915 provides a good example, tempered as it was with his constant theme of its value for tourism:

In this connection, perhaps it is not out of place to call attention to what the preservation of wild life in the national park at Banff has brought about. A few years of rigid protection has resulted in a very great increase in the wild life of the parks. To-day thousands of tourists make special trips to see the large herds of mountain goat, sheep, and other animals that are to be found roaming there in a wild state. These animals have become an attraction to the tourist that is perhaps not even second to the grandeur of the mountain scenery.

The protection of wild life in this park adds enormously to its recre-

ational value, and from the purely commercial standpoint it pays because it is to-day attracting and will continue to attract in the succeeding years the dollars of tourists. People love to look at wild animals. The crowds that constantly surround cages in zoos show this, but the attraction in their wild state is immeasurably greater.[15]

One of Harkin's most notable accomplishments in game preservation in Rocky Mountains Park followed a few years later, in 1919, when he was instrumental in reaching agreement with the United States Park Service to have a herd of elk that was being threatened with starvation moved from Yellowstone Park. While elk were native to the Bow Valley, they had virtually disappeared from their historic range by 1900 and the shipments of several hundred animals became the basis for their re-establishment in the park.

Harkin also had to fight a renewed battle on park boundaries, since the Dominion Forest Reserves and Parks Act that brought him to the position of Commissioner in 1911 also reduced the size of Rocky Mountains Park from 4,400 square miles to a mere 1,800 square miles. This reduction seems to have been a result of the belief of the new Minister of the Interior, Frank Oliver, that the park was too large and impossible to administer with the manpower available. In this regard he had some allies at Banff, including Howard Sibbald who was finding the task of having his wardens effectively patrol such an extent of wilderness virtually impossible. In any event, Harkin immediately saw the need to find some compromise for the amount of public lands now controlled by his department in comparison with the Forestry Branch and worked with the officials of what was now essentially a rival department to find a solution. In 1917 this led to an extension to the park to 2,751 square miles, including the re-incorporation of the upper Red Deer and Panther River watersheds as well as part of the Kananaskis River Valley.

While Harkin was making good progress on the ground, perhaps his greatest value to park conservation matters lay in his ability to project a vision for the park system that would appeal to both his political masters and the general public. As a former newspaperman, he knew the power of words and had a great mastery of both the written and spoken variety. Combined with an almost mystical belief in the value of parks for the nation and the betterment of mankind, he was able to successfully link the issues of preservation and park values with Canada's awareness of itself. His annual government reports were full of such references, carefully crafted and heartfeltly stated, but unfortunately never read by the common man. Recognizing this, Harkin created the Parks Branch's first tourist brochure in 1914 — entitled *Just A Sprig of Mountain Heather,* it was beautifully designed and illustrated, including tucking into the cover of each copy a pressed piece of red mountain heather meticulously gathered by park staff from the Simpson Pass area. Its intent was to acquaint the public with the true value of national parks, and although his name was not directly ascribed to the text, the rhetoric was unmistakably his: "This sprig of heather come to call to your attention Canada's National Parks, which have been set aside primarily to ensure to Canadians for all time those opportunities for recreation in the out-of-doors which humanity is more and more recognizing as vital to its well-being."[16] Ten years later, in 1924, he was offered the opportunity to write the chapter on national parks for the *Handbook Of Canada*, and, if anything, it was obvious that his passion and conviction had been honed to an even finer edge:

The swift onrush of settlement in the last half century has been pushing the wilderness farther and farther back, changing the face of primitive nature, sweeping out of sight much of the virginal beauty that once characterized the whole land. The great forests, the untainted rivers, the rich heritage of wild life of all kinds — these tend everywhere to disappear. To preserve out of its vast area, for the generations to come, a certain share of primitive nature is the meaning of the national parks movement. . . . Everywhere else, it is recognized, nature must gradually but inevitably give way to the economic pressure of civilization, but in the national parks, at least, primitive beauty may remain untouched and unscarred by the hand of man. The parks it may be said are the sanctuaries of the original and the wild.[17]

If there was one area of the preservation issue that had a direct impact on the Valley that seems out of character for Harkin, it was his direction and support of the predator control policy carried out by the warden service for many years. As pointed out, such a program was part of Whitcher's recommendations as early as 1886 and it had been followed without deviation from that time forward. Even though it incorporated a wide range of predators, action was basically directed towards coyotes, wolves, mountain lions and bears. The bear problem was mainly confined to black bear activities within townsites, but also sometimes extended to campsites. In fact, in July, 1915 Harkin and his superior, Deputy Minister of the Interior W. W. Cory, accompanied the Superintendent and Howard Sibbald on an excursion on the new auto road west of Banff and upon coming across a female black bear noted for her propensity to plunder camps, they armed Cory's young son and had him despatch her. In 1918 Sibbald, who was now responsible for the warden service in all the mountain parks, requested permission for wardens to be able to "destroy any bear found within any townsite in a national park" to avoid frequent criticism from park residents. In February, 1918 Harkin, noting the increasing number of incidents of bear-human encounters, gave permission for wardens to "kill all bears on the same being encountered, roaming at large, within any townsite in your park."[18]

While bears were regarded more as "nuisance" animals than predators and the "shoot on sight" policy only extended to townsites, destruction of coyotes and wolves was to be undertaken anywhere within the park confines and was to be vigorously pursued. The tools of destruction included leghold traps, poison and bullets and as late as 1918 Harkin was spurring the warden service onto greater efforts by officially recognizing an incentive that had long been practice on the ground — the pelts of all wolves, coyotes and mountain lions became the property of the warden who killed them. This lifted the campaign to new heights, as income from this activity could reach an equivalent bonus of ten to fifty percent of a warden's annual salary. It was not until 1924, after attending a conference of federal and provincial game officials, that Harkin began to re-assess the predator policy and was shocked to learn the extent of its application when he quizzed his superintendents (it included everything from magpies to porcupines in Rocky Mountains Park). Although the change was slow to occur, he thereafter consistently began restricting the policy's application, meeting head-on resistance from the warden in the field, many who had been brought up with an "only good predator is a dead predator" philosophy, had learned the ways of the trapline in their youth, and depended on the policy as a significant source of income.

J. B. Harkin, father of Canada's national parks

It has been said that the conservation movement in Canada was essentially carried forward by a dedicated group of public servants during its early years, and this statement certainly rings true in the case of Rocky Mountains and the other mountain national parks. Douglas, Harkin and Sibbald, all senior parks officials, helped develop an only vaguely understood concept for the first two decades of the century. But by the early twenties, their voices were joined by those from a new quarter. Arising from the significant and influential ranks of the Alpine Club of Canada and reacting to the demands for irrigation and electrical power in the growing rural and urban economy of western Canada, the 1920s saw the beginning of the first publicly-supported conservation movement, the Canadian National Parks Association. The focus of the movement was on two of the Valley's most significant water resources, Lake Minnewanka and the Spray Lakes.

Originally, the needs for electricity in the Valley were provided by coal-fired steam generation operated in conjunction with the coal mines at Canmore and Bankhead. However, the rapid pace at which Calgary was growing on the Valley's eastern flank and the strain it was putting on its own municipal steam-generated electric plant soon resulted in a call for more and cheaper power. This led to the formation of the Calgary Power Company and the construction in 1911 of the first hydro-electric generating plant on the Bow River at Horseshoe Falls, some fifty miles west of Calgary on the Stoney Reserve. Fundamental to the success of this project was water storage capability upstream, and in 1912 the Department of the Interior granted the company permission to install a control dam at the western end of Lake Minnewanka on Devil's Head Creek to regulate the flow of the Cascade River, a major tributary of the Bow. A few years later, the Kananaskis Falls plant was added to Calgary Power's generating capability, yet the appetite for hydro-electricity seemed insatiable, and by the early twenties new initiatives were afoot to increase the storage capabilities at Lake Minnewanka and to begin them at Spray Lakes.

By this time, another voice was being added to the call for water impoundment by William Pearce, the former federal government bureaucrat who had played an important role in the creation of the first park reserve. Now the CPR's major spokesman for the promotion of irrigation in southern Alberta, he believed that conservation implied use, a philosophy consistent with the work of the federal government's Commission on Conservation created in 1910 under the chairmanship of Clifford Sifton, a former Minister of the Interior. The Commission, formed by representatives of the federal and provincial governments as well as academics and specialists, believed that conservation meant scientific management of Canada's resources, be they mineral, water, forest, fish or wildlife, so that they could produce long term economic benefits. Opposing this point-of-view, as represented in Calgary Power's and the CPR's interest in seeing watercourses in Rocky Mountains Park dammed up, was none other than the hard-driving A. O. Wheeler.

After the creation of the Alpine Club in 1906, Wheeler had been given "time off" from his government survey duties to help organize and oversee the club's annual mountaineering camp, but with the creation of the Dominion Parks Branch this changed and he was no longer able to do club work on government time. Making a difficult choice, he left the government service to become the club's executive director, the small stipend he received in return being supplemented by private survey contracts gained from provincial and federal governments, one of the more important being work on the delineation of the Alberta-B.C. Boundary. In addition, he began to operate the aforementioned Mount Assiniboine Walking and Riding Tours from a lease he obtained at the Middle Springs, adjacent to the Alpine Club clubhouse. Wheeler saw no distinction between his own beliefs and interests and those of the Alpine Club, so it was not surprising that his strongly-held conservationist outlook, honed through years of activity in the mountains, should be adopted by many like-minded members.

The diverging philosophies of Pearce and Wheeler, two of the key players in the Valley's history who were pitted against each other on the water issue, has been well-captured by political scientist Leslie Bella in her polemic on the meaning of Canada's national parks, *Parks for Profit*:

Both Pearce and Wheeler claimed to support conservation. For Pearce, conservation was the economic principle advocated by the Commission of Conservation. Agricultural irrigation, his long term enthusiasm, now gained legitimacy. Hydroelectric developments were also entirely consistent with his idea of conservation. Pearce joined other more powerful interests, with influence in Ottawa and the provincial capitals, which wanted to maximize the economic exploitation of all

Canadian resources, including those which might by some mischance be found within national parks.

But for Wheeler, and others enjoying the mountains and other wilderness areas, conservation justified the preservation of natural wilderness. Wildlife protection became a general and popular concern. The idea of preservation took on an aesthetic and moral character. Wheeler, and other Alpine Club supporters, opposed hydro development in the parks. They wanted more and larger parks, managed with more attention to preservation.[19]

Speaking in favour of the impoundment schemes were the Province of Alberta, Calgary City Council and the Water Powers Branch as well as several other Alberta industries. Joining the protest with the Alpine Club were such diverse interests as the Banff Citizens' Association, the Calgary Automobile Club and the American Association for the Advancement of Science, all of whom kept Harkin regularly informed of their opposition.

Wheeler took steps to solidify his position as the leader of the voices in opposition at the annual camp of the Alpine Club held in 1923, suggesting the creation of the Canadian National Parks Association to protect park interests. One wonders if the fine hand of Harkin was not behind this idea, as he and Wheeler obviously shared philosophies, were in constant communication because of the Alpine Club's activities, and Harkin was present at the club's annual meeting in the Larch Valley when it approved the concept. A report of the action appearing in the "Official Section" of the *Canadian Alpine Journal* described it as follows:

The Director then spoke of the formation of a National Parks Association. The Club was vitally interested in defending the system of national parks from encroachment and despoilation of their scenery. A national organization should be formed with this aim. He would be glad to hear the opinion of the meeting.

Mr. Harkin, Commissioner of Dominion Parks, stated that the parks were a great commercial asset to the nation, bringing enormous amounts of money into the country. They were a business that earned a phenom-

enal interest on the capital expended. They also paid dividends of mental, physical and spiritual efficiency. Representatives from the Vancouver Island, Vancouver, Calgary, Saskatoon, Winnipeg and Toronto Sections spoke strongly against the spoliation of the parks.

It was then moved by A. S. Sibbald, seconded by F. C. Bell, that this meeting declares itself in favour of the immediate formation of a Canadian National Parks Association, whose objects shall be the conservation of Canadian National Parks. It was further resolved that the Club offer the facilities of the Camp and recommended that an organization meeting of that Association be held immediately following the meeting of the Club. This was duly carried.[20]

All this was undoubtedly music to Harkin's ears, and as the battle over the proposed Lake Minnewanka and Spray Lakes projects dragged on throughout the remainder of the decade he lent the new organization support where he could. But he needed to keep a low profile, given that another division within the Interior department, the Water Powers Branch, was in favour of the Minnewanka and Spray Lakes projects and because it was a matter in which his minister, Charles Stewart, was directly involved and spoke on frequently. He likely also wanted to keep some distance between Wheeler and himself, as the surveyor tended to make as many enemies as friends with his imperious demeanour and outspoken approach, something that was entirely anathema to Harkin's favoured *modus operandi.*

In any event, the protracted debate produced what Harkin would have seen as a benefit, engraining in the public's mind questions about the future of their country's park lands and, in particular, those in the Banff-Bow Valley. The issue would not ultimately be resolved until the discussions over the transfer of natural resources to the western provinces and the writing of the National Parks Act, 1930 took place at the decade's end. Harkin's long personal efforts and those of the incipient conservation movement towards enshrining a preservation ethic in the Canadian consciousness would become obvious in the dedication clause of that new act.

Chapter Eleven
Islands of Industry and Commerce

While it was the activities taking place in the wilderness areas of the Banff-Bow Valley that accounted for much of its heritage formation, it was, nonetheless, the townsites that would provide an important part of the story. Initially comprised of the resource-based centres of Canmore and Anthracite, as well as the more tourist-oriented Banff, they quickly carved out a key role in the unfolding tendency toward growth and expansion. And, the fact that after 1902 all sites of human habitation in the Valley were part of the the enlarged Rocky Mountains Park and situated in mountainous terrain meant that they developed in ways that made them distinct from other western Canadian communities. In the years after the boundary expansion other townsites and outlying development would also be added, exemplifying the philosophy of the times that saw no conflict in the ideas of industrial and commercial development within the confines of a national park.

It would continue to be coal-bearing lands that would have the strongest and most protracted influence on the life of the Valley from an industrial point-of-view. As we have seen, mining at Anthracite on some 1,600 acres of land held under lease by the Canadian Anthracite Coal Company (C.A.C.) of Eau Claire, Wisconsin was already well underway in 1887. By 1888 the accompanying Anthracite townsite had been surveyed into 337 lots, and it contained three hotels, a number of stores, a church, a company boarding house for up to 200 miners, and at the edge of town a famous "house of ill repute" operated by one Blanche Maloney, where a lonely miner could find both a good drink and female companionship. The population of the town at its height seems to be a matter of some dispute, with numbers ranging from 300 to

The village of Anthracite and the Black Diamond Mine, ca. 1900

1,500 inhabitants but likely being closer to the former. Mining was carried out at what was known as the "Black Diamond Mine" (near the ravine that goes up to today's Johnson's Lake) with two tunnels of 180 feet and 100 feet being in operation by 1887 and evidently proving quite productive. However, the seams were found to be steep and narrow, the coal friable (breaking into small pieces, fines and dust) to the extent than less than half of it was marketable, and the mine subject to flooding due to its extending under the water table of the near-by Cascade River. Frequent shutdowns plagued the operation and in 1891 C.A.C. leased its interests to the H. W. McNeil Company for a ten year period at the same time as those in neighbouring Canmore. In 1897 a spring flood of the Cascade River virtually wiped out the townsite and completely flooded the mine, killing all the livestock working in it, with the miners themselves narrowly escaping the same fate. By 1900 the McNeil company was losing money on the operation, and with the success of their workings at Canmore it no longer made sense to keep the mine open. By 1904 it was completely closed down and there were only seventy people left living in the village, many of the buildings being removed to Canmore and Banff.

Meanwhile, at Canmore the two segments of the community, townside and mineside (sometimes referred to as "Oskaloosa town" after its main hotel), essentially lived in their own worlds. There was not even a bridge to join the two settlements until 1892, but even it did not do much to shrink the gulf that had sprung from their different development histories. Each part of the community had its own infrastructure of stores, post office, hotels and other amenities throughout the 1890s. However, changes had begun to occur in railway technology that would affect Canmore's future development and history. As described by J. D. R. Holmes in his thesis *The Canmore Corridor: The Historical Geography of a Pass Site, 1880 to the Present,* these had to do with locomotive design:

During this time, however, the technological changes in the quality and variety of railway running-stock were creating a transition which would usher in the next sequence in Canmore's evolution. North American locomotive design was becoming less of a stereotype of the British counterpart. The trend for railways in the America's to handle much heavier loads than those in Europe was already evident in locomotive and freight car construction. These developments also resulted in equipment that did not require repair and service sheds at 125 mile intervals.

In 1898 repair sheds and full service installations for the new engines were constructed in Calgary to replace those in Canmore. Thereafter, Canmore's dependency on the railway altered. As fewer jobs were available around the Canmore roundhouse, Canadian Pacific Railway employ-

The early "townside" and "mineside" character of Canmore is evident in this view taken about the turn-of-the-century

ees either transferred to other divisional points or found alternate means of livelihood.[1]

All CPR shops were closed down in 1898 and Canmore's divisional point status was officially removed in January, 1899.

While Canmore's days as a railroad service depot were waning, the same technological forces that brought this to pass meant that its development as a coal mining centre became even more pronounced. Increasing introduction of coal-burning locomotives meant that there was a demand for good coal, and that coming from the Canmore mines was particularly well-suited for locomotives, leading to its use in all CPR engines from Medicine Hat to North Bend. And the McNeil interests, which now controlled virtually all coal-mining in the Valley, aggressively sought new markets, including an attempt to provide product for U. S. Navy steamships until blocked by a lobby of American coal producers. Nonetheless, just when it seemed that expansion of mining operations might alleviate some of the economic impacts associated with the loss of railway divisional status, the boundaries of Rocky Mountains Park were expanded in 1902 to include both the town and all coal mines in its vicinity. This had a further dampening effect due to the circumstance where any new coal mining could only be carried out on leased rather than purchased lands, and this restriction also applied to development of residential lots in the townsite. Then, to make matters still more difficult, in 1903 the CPR decided to open its own mines in the new Bankhead development at the foot of Cascade Mountain.

Despite these setbacks, mining activity in and around Canmore continued to hold its own for the time being. In 1901, the McNeil company renewed its lease from C. A. C. for a further ten years and in 1904 opened the new Sedlock seam. By 1908 there were some 300 miners at work, producing over 110,000 tons of coal annually, and the same year the new Number 2 mine was developed to the east of the existing works. This resulted in a subsidiary townsite, known as Prospect, consisting of some twenty dwellings to house the workforce nearby. In 1911 the original C. A. C. leases expired and were taken over by a new company, the Canmore Coal Company, headquartered in Pennsylvania and largely owned by American interests. Competitors appeared to the west of Canmore (immediately adjacent to today's park boundary) in 1910 in the guise of English interests operating as Georgetown Colleries supplying the steamship trade. A spur from the CPR mainline was run up to the mine and by 1913 a separate townsite known as Georgetown boasted some forty residences. But problems with the company's operations created by the First World War and high production and shipping costs led to its demise in 1916, after which its lands were acquired by Canmore Coal, bringing its holdings to over 8,000 acres. Regardless, by the end of the war the abundance of western Canadian coal (the Crow's Nest Pass branch line, with its huge coal resources, had opened in 1898) and the fact that it owned its own mines put the CPR in the driver's seat and kept coal prices low. During the 1920s the tendency for some of the larger CPR locomotives to begin burning oil put the delicate economic balance of the community at even further risk.

In the circumstances, the growth of the Canmore community was entirely dependent on the mine, mainly coming in the form of buildings that helped to improve resident life. In 1898 a significant amenity appeared in the guise of a bandhall that helped to serve as a social centre for local activities, constructed of logs brought down from the slopes of Chinaman's (Ha Ling) Peak by the mostly Italian members of the H. W. McNeil Co. brass band. It served its purpose well for many years, but was replaced as the main focus of community activity when a Union Hall was completed in 1910. That is until electricity came to mineside in 1915, at which time it received a new life as the town's movie house, being added to in 1922 and taking on the name of "the Opera House."[2] Local 7297 of the United Mine Workers of America was active in the town and even before building the Union Hall had set out to construct the community's first hospital, initiated in 1905 and completed as a two-storey structure in 1911. The first purpose-built school, a two-classroom frame building with two teacherages at the rear, was also completed in 1910 and in 1921 the Canmore Coal Co. opened its three-storey Memorial Hall as a tribute to Canmore's World War One veterans and to serve as lodging for single miners. That same year the original school building burned down and was replaced by a "model" six-room building, one of the first on townside to have electric lighting. As for housing, the closing down of the Georgetown Colleries in 1916 greatly improved Canmore's tight situation when all the houses were dismantled and moved to become new miner's residences in town.

Even though the major mining interests of Canmore and district were added to Rocky Mountains Park in the 1902 boundary extension, it did not preclude there being room for more. With the proviso that they were not to "in any way impair the usefulness of the park for the purposes of public enjoyment and recreation," mines were allowed by virtue of the Rocky Mountains Park Act and added considerably to government coffers in the early days of park development. Therefore, no deterrent and even some incentive existed for the expansion of the industry on park lands. While the coal from Canmore was of high quality and in good supply, its ownership resided in the hands of a private company that was not controlled by the CPR, a fact that concerned Thomas Shaughnessy, Van Horne's successor as CPR president. He did not want the railway to be at the mercy of others, particularly in an age of growing union activity, and accordingly in 1903 the CPR set up a subsidiary, Pacific Coal Mines Ltd., capitalized it with a million dollars, and began to acquire leases on coal lands at the foot of Cascade Mountain. By the next year some 5,000 acres were under lease and while the railway company started to construct a spur line to the minehead and build a station at the mainline junction, Pacific Coal began the task of opening the mines and laying out a company townsite. Named Bankhead, it was soon rivalling neighbouring Canmore and Banff in population and the amenities enjoyed by its inhabitants.[3] In perhaps one of the most optimistic of his reports, Superintendent Douglas in 1904 described it in glowing terms:

The new village of Bankhead, instead of being a detriment to the beauty of the park, will, on the contrary, add another to the many and varied attractions of the neighbourhood. Situated almost directly on the road to Lake Minnewanka, one of the most popular drives in the vicinity of Banff, and a little more than half way to the lake, nestling under the shade of Cascade with its beautiful homes and teeming industrial life, it has already become a popular stopping point for tourists.

Every possible provision has been made for the comfort of the men engaged in and about the mine. Already a large area has been cleared of timber, streets have been graded, and a modern waterworks system has been provided. Hand-some and commodious offices have been erected, which are now being used to house a large clerical staff. Rows of comfortable cottages have been built for the use of the miners and their families, and palatial boarding houses, provided with all modern conveniences, are in the course of erection.[4]

At the time, mining of two seams of coal extending westward at an angle of forty-five degrees under Cascade Mountain was already underway. Rather than mining the coal downwards in tunnels, as was done at Anthracite, Canmore and indeed at most coal mines, at Bankhead it was decided to begin at the mountain's base and work upward, avoiding flooding and using gravity to help bring the coal down. As there were twelve seams that were folded, faulted and variable in thickness, it was not an easy task and eventually it was decided that each seam must be entered at different levels to be effectively exploited. This resulted in three levels of mining at Bankhead, "A" level at ground and "B" and "C" levels each about seventy-five feet higher up the mountain-side. Initially the coal was moved down from the upper levels to ground level inside the mine, but in 1911 a clever outside tramway system, designed so that the loaded cars coming down would pull the empty ones back up, was put in place. These cars were unloaded into the massive tipple where the sorting of coal into its various sizes took place, a major operation employing some 135 men each shift at the height of the mine's production. Unfortunately, as at Anthracite, Bankhead coal was friable and although it burned very hot could not be used effectively in locomotives or for heating until it was briquetted. A briquetting plant, the first in western Canada, was set up next to the tipple in 1906 where the fine coal was sent on a conveyor belt and mixed with pitch (coal tar) imported from Pennsylvania, steam heated until almost liquid, and then poured into moulds for making into briquettes. Briquettes were not particularly well-suited to burn in steam engines, but were excellent for domestic heating and those from Bankhead were used to heat virtually every railway car and station between the Pacific coast and Winnipeg. In 1908 the company's name was changed to Bankhead Mines Ltd. and by 1914 a report of the Commission on Conservation identified an employee complement of 430, with 275 labouring underground, and 155, of whom forty were Chinese, working above ground.

As in all mining towns, the population of Bankhead was drawn from a number of ethnic backgrounds, making for an interesting, but in this case rather unique, story of community development. Given its location in a highly-visible tourist area and on the carriage road to one of Rocky Mountain Parks' most popular attractions, Lake Minnewanka, it is apparent that the company wanted it to be a "model" mining town, as Douglas's description would have us believe. The townsite was above and well-removed from the mine and carefully planned according to Ben Gadd's coal town "biography," *Bankhead, The Twenty Year Town*:

The place was built on a sunny, south-facing bench on Cascade Mountain, 30 metres above the mine buildings. Designed for a population of 1500, Bankhead was planned in its entirety, not allowed to grow haphazardly. The buildings were solidly made of fir. They varied in style and color, and sat on large lots. In those forward-looking days, the CPR did things with style. Bankhead was a model town.

Bankhead had a municipal water supply and a sewage system, with indoor plumbing in most homes. In 1905 the switch was thrown on the town's electric system, which provided domestic power as well as street lighting. All these comforts were the envy of Banff and Canmore residents, who had none of them.[5]

In 1908 there were 114 buildings in Bankhead, 100 which were residences. The road from Banff came into town from the south-east after passing the large, three-storey mine office and then split in two, with one branch going straight ahead to Lake Minnewanka and the other turning left and going up Boarding House Hill. This became main street, Cascade Avenue, and passed the hotel, the Cascade Boarding House, which contained the town's only bar. Not surprisingly, the small NWMP detachment and a Chinese laundry were right across the street. There was also a store, a post-office, a school, a butcher shop, a community hall, but, despite the size of the population, only one church. Holy Trinity was built in 1908 and used by the predominantly Catholic residents, be they Roman Catholic or Eastern Orthodox, while other denominations used the community hall for services or, like the Anglicans and Presbyterians, made the long buggy drive to Banff on Sundays.

As well as being a model of design, Bankhead appears to have been a paragon of tolerance for a mining community of the time, with one notable exception. This was partially due to the fact that the majority of the population was Catholic, but, again, planning also seems to have played a role. CPR officials responsible for housing in the community saw to it that there was no ghettoization, with Poles living next door to Italians living next door to Germans. There was also a great deal of mixing of racial backgrounds in Bankhead's famous brass band, which provided musical entertainment at all public events, on its hockey team, which had a strong rivalry with the Banff and Canmore sides, and with the children in the school. The exception were the Chinese, numbering some sixty men, who not only worked under their own Chinese boss but had their ramshackle quarters near the mine's slack heaps far away from the main townsite.

The mine itself was, perhaps, not quite so harmonious a place, since coal-mining was dangerous work and the economic situation at the time combined with a growing union movement to result in numerous work stoppages. During twenty years of operation accidents took the lives of fifteen miners, resulting in one of the stranger spectacles in the Valley when the subsequent funerals were held. For many years Bankhead did not have its own cemetery requiring the dead of Bankhead to be buried in the Banff Cemetery, with the mourners accompanying the coffin in wagons for the five-and-a-half mile trip and unloading for the final march into town accompanied by the brass band playing appropriate funereal dirges. After the service, a wake would ensue, usually in the bar of the Alberta Hotel, leading the Superintendent to complain of drunken Bankheaders causing an uproar and bothering the tourists. The annoyance of these wakes finally led the government to the open a cemetery at Bankhead in 1916, but even then a superstition that a family member of the first to be buried would soon follow meant that it remained empty. That is except for one Chinese worker, rumoured to be a murder victim, interred in 1921, for whom it was obviously felt the superstition didn't matter.

Despite the fact that the number of serious accidents at the mine were relatively few given the often dangerous working conditions, injuries were common and many miners were affected by respiratory problems. There was no compensation, but the union,

The massive tipple at Bankhead

as in Canmore a local of the United Mineworkers of America, did attempt to improve working conditions and wages. This meant that work stoppages occurred on a regular basis as miners joined their brethren throughout North America in attempts to improve their lot. Strikes occurred in 1907, 1909, 1911 and 1916, and after the First World War employer-employee relations underwent a serious deterioration as a result of a glut of coal on world markets combined with pressure from the miners to maintain a $1.18 daily bonus they had received during the war. A four month strike in 1919 exacerbated the bad feeling, and when the miners walked out again in 1922 the company issued an ultimatum that the mine would be closed if they did not return. The union believed it was a bluff, but to their horror the company made good on its threat, permanently closing the mine on June 15, 1922. Briquetting and power generation activities continued for some months, and many expected the mine to re-open at any time. That is until Commissioner Harkin stepped in and ordered the CPR to remove the entire mineworks and townsite from the park, something that took several years to accomplish but was clearly a sign that the compatibility of mining in a national park was beginning to be re-assessed by the mid-twenties. It was somewhat ironic that many of the buildings, which were sold variously at $25 to $50 per room, ended up in Banff, much like the citizens of "the twenty year town" who had deigned to die there.

Coal-mining was the major industrial enterprise and reason for the development of communities in the Valley in the early years of the new century, but not the only one. In the vicinity of Edwin Loder's lime works near the Gap, which he and his brothers had formally incorporated as Loder Lime Company, another new industry and townsite came to life that would also have a lasting impact on the region.

In 1904 a prospecting party from the Cement Company of Hull, Quebec, which had begun a survey of western Canada a year earlier to find a suitable location for the manufacture of Portland Cement, discovered exactly the combination of elements they were looking for at Lac des Arcs. An entire mountain bearing a high content of carbonated lime stood immediately adjacent to the CPR mainline, deposits of shale containing the necessary amounts of silica, alumina and iron needed in cement manufacture were located two miles east of Kananaskis at Radnor, and the abundant coal resources of Canmore provided a ready fuel for providing steam and electricity. The prospectors, Hugh Fleming and Daniel Diver, applied to the Department of the Interior for a lease of land and permission to construct a cement plant, and after an investigation by the superintendent, who found that "the operation of stone quarries would not be objectionable and would not conflict or interfere with the improvements made or to be made in the park," they were granted in June, 1905.

Immediately a new concern, Western Canada Cement and Coal Company, was created and the leases were transferred to it in August, 1905 while work began on the construction of six kilns and a grinding mill for the production of cement using a new, all-weather dry limestone process. The company also quickly began the laying out of a townsite, to be known as Exshaw, and by early 1907 it consisted of some twenty buildings including a hotel, a general store and a number of dwelling houses, with many more under construction, to house the expected population of some 500 people.[6] Like Bankhead, it was a company town, also built with all the amenities of the day, boasting a water and sewer system, a telephone exchange and electric lighting. Howard Douglas would likewise comment favourably on it in his annual report:

> *Beautifully situated on a gentle slope overlooking Lac des Arcs, the new town of Exshaw, the centre of a great manufacturing industry, has arisen out of the valley of the Bow River. . . . The erection of these large cement mills within the park will prove an important step in the building up of Western Canada. With an output of half a million barrels of cement a year they will not only circulate a large sum of money in this neighbourhood, but they will provide a most necessary material for the construction of railways and large industrial buildings through-out this country and supply cheaper and better building material for the settler than he is now able to procure.*[7]

Douglas's optimism was not immediately realized, as the new plant would experience its difficulties, mainly due to the great number of similar operations coming on stream in Canada at the time. Three of the six kilns were shut down almost immediately and by 1910 the company had ceased operations entirely. That year its assets were purchased by the Canada Cement Company, a conglomerate of virtually all similar plants in eastern Canada put together by New Brunswick entrepreneur Max Aitken, later Lord Beaverbrook, who would breathe new life into it. Thereafter it provided a steady output and employment for its thirty-odd workers until it underwent major expansions later in the century.

As indicated, the need for hydro-electric power to fuel the kilns at Exshaw as well as the needs of Calgary and other prairie communities had led to the development of Calgary Power's operations at Lake Minnewanka. Allowance had been made during construction of the dam for the addition of power-generating facilities for park development at a later time, and after the closing of the Bankhead Mines this became necessary for Banff's electrical needs. A small generator, or "thimble," was brought on stream in 1923 for this purpose, but in the meantime the construction of the original dam had disrupted one of the other small settlements in the park. In 1894 George Stewart had laid out a subdivision of six lots at Lake Minnewanka, all of them being taken up by B. G. Way, operator of a boat livery. A two-storey log hotel, known as The Beach House, was erected in 1898 by Charles D. Astley, who had acquired the subdivision and the boat livery, and the small settlement became a popular site for carriage outings by tourists from Banff. In 1909 a revised subdivision comprising five blocks of lots had been created with the idea that they would become cottage sites for wealthier Calgarians and Valley residents. Some cottages were erected between 1909 and 1912, but the building of the dam flooded two complete blocks, requiring Calgary Power to compensate the owners. A new survey laid out a plan of nine blocks containing eighty-seven lots and by June, 1913 these were being promoted for sale in regional newspapers, leading to twenty-three purchasers agreeing to erect a building of $300 value and pay the annual land rental of $8 to $10.

With virtually all of the settlement in the Valley during these years being oriented towards resource exploitation, these communities tended to develop and institutionalize in similar ways. Such was not the case with Banff, which had a completely different character and development history. As a resort town which quickly came to regard itself as an attraction to visitors from around the world, all interested parties, including the federal government, the CPR and local residents, had a stake in making it appealing to the tourist. Given its location on the western frontier far from the sophistication of the east, this did not prove an easy task, although most early visitors seem to have found the place agreeable. The Reverend Green stopped off on his way to Glacier House in 1888 and described his impression in his book *Among The Selkirk Glaciers*: "... there are shops selling articles of vertu, posting establishments, several smaller inns, two churches, a theatre, boats to hire on the river, provision shops, post office; altogether it is a most respectable little town."[8] This initial prosperity continued for a few years after Green's visit, but by 1893 the onset of the worldwide depression had begun to affect matters. A clear indication was the recall of E. A. Nash, Stewart's assistant as land agent, because of a lack of work. A residence for Stewart near the Banff Springs Hotel (today's parkade site) was under construction at the time but was discontinued and he moved his family into Nash's former home on Buffalo Street (the site of today's Superintendent's residence). The upper storey of his uncompleted home was dismantled and moved to the junction of the roads to the Banff Springs Hotel and Upper Hot Springs, where it became the first park museum (later incorporated into the building that is now Phil's Restaurant).

Disregarding the economic situation, there were a few confident individuals who would not be deterred. One was Dave White, who had come into possession of a small frame store on the first block of Banff Avenue when one of his sectionmen couldn't repay the loan he had made to him to purchase it. The section foreman turned businessman named his establishment The Park Store and initiated his business as a general store and "tourist outfitter," the beginning of what would become the town's longest-lived general merchandiser. Next to him was George Fear's small curio or "heads and hides" shop, originally operated in partnership with Tom Wilson, to which was added the new town post office. Across Banff Avenue, John Walker left his position as the caretaker of the Cave and Basin, which he had held from 1890 to 1897, and opened a clothing and dry goods emporium known as The People's Store. Business and life was not easy for these early entrepreneurs, as they had to work long hours on the thinnest of margins to sustain a livelihood, a fact borne out by a later description of Dave White's career:

The early history of the Park Store business could not be described as "booming" — far from it. Competition was keen, money was scarce, and the resources of the new merchant might be described as being tied up in "hard work and honesty." The business was practically a one-man show, Dave acted in all capacities around the premises during business hours, and for relaxation in the evening after the doors had been closed he wrote up his books, answered his business correspondence and baked the bread.

The Park Store was a busy one and it prospered during the first five years to an extent that it became necessary to build an addition in 1899. Dave, however, in the new premises still retained the title of the "whole show" until 1900 when a helper was hired. In 1901 it was necessary to enlarge the building still further.

In 1903, owing to the opening of the new mine at Bankhead, business was given a great impetus, White's store furnishing the bulk of the requirements in the new camp. In 1904 it was decided that the time was ripe for the opening of a store in Bankhead, so Mr. White took in with his as partner in this venture Mr. D. C. Bayne, and a business was started in the new camp.[9]

While the beginning of these businesses were important signs of life, the lifting of the depression towards the end of the decade signalled a real boom in Banff's development. In 1900 Ike Byers started publishing a newspaper on a press brought in by Dr. Brett's associate Dr. White, initially bearing the masthead of *National Park Gazette*, but changing to *Crag and Canyon* after two issues. Byers kept it going to for six months before departing for the coast, and Dr. Brett managed to take over and get one more issue out on Christmas Day, 1901. Publication then ceased until the paper was acquired at the beginning of 1903 by another entrepreneur who would have a lasting impact on Banff's future. Norman Luxton was the son of the founder of the Manitoba *Free Press* and initially came to Calgary as a young man to work as a reporter and bill collector at the Calgary *Herald*. Of an adventurous mien, in 1901 he went to Vancouver and, after an unsuccessful attempt to start a weekly with some partners, he met a similarly footloose venturer named Captain John Voss, with whom he hatched a scheme to buy an Indian dugout canoe, named the Tilikum, and sail across the Pacific. Their voyage of 10,000 miles ended in near disaster at Fiji, and when he returned to Calgary from Australia, Luxton was convinced to come to Banff to recuperate in the hot springs. Given his newspaper roots, it was natural that he should quickly find his way to the defunct *Crag and Canyon* and buy it for a song. Thereafter its weekly appearance, initially publishing only in the summer, documented the whirlwind of development taking place in the community, much of which he was involved in himself.

One area that fell under Luxton's gaze was the need for more hotel rooms with the rapid growth in tourism in the early years of the new century. Leonard Fulmer's small store at the corner of Wolf Street and Banff Avenue was acquired by the Anglican Church in 1900 with the intention of starting a school, but the project fell through and Mrs. Celia Lowther obtained the property and developed a boarding house on it. Luxton purchased this building from Mrs. Lowther and added to it, opening his King Edward Hotel to the public for the first time on May 15, 1904. Several additions followed, one in 1906 doubling its capacity, a further smaller one the next year, a third in 1908 which added a complete third-storey, and a fourth in 1912 that saw the first brick addition. A fire in October, 1908 destroyed the small livery on Bear Street run in conjunction with the hotel and in May, 1909 Luxton opened the new King Edward Livery, meant to compete with several others that had recently appeared. These included the Banff Livery begun by the Brewster Brothers in 1904 two doors down Banff Avenue from the King Edward, as well as the Bow Livery of Rattray and McDougall across Banff Avenue and the Sanitarium Livery of Dr. Brett, both appearing in 1906. But Dave McDougall, by this time Luxton's father-in-law, had more than a livery in mind for his prime corner location and in 1907 began construction of what was to become the major downtown hotel, requiring the moving of the Bow Livery to a location further down the street. Originally named the Banff Hotel when it was first opened in May, 1908, it soon became known as the Mount Royal and continually underwent expansion. When it was sold to Jim Brewster in May, 1912 for $100,000 it was reported as "one of the biggest real estate deals to date" in Banff. However, it and the King Edward by no means had the field all to themselves.

Numerous other hotel projects appeared in these years. In the downtown area an addition to A. S. Marsh's Alberta Hotel in 1904 (originally the National Park Hotel built in the 1880s and later the Cascade), the Alpine Hotel was opened in the new Brett Block in 1912 and construction began on John Locke's Homestead Hotel on "CPR Avenue" (Lynx Street) in 1910. The first of several additions to Brett's original Sanitarium Hotel at the head of Banff Avenue

Banff Avenue just prior to World War I, including Fear Bros. store and post office, original Harmon studio and store and Dr. Brett's Alpine Hotel on left as well as Mount Royal and Alberta Hotels on right

was begun in 1904, culminating with its new name of Chateau Rundle (later Bretton Hall) after the medical facilities were moved to the new Brett Hospital across Spray Avenue (the location of the present YWCA) in 1909. At the old site, one of Dr. Brett's most unique enterprises began operation in 1910 under the name Sanitarium Bottling Company selling "Banff Lithia Water." There was also major new development at the Upper Hot Springs involving the rebuilding and addition of a new bathhouse to the Upper Hot Springs Hotel in 1904-05, the re-building of the Grand View Villa (on the site of today's Rimrock) in 1905 and the opening of the Hydro Hotel in 1909.

Of course, what proved to be the most significant hotel development of this period concerned the major additions to the CPR's own Banff Springs, beginning in 1903, as a response to its inability to house all prospective guests. That year some half-a- million dollars was spent in essentially duplicating the original wing, involving the addition of 200 rooms to the south of the existing building. Further work took place in 1904 and 1905 when six-storey towers were constructed on both the north and south wings and over the winter of 1906-07 when a new boiler, engine and laundry were added. Despite these improvements, the hotel was immediately filled to capacity with 450 guests when it opened in May, 1907 and by 1910 some 400 guests had to be sent back to the CPR station to be housed in sleeping cars. In 1911 statistics indicated that over 22,000 people had stayed at the hotel in a little over four months. This led to a decision to begin what was described as a "new" hotel, at least one that was new in appearance, and chief CPR architect Walter S. Painter was sent on a tour of the Loire region of France to study the chateau style of architecture. However, the concept he evolved for a new eleven-storey Rundle rock and concrete centre tower owed much more to the Scottish baronial tradition, probably due to the fact that this design had itself grown out of the French chateau style and the desire of CPR management to celebrate the homeland of its founders. In any event, work on the new tower began after the end of the 1911 season, and the next spring the *Crag and Canyon* reported that the population swelled by the large numbers of Italian stonecutters and Scottish stonemasons had made the winter "one of the most active and full of life Banff has ever known." Work was halted for both the summers of 1912 and 1913 to allow business to proceed, but in the winter up to 600 men were engaged in work at any given time. The completed wing, along with new swimming pools and a full redecoration, cost some $2 million and was proudly opened to the travelling public at the beginning of the 1914 season.

In light of the major increases in accommodation becoming available, a number of ancillary businesses to provide goods and services to the swelling tourist population also appeared in Banff during the pre-war boom.[10] Dave White exhibited his personal belief in the town's future prosperity and stability in 1908 when he began construction of one of its first brick buildings, tearing down The Park Store and replacing it with the two-storey Dave White and Co. and then doubling its size in 1913 with the construction of an addition on a lot he had acquired to the north. Competition in his line of business had appeared in 1904 when Morrison and Bradford opened their Dominion Store between the Banff Livery and the King Edward Hotel, taken over and expanded by Brewster Brothers the following year, and John Walker commenced his new business in 1906 after his original store was taken over by Banff Mercantile. The new Brewster Brothers company was particularly active as they also constructed the Banff Opera House on Lynx Street (later moved to the site of today's Caribou Corner), meant to provide a meeting space for the local Masonic Order as well as an entertainment and dance hall. A few doors north of Dave White's, photographer Byron Harmon purchased the old Moore livery stable in 1909 and began the construction of a photographic studio, complemented by a movie theatre in 1912 and eventually rebuilt as the Harmony Block after a fire in 1917 destroyed the original building. South of White's, on the corner of Buffalo Street and Banff Avenue, Calgary meat-packing magnate Pat Burns built a new butcher shop in 1906 to replace the former Hull and Trounce structure, copying the rustic, half-timbered style of the new Banff Museum and government administration offices built across Buffalo Street near the river in 1903. Kitty-corner across Banff Avenue on part of Tom Wilson's old corral site, the Imperial Bank emulated a related architectural style for its new branch, also opened in 1906. Next door to it (the site of the present Legion) stood Norman Luxton's Sign of the Goat Curio and Fur Store, which a few years later was moved to a new location immediately adjacent to the bridge on the south side of the river.

New residential construction was equally in evidence as wealthy summer cottagers vied with the growing Banff middle class for prime locations on Beaver, Lynx and Buffalo Street. Others found new lots on the extensions to Otter, Cariboo, Wolf and Muskrat Streets when they were graded and cleared in 1906. The residences of the period were built largely in the cottage or bungalow style which was then popular in the United States, modified and given a more alpine or rustic look by the use of logs,

Rundle stone or river rock. Several examples from this period still form part of Banff's historic residential character: on Beaver Street are Norman Luxton's frame and Reggie Holmes's log residences; on Cariboo Street is Gair Lodge; and on Buffalo Street are Saskatchewan Senator A. E. Forget's prefabricated house shipped in by rail from Winnipeg, his neighbour Walter Painter's self-designed residence and the distinctive log Superintendent's house.

While the government itself was involved to some degree in the building boom — the construction of the new Museum in 1903, the opening of the first government hotpool at the Upper Hot Springs in 1905, and a rebuilding of the Cave and Basin complex based on a Walter Painter design in 1914 — its main role was to supply community infrastructure. With power available from Bankhead, a town arc light street-lighting system was put in place by September, 1904 between the railway station, the Banff Springs Hotel and the Cave and Basin. Electrical service was gradually extended to other parts of the community over the subsequent years, and in the meantime the government hired a Toronto civil engineer to begin design of a water and sewage system. The John Galt Engineering Company estimated the cost of a wood pipe gravitational water system with iron service mains fed from Forty Mile Creek at $62,000 and a complementary sewage system draining into the Bow River near Bow Falls at $33,000 (amazingly, with several upgrades the latter would remain in place as Banff's sewage disposal system until well into the 1960s). Construction started in May, 1905 but was not completed until the summer of 1906, with Superintendent Douglas expressing particular pleasure at being able to use the new fire hydrants as a source of water to keep down the dust on the roads. Of even more importance was the fact that these hydrants, originally located only in the commercial district, for the first time provided adequate fire protection. This allowed the formation of Banff's volunteer fire department in September, 1907, consisting of twenty-eight men equipped by the government with 1,000 feet of hose and a chemical engine. Other services included a new police barracks to house Banff's small (some residents claimed too small) Mounted Police detachment, built adjacent to the new Museum site in 1902, and the provision of telephone service in 1905.

During the period from 1900 to 1910, Banff's population almost quadrupled, and with a commercial, residential and government building boom in full flower, planning of the town took somewhat of a back seat. A British visitor, E. W. Elkington, provided his view on this situation in 1910:

The town is all out of proportion to its surroundings: if it were not rather quaint, it would seem silly; there is one main short street of small uninteresting houses and shops. No attempt has been made to beautify the place. The road to the mountains is generally in an almost impassible state, and hotel accommodation, with the exception of the Sanitarium and the magnificent CPR hotel, is poor. . . .[11]

If Elkington had visited twenty years earlier and seen how much greenery had replaced the barren, burnt over landscape of the original townsite through government beautification efforts, he might have had a different opinion, at least about the attempts "to beautify the place." But he did make some points in his remarks and by 1912 the problems he mentioned had begun to be dealt with by the tightening up of building regulations, requiring plans and cost estimates to be submitted to the Superintendent for approval before any construction could commence. In an attempt to eliminate the somewhat haphazard pattern of development, the government also commissioned a noted English landscape architect, Thomas Mawson, to come up with a plan for improvement "so as to enhance the scenic beauty of the place and develop its character. " Mawson, a disciple of the popular City Beautiful Movement that sought to replace thoughtless development with community planning stressing parkland and recreation facilities, produced his report in December, 1913. In it he called for a large recreation centre north of the Cave and Basin road on reclaimed marshland and linked to the townsite by a new road and bridge near the confluence of Echo Creek and the Bow; a racetrack, pavilions, a baseball diamond and football pitch at these new grounds for summer use as well as a toboggan slide coming down from Sulphur Mountain for winter entertainment; the opening of bathing establishments at the Middle Springs; a traffic circle and new administration building on Banff Avenue at its intersection with Elk Street; the moving of the zoo to a new, larger location near the railway station; a new access to the town following the benches on the east side of Tunnel Mountain and crossing the Bow River just east of its junction with the Spray; the construction of a new concrete bridge to replace the existing steel one on Banff Avenue; and the straightening of Lynx Street.[12] Due to the fact that Mawson's plan appeared on the very eve of the First World War, during which Parks appropriations were slashed by more than half, few of his ideas saw the light of day. But two that were realized would henceforth form important parts of Banff's community character — one being the building of the recreation grounds, complete with sports facilities and the provision of a pavilion designed by Francis Sullivan, an associate of Frank Lloyd Wright, and the other the construction of a new bridge over the Bow designed in a handsome river stone motif adorned with beautiful Indian heads, modelled on Stoney chief John Hunter, wrought by Calgary mason James Thomson.

The First World War brought an end to Banff's rapid era of growth, but in that period its character and architectural heritage was largely defined. One only has to examine the modern inventory of the Town of Banff's heritage resources, including such buildings as the White Block, Harmony Block, King Edward Hotel, Park Museum, Sign of the Goat Curio Shop and variety of pre-war residential homes to understand how important this epoch was. Although the town would undergo some further minor development periods, such as when some sixty residences were moved to town in the late-twenties with the dismantling of Bankhead, another age of growth as significant as this would not occur for more than a half-century. And by that time, the Valley's other remaining major townsite, Canmore, would also have begun to reinvent itself and leave behind its mining community roots.

Chapter Twelve
The California-Banff Bee Line

The era of prosperity announced by the new century was in many respects the golden age of CPR tourism in the Banff-Bow Valley. Affluent international visitors stepped off the westbound Imperial Limited at the Banff station and were greeted by drivers of CPR carriages and hotel coaches, with those representing the liveries of the downtown hotels having to take second place further down the platform. During sojourns at Banff or Lake Louise, these travellers most often stayed at the CPR hostelries and employed their trail guides, liveries, Swiss guides and other services. By the century's second decade these were complemented at the Banff Springs with such diversions as swimming pools, tennis courts and links on which to indulge in the growing popularity of golf. At Lake Louise, Chinese boatmen plied sightseers across the aquamarine waters of the famous lake in front of the rapidly expanding Chalet. It was a time when the company enjoyed a near monopoly in the upper middle-class and wealthy segment of the tourist trade. In order to sustain it, those charged with marketing began to advertise the mountains from the perspective of destination resorts rather than merely a stop along the Imperial Highway, initiating the extremely successful "Canadian Pacific Rockies" campaign. But these idyllic times for CPR tourism would not last, for in the years preceding the First World War changes were afoot in the Valley that would place tourism on a different path, one that democratized it and wrested it away, at least partially, from the tight grip of the railway. The turning point came when the company lost the sole means of transporting visitors to the area, as the coming of roads and automobiles to the Rockies and their championing by parks administration would forever change the face of Valley life and the way tourists experienced the mountains.

Early issues of the *Crag and Canyon* ran a weekly notice that trumpeted: "The Canadian National Park. A natural watering place and pleasure resort. Seventy-five miles of good roads and bridle trails." The roads being pitched in this advertisement were mainly those that had been built in the first few years of the park's existence to allow tourists to reach local attractions, such as the Upper Hot Springs, Cave and Basin, Buffalo Paddock, and Lake Minnewanka, or simply enjoy sightseeing outings over the Corkscrew and Loop Drives. They were utilized by various livery concerns in Banff, the major one always being that associated with the Banff Springs Hotel. The company had taken back the operation of its own livery services from the CPR Transfer Company in 1897 and had continued to add to its stock of democrats and carriages for sightseeing and enclosed Concord coaches, known as "hotel busses," for transporting its guests between the station and the hotel. In the summer of 1903 it proudly took possession of its first tally-ho, or "English drag," a multiple-seated, high-rigged carriage drawn by a four-horse team capable of carrying up to twelve passengers on the tour to Lake Minnewanka.

In 1902 the CPR had contracted out its livery at Laggan and Field with Tom Wilson at the same time they had reached agreement with him on an outfitting concession. The contract stipulated that he would "accommodate and supply the requirements of the Company and its guests in connection with the transfer and conveyance of baggage and passengers and furnishing and supplying of horses, conveyances, drivers and attendants at the said stations and in connection with their said Hotel at Field and their said Chalet at Emerald Lake and also between Laggan and their said Chalet at Lake Louise. . . ."[1] While the arrangement with Wilson worked well, it was not immediately extended to Brewster Brothers when they were awarded the outfitting concession at Banff in 1904. However, by June, 1905 the CPR had created a new Hotel Department, and its first manager-in-chief, Hayter Reed, decided he wanted securely contracted services at all hotels. The Brewster company eagerly accepted the offer for Banff. As part of the arrangement they received all the CPR's stock-in-trade, includ-

Jim Brewster and his daughter Fern in a Brewster tally-ho at the CPR hotel livery stables, ca. 1910

ing the right to use their livery stables near the Banff Springs Hotel (the area later developed as Glen Crescent), and sole rights to solicit conveyance on the railway platform and at the Banff Springs Hotel. In return for the privilege they submitted an annual fee of $1,500 for 1905, paid $8,000 for the stock-in trade of carriages, buggies, harness and forty-three horses, promised to make two wagons with drivers available for the exclusive use of the hotel, and agreed that the business was "generally to be subject to the CPR's control and direction." Immediately after entering the contract, their mettle was tested in providing services to one of the first group tours ever to appear at Banff, organized by the large Boston-based travel agency Raymond-Whitcomb Touring Company. The *Crag and Canyon* enthused: "Visitors poured into Banff in a steady stream yesterday, 162 going up to the big hotel. So heavy was the traffic that No. 96 came in in three sections. . . . Every one of Brewster Bros. rigs was engaged yesterday afternoon for the service of this large party."[2]

The Brewsters quickly began to expand the beach-head they had established in Banff by acquiring outfitting and livery concessions at the other CPR facilities throughout the mountains. At Lake Louise there were some sixteen miles of carriage roads by 1908, mainly connecting Laggan with Lake Louise and Moraine Lake, and at Field some thirty miles, leading to Emerald Lake, the Yoho Valley and along an abandoned railway roadbed to Ottertail. In 1904 Bob Campbell had acquired Wilson's interests at these locations, and in April, 1908, upon the expiry of his concession agreement, it too was offered by the CPR to Brewster Brothers. This new contract required the company to keep vehicles and teams capable of carrying fifty passengers at Laggan and thirty passengers at Field. In order to handle the increased demand, by the end of 1908 the company's assets included seven "bus" coaches, two touring coaches, one tally-ho, fourteen three-seaters, two two-seaters, twelve surreys and buggies, one single rig, numerous wagons, sleighs and cutters, as well as 205 head of livestock. Reorganized as the Brewster Transfer Company in 1910, Jim Brewster had by that date hired some key company personnel, several of whom would play important roles in the Valley's future. They included Lou Crosby as accountant and financial manager, Jim McLeod as manager of the Lake Louise operations, and Earl Gammon with similar duties at Field. By 1917 the company, again renamed as the Brewster Transport Company, gained a complete stranglehold on CPR mountain concessions when it bought out Syd Baker's interests at Glacier.

Since it worked to their advantage, the Brewster company and all of the other smaller livery interests in the park undoubtedly were quite happy that the only connection to the outside world was by way of rail in the new century's early years. This would begin to change after 1905 when the Public Works Department of the new Province of Alberta announced its intention to build a "coaching road" from Calgary to the eastern park boundary and the federal government agreed to upgrade the basic carriage road that already made its way intermittently up the Bow Valley to Banff. This was expected to be a road available only for horse-drawn conveyance, as the year previously an Order-in-Council had been passed banning automobiles, the new invention of Henry Ford that was rapidly gaining worldwide popularity, from any part of the park. The ban had originated in a request made of Douglas in 1903 from an early Calgary automobile owner wanting to ship it into Banff by rail and be allowed to use it to carry tourists over park roads. The CPR and local livery owners had expressed their opposition when consulted by Douglas, and William Pearce, one of the government officials asked his opinion, expressed the belief that horse and automobile use of the roads would not be compatible as the autos would frighten the horses and seriously endanger life.

There matters rested for a few years until the automobile lobby, largely represented by the affluent and influential members of the Calgary Automobile Club, began to press for a less heavy-handed approach as the Calgary-Banff Coach Road neared completion. By September, 1908 Superintendent Douglas was reporting that "in another year or two it is hoped to have that part of the road in the National Park in such condition that automobiles and carriages may be able to pass between the two points." It didn't take that long, for on August 14, 1909 Norman Lougheed of Calgary became the first recorded motorist to complete an eight-and-a-half hour marathon and drive his car over the partially-completed road into town, where he was immediately charged by the local police. However, he was quickly followed by a Mr. Downey of Calgary and a Mr. Gooderham of Toronto, as well as by Mr. and Mrs Richardson of Calgary who made the same trip by buggy. By the next summer a deputation of Calgary automobile owners was meeting with Minister of Interior Frank Oliver seeking approval to bring their machines into the park on the condition that once they arrived they would be parked and not driven over town and area roads. Permission was granted in the spring of 1911, with the proviso that the vehicles be left at the police barracks while in town. To the chagrin of local residents, a cavalcade of the Calgary Automobile Club arrived in town on July 15, 1911 and drove their "buzz wagons" everywhere, including over the Spray bridge and onto the Loop Drive to the official opening of the Banff Springs Golf Course being held that day. The Banff Board of Trade protested to Ottawa about these and other infractions, but as the Calgary press claimed this was just an attempt by livery concerns to protect their interests, little was done. Some 150 motorists were recorded as having made the trip to Banff in 1911 and subsequent Orders-in-Council gradually whittled away remaining restrictions. In 1913, at the instigation of, among others, Senator James Lougheed, himself a summer resident of Banff who preferred to drive, autos could be used on town streets and to the Banff Springs Hotel during daylight hours. By 1914 the Lake Minnewanka road, Cave and Basin road and Loop Drive were added to the permitted list, and in 1915 virtually all restrictions were lifted, but with the provisos of an eight-mile-per-hour speed limit on town streets and the right-of-way remaining with horses and horse-drawn vehicles.

Nonetheless, getting to Banff at the time was an adventure, as witnessed by the account of W. R. Marshall of Syracuse, New York. He was part of a two-car expedition of Moyer automobiles to Banff in September, 1912, one of the first of the tens of millions of motorists who would follow to be struck by the experience of reaching the Valley by road. Marshall observed on setting out that the prairie roads seemed, on first glance, to be barely passable as "they are, on the whole, nothing more or less than old trails, with the two rather deep ruts into which the wheels of the car fit very nicely, requiring very dexterous work on the part of the man at the wheel." He soon learned to enjoy them, however, and marvelled at how the driver would divert through a field of grain if the way appeared better than on the road allowance. Several hours of travel brought them to the Gap, where he commented on the changing character of the roads and the work that the Calgary Automobile Club had done to improve safety:

A little station on the Canadian Pacific Railway, called The Gap, is the first sign of civilization we see as we enter the pass. Just beyond this we commence our real mountain experiences. The roads begin to wind and every now and then we are confronted by a sharp curve bringing us

Early automobile party at Lac des Arcs on the Calgary-Banff Coach Road

out to the edge of a precipitous incline, two thousand feet to the bottom on one side of the car and five thousand to the top on the other side, with a track ahead scarcely wide enough for one car to drive with safety. Only once did we encounter a team, and that fortunately happened to be in a convenient place to pass.

If there is anything the Calgary Auto Club did not forget to do it was to furnish plenty of signs when covering this trip. It seemed that every ten feet we would turn a corner way up on the side of a mountain and suddenly bump into one of those ominous signs reading, "Slow," "Danger," "Blow Horn," or something just as cheerful, and we soon learned that it would not pay to disregard the warnings.

Once of twice in making a hairpin or letter "S" turn we would feel the rear wheels take a sudden lurch in the direction of the yawning canyon and instinctively shift to the other side, but the mountaineers in the party kept up the encouraging: "Don't mind that, you'll get used to it," so we tenderfeet took what consolation we could out of it and pretended to admire the scenery. But it was not until the trip home that we really did feel enough at home to drink in the wonders of the country.[3]

Marshall's party was concerned about getting to Banff before six o'clock, as "to reach Banff after six in an automobile meant a fine." They didn't quite make it, but were able to convince the police constable to forego the fine, only to find, like so many future generations of unsuspecting motorists reaching the park, that "another fee awaited which no one could sidestep." Marshall found that "Banff is federal property, and as such does not recognize license numbers from any other part of the world, regardless of flag or nation," and had to pay the prescribed $2 fee.

Undoubtedly the government's changing attitudes about the use of automobiles in Banff emanated from a decision concerning a much larger, and ultimately more important, transportation scheme. On April 1, 1911 Commissioner Douglas for the first time reported on plans to extend the Calgary-Banff Coach Road westward to Castle, indicating that Parliament had already passed the necessary appropriations. From there, he stated, construction could be carried some nine miles to Vermilion Pass "to connect with the road now under construction by the B. C. government from that pass through the Windermere Valley to Ft. Steele and Cranbrook." The idea of a road connecting Calgary and Banff with the Columbia Valley was the brainchild of Randolph Bruce, an Invermere mining engineer who had originally worked for the CPR and believed that such a road would unlock the commercial and tourism potential of the region. Through his railway connections he was able to convince CPR President Thomas Shaughnessy of its value, likely because it would link the Crow's Nest Pass line with the CPR mainline, and eventually enlisted the support of B. C. Premier Richard McBride and the Dominion Government. J. B. Harkin, in his first report as the new Commissioner the following year, provided details which showed this to be a project of major proportions and far-reaching consequences:

This road is a link in an automobile scheme in which the Canadian Pacific Railway, the Government of British Columbia and the Dominion Government are jointly interested. The scheme involves the completion of an automobile road from Calgary to Vancouver. The Dominion is building that portion of the roads through the parks and the railway company and the province are responsible for the balance. The Dominion has already built sufficient roadway to enable automobiles to travel from Calgary to Banff and several miles beyond. Work is to be proceeded with during 1912 from the present terminus to Castle. . . . From the Vermilion Pass the road is located via the Windermere lakes to Wardner, on the Crowsnest line. From this point the road, linking up with existing roads, will reach Vancouver. Going eastward it will proceed via the Crowsnest with Lethbridge. Thus in a short time, not only will it be possible to go to Calgary and other points east to Vancouver by auto but there will also be provided a round trip — Calgary to Banff, to Castle, to Vermilion, to Wardner, to Lethbridge, to Calgary — of 500 miles during which the autoists will at all times be either in the Rockies or in full sight of them.[4]

Finally it appeared as though Palliser's assertion, stated over half a century previously, that the Vermilion Pass route was "the most favourable and inexpensive to render available for wheeled conveyances" would be proven true.

Harkin's obvious relish for the idea of a road eventually connecting to the coast running through the middle of Rocky Mountains Park may seem like a contradiction given his previously described growing conservation consciousness. Yet he was a pragmatist at the same as being a philosopher, grasping the realities of political life and of widely-held views about resource exploitation at the same time as he understood, and to a degree led, the changing climate of opinion in the country. As such, he became a strong advocate of tourism in the park:

There is another way in which national parks prove advantageous to the people of Canada. They attract an enormous tourist traffic and tourist traffic is one of the largest and most satisfactory means of revenue a nation can have. The tourist leaves large sums of money in the country he visits, but takes away with him in return for it nothing that makes the nation poorer. He goes away with probably improved health, certainly with a recollection of enjoyment of unequalled wonders of mountain, forest, stream and sky, of vitalizing ozone and stimulating companionship

with nature but of the natural wealth of the country he takes nothing.
. . . Extraordinary scenery is one of the greatest assets a country can have. Canada has twenty Switzerlands in one. . . . With the natural advantages Canada possesses in her national parks there appears to be no reason why she should not get a good share of the hundreds of millions of dollars that tourists annually spend.[5]

That he believed this would be accomplished by an increasing use of the automobile was evident in 1912 when he predicted "what motorist will be able to resist the call of the Canadian Rockies when it is known that he can go through them on first-class motor roads. And what a revenue this country will obtain when thousands of automobiles are traversing the Parks."

In the years after his first report, Harkin continued to play the tourism card, realizing it would be far more effective in securing appropriations needed for development than arguments about the intrinsic value of wilderness. In 1915 he came up with a novel approach to its financial benefits, bringing forth elaborate statistics to show that while tourism was the country's fourth largest revenue generator, Rocky Mountain scenery actually produced more income per acre in export value than did an acre of wheat ($13.88 per acre compared to $4.91 per acre). He also began strongly promoting the humanitarian value of parks, stating that they would serve to make the Canadian people "physically fit, mentally efficient, and morally elevated." In this argument he was following the lead of the "Recreation Movement" which was flourishing in the United States and Europe. It postulated that man's "play spirit" had been subverted by the pressures of work and society in the modern industrial age, one American writer summing it up by stating that "in country-side and city we have cherished the ideals of work, not play; we have apologized for leisure instead of making it divine." Harkin married this thinking with polemics about the necessity of national parks, where mankind could indulge this "play spirit" through healthful outdoor recreation amidst nature's grandest beauty. He spoke of the parks as having a dual function in their tourism and humanitarian aspects, best summed up in this

1915 annual report where he referred to them as producing "dividends in gold and human units."

Insofar as the role of the automobile would play in achieving such "dividends," Harkin's initial optimism about the new highway through Vermilion Pass was tempered by the experience of the exigencies of mountain construction, but with an unforeseen benefit for the park system he headed. Estimates for construction of the highway were initially $150,000, but by 1913 some $277,000 had already been expended and only seven miles of road had been built easterly from the Columbia Valley up Sinclair Creek and five miles westerly from the summit of Vermilion Pass. Construction of the B. C. portion was halted at this point, although the federal government continued with its stretch through the park, reaching the summit in November, 1914. The outbreak of the war and its financial challenges precluded the B. C. government from considering continuing the project, but by 1916 Bruce had come up with an idea to overcome this roadblock. The solution was to trade the cost of the Dominion Government completing construction for lands which would allow them to create a new mountain park. The scheme was perhaps best described in a letter from Bruce to Harkin when the issue of highway's name was being debated:

One might say that the calling of this park 'Columbia' might be pandering to our cousins across the line. Well, we want to pander to them all we can. We want their cars and their money and their business, and that is a good deal why this road was started originally. I know because it was me who started it. I got the C. P. R. interested and the provincial government, away back in 1910. The former put $75,000 into it and the latter about $200,000. Then came evil days in B. C. Our government had no more money. What had been built was falling into decay and I bethought myself of the Dominion Government and in conjunction with your good self, I suggested to Dr. Roche, the Minister of the Interior, that he should take over the road as then constructed, as an outlet for the national park. At that time you will remember he said the Dominion Government was willing to pay for the necessary right-of-way, which we then talked about as extending a mile on either side of the road. From

Ottawa I went to Victoria, and asked the Government for five miles free right-of-way on either side of the road, and I got it for you. So I humbly think I am entitled to express my opinion as to what this area should be called.[6]

The deal Bruce brokered came in the form of the Banff-Windermere Road Agreement, signed by the British Columbia and Dominion governments on March 12, 1919. It provided for the road right-of-way, title to a ten-mile-wide belt surrounding it, as well as solving a long-standing dispute about federal legislative jurisdiction in British Columbia national parks. On April 21, 1920 the new Kootenay National Park, named to honour the original Kootenay habitation and use of the area, was created by an Order-in-Council. The Agreement had called for the federal government to complete the road in four years and the work of doing so proceeded throughout the summers of 1920, 1921 and 1922. The Banff-Windermere Highway, as it had become known, was officially opened to the public at an elaborate ceremony held at Kootenay Crossing on June 30, 1923 with a reported 1,200 persons in attendance to watch Lieutenant-Governor Brett of Alberta and Lieutenant-Governor Nichols of B. C. cut the ribbon. Many Banff residents were among the throng, some who had expressed their strong opposition to automobiles only ten years before. During the following season, more than 4,500 automobiles passed over the new route, and Harkin rejoiced in his annual report that the new road completed a six-thousand-mile highway system through Canada and the United States creating the "California-Banff Bee Line," and providing access to three Canadian and twelve American national parks. He also understood the historic significance of the creation, giving voice to it in a new pamphlet, *The Banff-Windermere Highway*, produced for its inauguration:

The building of a motor highway across the central Canadian Rockies adds one more thrilling chapter to the romance of modern engineering. It is the record of one more of those victories of the peaceful but daring imagination that should be no less renowned than those of war. Since that

Alberta Lieutenant-Governor Dr. R. G. Brett cuts the ribbon to open the Banff-Windermere Highway, June 30, 1923

rainy November morning in 1885 when Donald Smith, later Lord Strathcona, drove the silver spike which completed the construction of the Canadian Pacific Railway, there has been no event in the history of road construction in Canada of more dramatic significance. The ringing blows of Lord Strathcona's hammer, echoing among the lonely solitudes of the mountains, announced that the Canadian Rockies, so long an impregnable barrier between the East and the West and a terra incognita to all but the most intrepid explorers, had at last surrendered to the ingenuity and persistent courage of man. . . . The cutting of the ribbons on the Banff-Windermere Highway on June 30, 1923, will mean that a new triumph has been won over the physical obstacles of nature, a magnificent preparation made for the new and fascinating mode of travel which has already revolutionized modern life, and a new open-air and open-sky way provided to the scenic treasures of Western Canada.[7]

At the same time as the Banff-Windermere project was making

its way through its rather tortuous history, work had been quietly proceeding on extending the growing network of roads west from Castle towards Lake Louise and beyond. Some of the labour on this extension came from a source that provided one of the black marks on the Valley's history — alien internees. At the beginning of the war there were a large number of immigrant industrial workers who had come from the former lands of the Austo-Hungarian Empire, mainly the Ukraine, who found themselves without employment in the immediate pre-war period when the boom in western Canada came to an abrupt end. The fact that many of these men were on relief, tended to gather in urban areas, hadn't applied for citizenship and were often lacking skills in English, combined with the fact that they came from lands with whom Canada was at war, resulted in many being interned by the government. The Canadian populace expected that these internees should have to work while in detention, but finding suitable labour camp locations was a difficult task for the Director of Internment, Major-General Sir William Otter, given the anti-German hysteria of the day. In this situation officials in the Department of the Interior saw an opportunity to have a force of labourers at their disposal at little cost to the Dominion Parks Branch in a period when appropriations were rapidly shrinking.

In May, 1915 Harkin was informed that employment of enemy aliens in national parks had been approved, with the Militia Department providing the guard, the Parks Branch equipment, materials and supervisory services, and the Internment Operations Branch and Department of Justice costs of prisoner welfare, including the 25 cents a day they were to be paid. Harkin immediately had Park Engineer J. M. Wardle (the man later responsible for the Banff-Windermere Highway project) draw up a plan for highway construction projects and secured the approval of Sir James Lougheed and R. B. Bennett, Calgary law partners and members of the Borden government, for his idea.

The first contingent of internees arrived in June from a detention camp in Lethbridge and were placed in a camp near Castle Mountain in preparation for being put to work on the extension of what was now being referred to as the Banff-Laggan Road. By the middle of July close to 200 were behind the ten-foot-high barbed wire stockade surrounding their tent camp and being marched out each day under the guard of the 103rd Regiment, Calgary Rifles to perform their roadwork using the most basic hand tools. It was felt that they should be able to complete the road in two years, and, indeed even extend it to the lake itself and around its shore to the foot of the Victoria Glacier. Work continued through the summer, four miles of clearing and grubbing and one mile of gravelling having taken place by the end of August, but with the approach of winter the men were moved into a temporary camp using former construction crew bunkhouses next to the Cave and Basin in Banff. During the winter they worked at clearing the new recreation grounds, brushing the Buffalo Paddock and building a new bridge five miles up the Spray River. Internees complained about mistreatment, lack of food and poor living conditions, leading many of them to try escape, but despite these problems more prisoners were shipped in and by the end of the year the camp's population stood at over 400. This number quickly diminished the next spring when shortages of manpower caused by the war led authorities to begin releasing the "non-dangerous" prisoners, although road work did continue through the following summer, aided considerably by the addition of a steam-shovel. Other camps in the west were rapidly closing by this time, and all remaining internees were sent to Banff because of the perceived importance of the Lake Louise road.

During the 1916 season, an additional four miles of the highway was completed, and over the following winter the internees continued to do improvements around Banff townsite, including building an ice palace and toboggan run for the first Banff Winter Carnival. By the next summer, the Banff camp had been disbanded and although Harkin expressed disappointment at the amount of work accomplished, he did recognize it was a question of little work being done by the prisoners or none at all without them, as resources would not have otherwise been available during the war.[8] Thereafter the task of completing the road moved at a slow pace and it was not until 1920 that the link to Lake Louise was made. Further extensions continued through the early twenties, reaching Field in 1926 using part of the railway grade abandoned with the building of the Spiral Tunnels, and ultimately becoming the "Kicking Horse Trail" when a link to the provincial road to Golden at Yoho's west boundary was made the following year.

The completion of these major road construction projects joining the Banff-Bow Valley with Calgary, Lake Louise and Yoho, the Columbia Valley and the United States, led to a revolution in the provision of amenities, forever altering tourist offerings. One of the first requirements to accommodate the increasingly lower budget tourist was campgrounds. Banff already had a unofficial campground on the CPR station grounds in the years around 1910, but in 1914 it was disbanded and campers were allowed to pitch a tent anywhere approved by the chief warden. One of the areas they favoured was near the bridge over the Spray River and when the Parks Branch determined in 1915 that an "official" motor campground was needed they laid it out along the Loop Drive close to the confluence of the Spray and Bow Rivers. The Rundle Campground was found to be spacious in its first few years of operation when visitation numbered in a few hundred, but it quickly became inadequate and underwent several expansions as the trickle of motor traffic turned to a flood. By the early 1920s the area around the Loop Drive was becoming crowded and congested, not only because of the growth of the campground but equally as a result of the popularity of the near-by Banff Golf Course.

Harkin eventually found an answer to this problem in a deal with the CPR in 1927 when they requested the area occupied by the Rundle grounds be made available for the new golf course being designed for them by Canada's foremost golf architect, Stanley Thompson. Agreement was reached to add this and several other small parcels to the golf course lease in return for the company paying the relocation costs of the campgrounds and its associated facilities to a new site on Tunnel Mountain, which would have ample room for later expansion. Although the good burghers of Banff howled in protest that the new grounds were too far from town (and, perforce, their businesses), Harkin was undoubtedly pleased to find any solution and particularly one that someone else paid for in a time of great demand on park financial resources.[9]

The next level up on the accommodation scale resulting from the Valley's capitulation to the internal combustion engine was a variation on the campground — the back-yard tent cabin. The regulations of 1914 had allowed for the erection of more permanent "shack tents," including those that could remain at any approved location for an entire season and those located in residents' yards. The latter trend soon caught on when Banffites realized that they could participate in the expanding tourist trade by providing some basic habitation to value-conscious travellers. Many town homemakers made a few dollars by having back-yard tents and these basic habitations soon began to take on a more substantial air when they were built with permanent wood floors and half-walls with a canvas top. These tent cabins were just the forerunners of full back-yard cabins as these informal operations got more fully into the "approved accommodation" business, changing dramatically the built landscape of the town and creating some major regulatory headaches for park administrators in the years ahead.

While camping, be it of the campground or back-yard variety, was an important outgrowth of the automobile age, even more far-reaching was the effect that the change in travel habits had on the *modus operandi* of the CPR, the major provider of accommodation in the Valley. The double whammy of the appearance of the automobile in its hitherto monopoly field of transportation and the reduction of tourist passenger traffic caused by the war were keenly felt. The company's first reaction was to participate in the phenomena, as seen in Shaughnessy's involvement in the Banff-Windermere Highway scheme, but it also played a more direct role through its transportation concessionaire, Brewster Transport. Jim Brewster had been among the first to see the writing on the wall with respect to the replacement of horse and buggy livery by the motorized kind, and despite his hugh stock-in-trade in the former had begun to experiment with vehicles for his company as soon as his CPR concession and government livery regulations were amended to allow it. When a new concession agreement, including auto livery, came into effect on January 1, 1915 and government regulations including licensing of motor livery vehicles followed in June, Brewster took possession of a Baby Overland and became the first resident of Banff to own a motor car. He spent the summer of 1915 satisfying himself with the Overland's capabilities and in the spring of 1916 turned the Bow Livery into the Mount Royal Garage. In early May, 1916 the company sold off twenty-eight head of horses and unloaded four 7-passenger and one 5-passenger Overland touring cars from a CPR flat-car, signalling the beginning of the modern age in the Valley's tourism history. Still burdened with many carriages and tally-hos, which were not as easy to sell off as livestock, Brewster took a cue from John Locke, the proprietor of the Homestead Hotel, who the same month brought in a char-a-banc (open excursion vehicle with transverse seats) mounted on a Ford chassis. Brewster similarly mounted his three tally-ho frameworks on the chassis of used Kissel trucks and early in 1917 unveiled his "auto tally-hos." The largest of the three, seating eighteen passengers, was soon to be seen on the sightseeing run to Lake Minnewanka with the park's first bus driver, wearing a new top hat and jacket, at the wheel.

Despite financial setbacks in the later war years and the post-war recession, Brewster Transport had recovered sufficiently by the mid-twenties when the new roads were coming into their own to assist the CPR in coping with the changing market. By 1925 the Brewster company owned thirty-five passenger vehicles with a carrying capacity of 320 passengers, many of them recently purchased White buses, most with 18-passenger seating and one with a 30-passenger capacity. Along with its recently-purchased fleet of Studebaker and Packard touring cars, these vehicles were put to work on a scheme the CPR and Brewsters jointly promoted as "Twenty-Four-Hour Motor Detour Tours." The concept was to offer train passengers the opportunity to see more of the Rockies by detraining at Banff and spending the day touring the mountains in a Brewster vehicle before overnighting at the Lake Louise

Chalet and then driving to Golden to catch the westbound train the next day. These tours proved so successful that the companies worked out several other options as the twenties progressed and by the end of the decade even offered one that allowed an interchange of passengers between the Great Northern lines in Glacier Park, Montana and the CPR lines at Banff.

Another means whereby the CPR adjusted to changing circumstances was in the policy it pursued with respect to new accommodation facilities in the post-war period. Hayter Reed retired as manger-in-chief of hotels in 1915 and was replaced by Frank L. Hutchinson, who had been his assistant in charge of Alberta and British Columbia hotels since 1912. Working for Hutchinson at Lake Louise was an innovative young man named Basil Gardom who was about to change the face of hotel operations in the mountains. Lake Louise hotel facilities had been in an almost constant state of development since 1893 when a modest frame building replaced the first log chalet that had burned down. A second storey was added to this structure in 1898 and the next year Thomas Sorby, the designer of the original CPR railside hotels, was engaged to plan an addition. Noted Victoria architect Francis Mawson Rattenbury was the next to be commissioned, designing a wing built in 1902-03 placed at right angles to the existing building and exhibiting a "Shingle Style" that helped retain the complex's rustic appearance. Finally, chief CPR architect Walter Painter had his turn, in 1906 originating a "Tudor Revival Style" addition to replace the Sorby wing, and in 1910 realizing a major concrete "fireproof wing" in an "Italianate Style" somewhat incongruously attached to the smaller wooden chalet but adding 350 guest rooms. Meanwhile, the road between Laggan and the Chalet, being steep and tortuous, had been the source of many complaints about the treatment of livery horses used to convey passengers and baggage to the lake from the station. A solution was found in the construction of a narrow-gauge tramway line for the three-and-a-half mile trip, completed in 1912 and operating with two twenty-eight foot open-bench passenger cars with internal combustion engines. Gardom initially worked as the manager of the tramway line but was soon promoted to the position of superintendent of hotel construction and maintenance, where he was given free rein by Hutchinson to make good on his belief that many post-war tourists would prefer to stay in smaller, quieter and more out-of-the-way accommodation.

The CPR had already begun development of small camps in the pre-war period at Emerald Lake in 1902 and at Moraine Lake and in the Yoho Valley in 1906. With these locations soon connected by motor roads, Gardom began expanding them into full "bungalow camp" operations with individual rustic cabins for overnight use and a central log lodge for meal services, social interaction and, in some cases, additional accommodation. Gardom's first totally new camp was placed at Wapta Lake in the Kicking Horse Pass in 1921, already accessible by road from Field and soon to be joined to the roads being developed to the east and west with the completion of the Kicking Horse Trail. The next year two similar camps, one at Lake O'Hara (accessible only by foot or horse) and the other in the Yoho Valley at the foot of Takakkaw Falls, were added, and the concept was soon in full flower on the Banff-Windermere Highway after its completion in 1923. A bungalow camp was erected on the shore of Windermere Lake prior to the highway's completion and additional ones were added, convenient distances apart, as the decade progressed. These included Castle Mountain (later renamed Storm Mountain) and Vermilion River (today's Kootenay Lodge) Bungalow Camps in 1923 and Radium Hot Springs Bungalow Camp in 1926. Supplementing these camps was a system of resthouses and teahouses devised by Gardom meant to provide for the needs of trail riders, hikers and climbers who were prepared to penetrate a little further into the backcountry. Rustic log tea houses were built at Summit (Yoho) Lake above Emerald Lake in 1922; at Lake Agnes above Lake Louise, at Twin Falls in the Yoho Valley, and at Nakimu Caves in Glacier Park in 1923; at the Plain of Six Glaciers near the foot of Mount Victoria and in the Kicking Horse Canyon in 1924; and at the Natural Bridge on the Kicking Horse River in 1925. In 1922 a resthouse for hikers was erected on the Saddleback above Lake

Brewster Transport touring car on the Banff-Windermere Highway at Radium Hot Springs Bungalow Camp, ca. 1930

Louise and the same year the company constructed the sturdy stone Abbot Pass Hut, probably the first of what was meant to be a series of high altitude mountaineering huts.

By 1927 the CPR was issuing individual brochures on its main camps and a more elaborate one, *Bungalow Camps in the Canadian Pacific Rockies,* to describe in totality the new services available:

At several points *in the Canadian Pacific Rockies, bungalow camps have been established which make a special appeal to the trail-rider, the hiker and the climber. A "bungalow camp" consists, speaking generally, of a cluster of buildings of log or other wooden construction — the principal one the club building, used for dining and recreational purposes, the other being individual sleeping cabins of various sizes. These bungalow camps — which are supplemented by many outlying "tea houses" — combine comfort, simplicity, and good food with moderate charges — and always they have the magnificent background of wild Nature.*[10]

The appearance of bungalow camps also allowed the CPR to begin tying together packages using their hotels, camps and transportation services. "All expense tours," the first of what would become a popular tourism option, were being offered by 1927 beginning from Banff or Lake Louise at the rate of $25 per person for a return drive to Lake Windermere with overnight lodging at the Lake Windermere Bungalow Camp and meal stops at Storm Mountain, Vermilion River and Radium Hot Springs. A few years later Brewster Transport was offering a "Scenic Lariat" trip of three days duration "through Rocky Mountains National Park, Kootenay Park, the Columbia Valley, the Kicking Horse Canyon, Yoho Park and the Great Divide," and a "Rawhide Trail" trip of two-and-a-half days with overnight stops at Radium and Blairmore. A second package concept involved the CPR-sponsored Trail Riders of the Canadian Rockies wherein "Circle Trail Rides" were offered after the annual Trail Riders outing utilizing bungalow camps and other company facilities. In 1927 the six-day circle rides were under the direction of Phil Moore, manager of the Yoho Bungalow Camp, and were "operated during July and August from Lake Louise around those of the Bungalow Camps which are situated in Yoho National Park" priced at $10 per day.

Certainly the CPR and its concessionaire, Brewster Transport, were quick to adjust to and benefit from the coming of the motorized age, but many other individuals and companies in the Valley did likewise. While the towns of Canmore and Anthracite were largely unaffected, other than to make transportation and communication more efficient, the face of commerce in Banff was markedly changed. As was to be expected, the most profound influence was to be in the provision of infrastructure to support automobile use and in the commercial fields of livery service and automobile service and repair. As early as 1913 the government had purchased a large new steam-roller and had begun to use compacted crushed rock, known as "rocmac," to replace the former loose gravel on the road from the bridge to the CPR station. In an effort to beautify the main street, at the same time a centre island was created to separate traffic and planted with grass and asphalt sidewalks were laid. In September, 1914, just at the beginning of the war, Fred Ballard opened Banff's first garage and in 1915 it was joined by one operated in conjunction with William Mather's boathouse, connected to Cave Avenue by a small road, one operated by Bert Sibbald on Lynx Street (today's Standish Service) and by the town's first car dealership, a Ford agency owned by J. E. Deegan & Sons.

Major changes in motoring services thereafter awaited the end of the war, but by 1919 the proverbial "lid came off," with numerous new garage and livery schemes. One of them, fronted by former guide William Warren, who had married the wealthy Mrs. Schäffer, was to be called the Cascade Garage located on Banff Avenue (today's Imperial Oil site) and was complemented in 1921 by the similarly named Cascade Dance Hall built next to his Cascade Hotel. Within one month of opening, the Cascade Garage was reporting fifty-two cars being parked overnight and daily sales of 900 gallons of gasoline, leading to the doubling of its size the next year. This operation would form the nucleus of the second largest transportation company in town and Brewster Transport's major competitor when Warren and Jim McLeod, a former Brewster manager, joined forces in 1921 to create Rocky Mountain Tours and Transport. Purchasing Norman Luxton's King Edward Livery, and working out of a garage across the street from Warren's building (today's Grizzly House), the company began with three small Fords and two "auto tally-hos," but by 1924 had a substantial fleet of McLaughlin and White touring cars.

It was not only Banff where the effects of motorized tourism were felt, as it also gave the first impetus to the non-CPR development at Lake Louise. In June, 1917 the road from Lake Louise townsite (the former Laggan) to the lake was opened to automobiles for the first time. By 1921 the Parks Branch had decided to open for lease three blocks of villa lots (about thirty lots) down the road from the lakeshore for commercial development, and Brewster Transport acquired several of them, one for the operation of a drug store, a lucrative business in prohibition times. Because of their knowledge of the site, Brewster financial manager Lou

Crosby and his wife Gertrude, who had worked as a telegrapher and telephone operator at the Chalet before their marriage in 1911, were also in a good position to benefit. In 1922 the Crosbys erected a sturdy sixty by forty foot log building known as the Lake Louise Trading Company, one third devoted to a small store and two-thirds to a cafe. Their neighbour, Maggie Stephens, built a small inn which she named Deer Lodge on the lots to the north and in 1924 this too was acquired by the Crosbys. Further to the north was the leasehold of Robert Colebrook who, with the backing of the Calgary YWCA, built a dormitory-style hostel on it in 1926, the building eventually being acquired by the Y and added to with a two-storey wing in 1930. To the south of the Crosby's holdings were two other small accommodation operations, known as Triangle Inn and Inglenook Lodge. All of these facilities were gradually acquired by the Crosbys, the complex eventually becoming known as Deer Lodge, and after 1926 they also ran the Brewster service station, which replaced the old drugstore after the repeal of prohibition, as a matter of convenience.

In their totality, all of the influences and developments growing from the beginning of the motorized age would fundamentally change both tourism and the Valley itself, much as the completion of the railway had three decades earlier. The automobile would ultimately allow a broader scale of the social spectrum to become tourists, would dramatically increase their numbers and would result in them experiencing the Valley from an entirely different perspective and pace than had earlier railroad and horse-conveyed visitors. Roads would now begin to penetrate areas that had formerly been virtually inaccessible and tourist amenities to accommodate them would soon follow. The growth of roads and automobile traffic would start to overwhelm the area in the decades ahead, leading to the consideration of their existence as somewhat of a mixed blessing. In the final analysis, managing the benefits and the problems associated with the internal combustion engine would become one of, if not the greatest challenges of the Valley's future.

Chapter Thirteen
Making Fun of Winter

While the appearance of automobiles and roads in the Banff-Bow Valley began to revolutionize residents' and tourists' lives, the years around the First World War and immediately after saw another fundamental change in how they dealt with their environment. Until that time, the reality of winter in the mountains meant that commercial activities centring on the tourist trade almost completely halted for eight months and residents' lives turned to traditional activities, several of them outdoor-oriented, that would sustain their economic and social well-being through the quiet times. However, the change that occurred set the Valley off on a new course which would lead to a major extension of the tourism season and greater enjoyment of the long season of snow that was a fact of Canadian Rockies existence. It was the beginning of a transformation that would become a defining aspect in the Valley's life.

The closing of the doors of the Banff Springs Hotel and the *en masse* departure of the staff on an east-bound train at the end of September signalled the finish of the tourist season, just as their opening on the Empire Day weekend (May 24th) announced its commencement. For many of the town's businessmen, the fall provided an opportunity to enjoy some of the mountains' delights that had been the sole preserve of tourists for the previous four months. Back-country horse trips, fishing and mountain sheep and goat hunting were popular relaxations, and trips to the surrounding foothills and prairies in pursuit of waterfowl and upland game birds were equally well-enjoyed. Some families also savoured a quick train trip to the west coast, or after the war an automobile trip to the Columbia Valley, before winter set in. For the men of the trail, the season's work was not yet completed, as some of the outfitters' most lucrative business came from wealthy American hunters who were outfitted out of Banff and Laggan for hunting trips beyond the parks' boundaries, the Brazeau country being a particular favourite. But by early November all hunting and back-country pleasure trips were finished, the livestock moved to their winter pasture, and the town girded itself to celebrate another Packer's Ball. Begun in 1902, it became **the** social event of the year featuring dancing till dawn at the Brewster Opera House with punch bowls made from washtubs placed at convenient locations for all to enjoy. After the cobwebs cleared, Banff residents knew it was time to prepare for the onset of winter.

Except for those working in the coal mines, where seasonal aspects of employment were not a major consideration, finding gainful employment in the winter was a challenge for Valley folk. Some of those working for the warden service were kept on over the winter doing back-country patrols on snowshoes, actively trapping and hunting predators or assisting closer to town in clearing brush and trails and feeding the animals in the Buffalo Paddock. Of those who gained their summer wages on the trail, many made their way to prairie ranches to find winter work while those who stayed sometimes found a calling labouring in the mines or for the Eau Claire Lumber Company. The original Eau Claire timber berths in the park had been gradually eliminated by the government, but the 1902 boundary extension brought a number of operations back within its limits. The largest of these was on the Spray River where the experience of guides and packers working with horses made them valuable for employment as skidders, hauling out logs on the snow from the bush with two and four-horse teams. The logs were stacked on the river in preparation for break-up, and when floated down in spring when the ice went out caused considerable havoc with the Spray River bridge.

Perhaps the most fortunate employees were those working for the Brewster company, as their regular men had the best chance of being kept on the payroll over the off-season. Some of them were assigned to the care of the company's considerable herd of horses, originally kept on a variety of foothill ranges around Morley and on the Kananaskis River, but after 1905 mostly on the large grazing lease they acquired from the government at the subsequently famous Yaha Tinda Ranch on the Red Deer River. Although this land had been included in the park by virtue of the 1902 boundary revision, the Brewsters' close connection to the CPR likely led to the granting of a lease on one section of grazing lands in 1905 and a further section on which ranch buildings could be constructed in 1907. Three or four company men held a lonely winter vigil guarding the horses from marauding wolves and coyotes, but undoubtedly glad for the work. Other company winter projects included hauling construction materials to the building contractors involved in the frequent additions to the Banff Springs Hotel and carrying out an ice-cutting contract to supply the needs of Canadian Pacific's western hotels. The latter activity usually began in January, when the ice on the Bow River had attained a thickness of about two feet, and employed up to fifty men and twenty teams of horses. Weighing up to 700 pounds, the ice blocks were loaded on sleighs to be hauled to the nearby railway where a hoist was used to transfer them into boxcars. The job could take up to six weeks to complete involving the loading of some 700 cars, but the dangerous conditions and subzero temperatures often made the work hazardous.

One of the most favoured winter occupations in the years before the war was the running of a trapline. Many of the men familiar with back-country travel identified suitable trapping territory outside the park in the course of their wanderings, with pine marten, lynx, coyotes and wolves being the most frequently harvested furs. Men such as Jimmy Simpson, Bill Peyto, Sid Unwin, Elliott Barnes and Fred and Jack Ballard spent many lonely months on the trapline using a variety of rough trapping cabins and wickiups to provide basic shelter in the often extreme weather conditions. In his book *Climbs and Explorations in the Canadian Rockies*, J. Norman Collie described one such cabin he visited in 1902 near the mouth of the Mistaya River belonging, he said, to "two young trappers from Banff, Ballard and Simpson" and cogitated on "how great must be the courage of the hunter or trapper who, in the depth of winter, ventures forth alone for weeks or months together in the woods, pack and blanket on back, dependent largely on his gun or rifle for food, and with none near to succour in case he falls ill or meets with an accident!"[1]

Consideration of such an accident was a very real concern, as the annals of winter travel in the area are replete with stories of Valley residents who cheated a cold death. After selling his outfitting interests to Bob Campbell in 1904, Tom Wilson spent a considerable amount of his time at a horse ranch he had established on the Kootenay Plains near the headwaters of the North Saskatchewan River, and then added a small stock of goods to trade with the members of the Wesley band Stoney who frequently hunted and trapped the area. For the next several years he spent about ten months of the year trading from this cabin and caring for his increasing herd of mountain ponies, the practice only coming to an end when he, like many other tough outdoorsmen, almost fell victim to treating the harsh winter environment too lightly. The near-tragedy is recorded in E. J. Hart's book on the exploits of early trailmen, *Diamond Hitch, the early outfitters and guides of Banff and Jasper*:

The incident occurred near Christmas when the desire to spend the festive season with his family at Banff led him to set off on snow-shoes in less than ideal conditions. Beset by a blizzard with plummeting temperatures, he had the misfortune of breaking a snowshoe, and for several days he struggled through waist-deep snow down the Pipestone in a desperate attempt to reach the railroad. Nearing his destination fate once more struck him a cruel blow when he broke through an ice bridge and fell into the river's numbing water. Normally Tom would have built a fire to dry himself out in such circumstances, but exposure had dulled his mind and he stumbled onward in frozen clothes. Several hours later he had all but resigned himself to his fate when he heard the whistle from the daily passenger train pulling into Laggan. As close as he was, he barely made it to the station, and had to be immediately transported to the hospital in Banff.[2]

Even a veteran mountain man like Tom Wilson almost fell victim to the harsh conditions of mountain winter travel

Wilson lost four of his toes and part of each of his feet to frostbite as a result of this experience, although he later claimed the doctor had enough sense to take the same amount from each foot so that he wouldn't be unbalanced. He was not the only one to have such a close shave with the grim reaper, Jimmy Simpson falling victim to an avalanche while out on the trapline and only saving himself by seeing how his dog buried its nose in the snow to make a breathing cavity, and Sid Unwin having to endure a painful journey in the opposite direction to Wilson's during the winter of 1906-07. On this trip the snow condition were so bad that it took Unwin ten days to reach the Saskatchewan and he was so dog-tired he fell asleep in front of his campfire and only awoke when his mackinaw pants and underwear caught fire and burned into his flesh. He made the rest of the way to Wilson's ranch in excruciating pain, but was too exhausted to even eat when he reached safety and simply rolled into a bunk and slept for twenty-six hours. A week later he joined Simpson at the cabin described by Collie at the mouth of the Mistaya with a piece of cloth the size of a hand still attached to the burn. Jimmy slowly cut away a bit of the cloth each day with Unwin's only painkiller being a few swallows of rum.

Snowshoes had been the traditional implement of mountain winter travel since David Thompson and members of the fur trade brigades had made their way over the snow-bound Athabasca Pass a hundred years earlier. Jimmy Simpson recalled hearing about some Swedish trappers who had been active north of Laggan in the years before the turn-of-the-century who used skis on the trapline, and on one occasion decided to try them himself. These he made from white pine in one of his cabins "with axe and drawknife, bent and dried before an open fire, waxed with four candles I hated to use." They worked well until he had the misfortune to become snowblind, one of the hazards of winter travel, and ran into a stump breaking off a tip. For the fifteen miles back to his cabin he was unable to distinguish the dips and rises in the snow and the "broken blade would go straight down while I went straight ahead and down so often that I ought to have contracted water on the brain."[3] Thereafter, he stuck to tradition, using the store-bought "Hudson's Bay variety" of snowshoes that he modified for use in the dry snows of the Rockies by gradually replacing the original caribou hide "babiche" with strips of goat skin that he carried for purposes of repair. The larger holes he thereby created allowed the snow to sift through more easily, preventing it from balling up and assisting him in perfecting the rolling gait that fast travel on snowshoes in deep snow country required. Simpson so mastered this technique and moved so swiftly that the Stoney honoured him with the name *Nashan-esen*, "wolverine-go-quick."

Snowshoes were the one implement that served double duty for winter work and winter leisure. This tradition also extended back to fur trade times when inhabitants at the fur posts used snowshoe tramps as a diversion to the long winter period of inactivity. In some western centres, such as Winnipeg, snowshoe clubs had been organized as early as the 1880s, and this was an institution copied in Banff. While many Valley residents undoubtedly participated in unorganized snowshoe outings in the early years, at Banff they also indulged in an unofficial "club" led by museum curator Norman Sanson. Sanson, who had come west after participating in the Riel Rebellion of 1885, was an extremely active individual who undoubtedly had previous snowshoe experience. A government weather observatory was built on top of Sulphur Mountain in 1903 and taking regular recordings was added to his curatorial duties, eventually leading to over one thousand ascents of the peak up a switchback trail. In wintertime he invited some of the younger Banff residents to accompany him, leading to the organization of frequent club outings to the top of Sulphur as well as to other destinations such as Edith Pass and Hole-in-the-Wall.

Other winter diversions engaged in by early Valley residents revolved around the use of ice. Ice-boating at Lake Minnewanka was one of the area's most exhilarating activities, particularly after Captain Jack Standly returned from a trip to the Klondike and took over the boating operations at the lake about 1900. Standly had been a carpenter for Dr. Brett before heading north and built two iceboats for winter operations, one of them a sloop capable of carrying several passengers and named *The Gibson Girl*. Sixteen feet long at the beam and so low-slung it only cleared the ice by a foot, it was sleek and fast. If it caught a good running wind it could cross the lake in forty-two seconds! Ice-boating became extremely popular after the opening of nearby Bankhead provided a large population intent on using the lake for winter recreation, and Standly built several other boats on order. Those who could not afford his services made their own craft, described by one observer as "anything of a triangular nature having three pieces of iron as runners, and a pole sufficiently strong to carry a blanket, a sheet, or mother's tablecloth. . . ."[4]

Skating was also an activity that lent itself well to the area because of large number of rivers and lakes and the frequent chinooks that would sweep their surfaces clean or release water to flow over top in a natural flooding, allowing them to be used for the sport. A 1911 CPR advertisement for winter activities reported that "James Simpson, a trapper and guide of Banff, skated twenty-five miles in one day over a British Columbia lake." However, skating was also done on a more formal basis, perhaps qualifying as Banff's earliest sporting activity. Small rinks in a hollow beside Banff Avenue where it left town had appeared in the late-eighties, and in 1893 a number of guests at the Sanitarium Hotel banded together and cleared a section of ice at the bend of the Bow River just above the Banff Avenue bridge. In 1894 Walter Garrett, a summer teamster at the Banff Springs Hotel, was engaged as the ice-keeper and set to work to upgrade the cleared space, surrounding it with five-gallon oil cans and strategically placed pieces of canvas to break the wind. Lighting for evening skating was initially provided by two poles supporting kerosene lamps placed in the middle of the rink, so that the skaters could do a figure-eight around them, and later by lights illuminated by the Bankhead power plant. The rink operated intermittently during the nineties, but by 1897 William Mather, a Scottish immigrant and employee of the Eau Claire Lumber Company, had taken over Garrett's position. In 1899 he bought out Raymond Rooper's boat business and boathouse at the site and began to run the rink in conjunction with it. Mather's rink quickly became a community institution and generations of Banff children learned to skate there.

One of the most popular skating events of the time was the "fancy dress carnival," essentially a dress or masquerade ball on ice. These affairs had been popular in Montreal as early as 1859 when the first indoor rink was built and provided the focus of the winter social season. By the turn-of-the-century they were becoming frequent in the west, and in the Valley served essentially the same purpose, being held to mark special occasions or provide a focus for community activities during the long winter months. In February, 1897 the Canmore populace turned out in force to the local ice, known as "Sifton's rink," to hold a carnival as a fundraiser for the "Indian Famine Fund." On New Year's Eve the same year the citizens of Banff celebrated the appearance of Father Time with a masquerade carnival:

The most successful skating carnival ever held in Banff took place on New Year's eve. The ice was in good condition, the weather perfect, the thermometer being a few degrees above zero. The rink was lighted by a huge bonfire and lamps. There was a large number of people present and the costumes were pretty and well chosen.

Almost the most effective was that of an Indian chief in feather head dress and beaded buckskin worn by a visitor at the Sanitarium, who with his painted face looked like a red man indeed.

A young Englishman whose skating was much admired personated "Folly" gorgeous in brown and yellow. There were men as chefs, a well dressed clown, a nigger and a negress; a Banff lady as Red Ridinghood looked charming; a young lady visitor as Daughter of the Regiment in correct scarlet military coat with yellow braiding and forage cap, made one of the most striking figures on the ice. Another visitor was well disguised as a nun and a gentleman resident, as the New Woman, deceived many. A tall young member of the Mounted Police gyrated on his skates in the garb of a most up to date hospital nurse and a well known visitor was a darky dude.[5]

The first figure skating on the rink was performed by Dr. William White and a Miss Rickerd, but the most enthusiastic proponent of "art skating" was George Paris, one of Banff's foremost winter sportsmen. Paris was originally from London, England and had come out to Banff while working for the CPR at the end of the eighties. He initially found employment with Dr. Brett as an attendant at the Grand View Villa bathhouse, but after a customer showed him how to cut hair he opened a barbershop at the Sanitarium Hotel. After marrying his wife Ida in 1903, they began the Paris Tea Room, one of Banff's subsequently most popular businesses serving tea and ice-cream to the weary tourists shopping in the curio and outfitting establishments of Banff Avenue. Although he had been one of the early stalwarts of the snowshoeing club, his real passion was skating and he often practiced on Vermilion Lakes. As the only resident with proper figure skates, all others interested in the sport learned from him. One of his keenest students was Jimmy Simpson's young bride Billie, who had seen the figure skating toast of Europe, "The Great Charlotte," skate at the Hippodrome in New York during their honeymoon trip in 1916. Her eventual devotion to the sport would bring Banff its greatest moment in the skating world in the years ahead when her daughters, Margaret and Mary, would themselves become famous in New York as "The Simpson Sisters." In the meantime, another individual skating sport that caught on in the years before the war was speed skating, Brewster manager Lou Crosby being its foremost proponent and soon passing its secrets onto his active young family on the ice in front of their Bow Avenue home.

While individual skating sports had their aficionados, it was the team sport of hockey that really caught the public imagination. In Banff, the first games had been played on the rink cleared by the Sanitarium guests in 1893, their competition being the local constables of the North West Mounted Police. When a stick was broken, the player would simply go into the nearby willow bushes and find a suitable replacement, but as the competitions were often played after an all-night carousal and the participants were, as one player recollected, "three sheets in the wind," the going could get rough. One memorable game played on Christmas Day sometime in the nineties began early in the morning after the players returned from an all-night dance at Anthracite and ended when the Sanitarium team's captain was arrested by the Mounties because his teammates were thought to be ganging up on the police's best player. Town residents soon replaced the Sanitarium habituees on the local side and by the late nineties included such stalwarts as Paris, Mather, Arthur Saddington, and the young Bill and Jim Brewster, who were regarded as having real hockey talent. There were many informal matches played on the Mather rink, the game being so popular they included everything from ladies' hockey, to mixed hockey, to men's pick-up games.

Hockey was popular in all the region's towns, and it would become the most visible form of inter-community rivalry in the Valley's complexion. By the end of the nineties, area teams frequently travelled to play each other on holidays and in district competitions. The most hotly contested of these was the Sifton Cup, put up by local Liberal politician A. L. Sifton for competition "in the Banff district," which included Banff, Canmore and Anthracite. Teams at the time were made up entirely of those of

Ladies' hockey on Mather's rink, ca. 1905

Anglo-Saxon heritage, the later tendency towards those of different ethnic backgrounds to dominate the sport in the mining communities not appearing until second generation offspring adopted the game. Teams were made up of seven players — a goal keeper, a point, two covers, and three forwards — and the game was divided into two halves. A newspaper report on the March, 1899 final between Banff and Canmore provides a good picture of one such event:

Accompanied by their brass band the Canmore Hockey team visited Banff today to do battle for the championship of this district and for possession of the Sifton trophy. The game was a lively due and the visitors played to win, but were slightly outclassed. . . .

At 2:48 the puck was faced and after a little band stand play Lindsay scored, time 2 minutes. Then W. Brewster took a hand and in 15 seconds had scored the second goal. This was fast time and some of Canmore's men began to waken up but after J. Brewster had done some clever dodging he passed to Lindsay who shot the the third in 3 minutes. Then McMahon for the visitors was fortunate enough to score the next in 1 minute. From then on the scorer was kept busy, the goals coming in fast and furious. . . . At half time the score stood 7 to 1 in Banff's favor. During the second half the home team continued their good work and

Members of the Canmore hockey team with the Sifton Cup, ca. 1925

added four more to their credit.

After the match the two teams and their friends repaired to the Sanitarium where Dr. Richardson on behalf of the visitors formally presented the Banff club with the trophy. Dr. Brett replied in their behalf. Messrs. Fidler and T. Douglas then gave short addresses, after which the assembly adjourned en masse to the Basin and there had the most pleasant time. In the evening a pleasant dance was given in honor of the visitors in the Foresters Hall.[6]

As time went on the Valley's hockey players became far more accomplished, and the calibre of play improved. When Canmore's native sons began to play in the years after the war, the town's teams went on a rampage in Alberta hockey. Canmore's first indoor rink was built in 1905 by the Canadian Anthracite Coal Company, giving its teams the advantage of more playing and practice time and in 1911 the Canmore Boys' Hockey Team bested the Banff team coached by Jimmy Simpson and won the Williams Cup. The original rink burned down, but hockey was so important to the community that the mining company immediately rebuilt it, and in 1921 the Canmore Intermediate Hockey Team won the provincial championship. In 1926 Canmore joined the Alberta Senior Hockey League and with players such as Joe,

Frank and Art Jerwa, Art Schivan, Vic Riva, Gonna Mackie and Joe and Johnny Bleskan won the provincial championship for three successive years from 1926 to 1928. It was said that during those glory days "on hockey night there was barely a light on in town; everybody was at the rink."[7]

Curling was not far behind hockey in the hearts of Valley sportsmen, particularly those goodly number of Scots origin. At Banff, the first curling stones were brought into town in 1896 from Calgary, where curling had begun in 1889, by a Mr. Winn and "diagrams" were drawn on the ice near the boathouse to allow interested locals to play. In 1897 a sheet of ice was made on the tennis courts at Dr. Brett's Sanitarium, although it lasted only one year before being replaced by a more permanent site created on a small backwater of the river at the boathouse. This was dammed up and flooded by Mather to create four sheets of ice, a small clubhouse was constructed and in 1899 the Banff Curling Club was formed by such local enthusiasts as Dr. Brett, Dr. White, Howard Douglas, D. D. Galletley, John Walker, Tom Wilson and Dave White, with a ladies' division being added in 1908. The first draws were confined to local sides, but by 1901 Banff curlers were playing Anthracite and Canmore teams. It was reported in January, 1901 that "an interesting inter-club series between the curling clubs of Anthracite and Banff has just been completed," with the winning rinks of each town playing off in Banff "for four handsome pipes put up by the Banff club." As in hockey, Anglo-Saxon names dominated curling, the Anthracite rinks of the day being led by Anderson, Lindsay, store manager W. F. Little and trail guide Harry Lang.

By 1904 curling in the Provisional District of Alberta was being governed by the Alberta District, Royal Caledonian Curling Club and organized bonspeils were the order of the day. In 1903 Banff had sent its first rink to the Calgary bonspeil and performed well enough to repeat the entry in succeeding years. The growing confidence of the town in the sport led to the decision for the Banff Curling Club to sponsor its own bonspeil in 1908, and under the leadership of Bob Campbell an event was organized with seventeen rinks from the Valley, Calgary, Cochrane and elsewhere in Alberta attending. Several trophies were awarded, the most coveted being the Grand Aggregate, symbolic of the spiel's championship, and the Visitors' Trophy for the best out-of-town team. Banff teams dominated the first few years of the competition, with Ralph Edwards' rink winning the 1908 event and two subsequent championships, while other Banff rinks led by James McRavey, Arthur Saddington and Harry Brett also had success. The ethnic mix of Canmore and Bankhead made putting a strong team together more difficult, but Alec Watters' team from Bankhead managed to grab the Grand Aggregate in 1915.

Banff rinks had by this time become a powerhouse in provincial curling circles and on February 15, 1915 won the Wiser Cup, emblematic of curling supremacy in the Royal Caledonian's Alberta Branch. The trophy was played for in a two team, total point format, with the rinks of Dr. Harry Brett and D. C. Bayne representing the Banff club. Having wrested it from the Victoria Curling Club of Calgary, Banff defended the Wiser four times against Calgary, Edmonton and Golden rinks before losing it to the Granite Club of Calgary on December 17, 1915. They in turn lost it to the Victorias, and on January 19, 1916 the Banff teams travelled to Calgary to bring it back home. The *Crag and Canyon* proudly reported that their "firm determination to bring the premier curling trophy of the northwest back to its home" had "turned the trick by a score of 33 to 28," gloating that the Victoria rinks were "composed of the flower of Calgary curlers, and their signal defeat on their own ice places Banff in the top notch of Alberta curlers."[8]

Curling notwithstanding, it would be the last major winter sport to catch on in the Valley — skiing — that would ultimately lead to its transformation. Apart from Simpson's recollection of Swede trappers employing skis on the trapline prior to 1900, Walter Fulmer, who accompanied George Stewart to "Old Banff," remembered Norwegian and Swedish tie cutters working for contractors Carlin and Lake at Castle Mountain in 1887 who "used skis for speed and were very adverse to the more cumbersome snow-shoes." The first pair of what appear to have been manufactured skis followed a few years later when George Paris acquired them through one of the customers at the Grand View bathhouse:

When Mr. Paris came to Banff as a young man he met a man from Montana who told him of the mail carriers in Montana who used skis and Mr. Paris was so interested that he had him send him a pair. It was in 1894 that he first used them; they were of oak with a single strap run through a mortise and over the toe. With no instructions or information about skiing to help him, he chose moccasins as the warmest footwear to ski in. There was no idea of any kind of binding, other than the single strap, and no poles were used. At that time, because of a winter forest fire that had swept through the valley some years earlier, there were no trees on the whole side of Sulphur Mountain and Mr. Paris found splendid running from the cliffs on that mountain down to the Banff Springs Hotel. A bad spill among the stumps one day wrecked Mr. Paris and one ski. He never went back for the other ski.[9]

The story of George Paris and these skis went on to relate that "after this mishap he took up snowshoeing which. . . really marks the beginning of the Snowshoe Club, a very active organization in Banff for many years." Indeed, his misadventure seems to have put an end to an interest in skiing for quite a period. It was not until 1910 that it would again receive an impetus as a result of the appearance of an interesting mountain guide in Banff named Conrad Kain. Unlike all other contemporary climbing guides, Kain was Austrian, not Swiss, having been hired by A. O. Wheeler in 1908 as an official guide for the Alpine Club and as an assistant on his own topographic surveys. He had spent two years in such work, including a winter survey near Banff in early 1910, and in late February left for town and went to work for Brewsters on the ice harvest at $2.50 per day. Having used skis as part of his guiding activity in Austria, he noted the lack of skiing in Banff and soon found an opportunity to rectify it. In his journal of March 8, 1911 he recorded:

Several weeks ago I founded a ski-club in Banff. The people seem to take to this sport. We practice very Sunday, jumping as well, and many people assemble. My longest jump is fifty feet, about twelve feet beyond the last record[10]

Most of Kain's followers appear to have been the young folk of Banff, such as Cyril Paris and Peter and Cliff White, who soon made a small ski jump on the side of Tunnel Mountain with his assistance. Kain had Norwegian telemark skis which were not available to his students, but he convinced Jack Standly to make a few pair at his small mill at Lake Minnewanka with his own as the pattern. Some used the home-made variety, fashioned from the rounded parts of wooden cheese boxes secured to the feet with a leather toe-strap while old broom handles served as poles. With this basic equipment the young skiers were soon beginning to explore some of the nearby valleys in the first recorded ski touring outings at Banff.

In another journal entry made a few weeks later, Kain noted his involvement in a "winter-sport festival" that had recently been held in Banff and had attracted 400 participants. He closed the entry with an interesting comment: "Yesterday a lady, sent by the railroad, came to me for information as to the possibilities here for ski and toboggan. I talked to her about sport for nearly two hours." The unidentified railroad representative had things on her mind, for the CPR had recently decided to begin promoting the Rockies as a winter resort, a result of decisions made concerning the Swiss guides. By 1909 the number of Swiss guides being brought out from Interlaken each year had increased markedly, including the sons of Edouard Feuz — Edward jr., Walter and Ernest and a cousin Gottfried — and the son of Christian Häsler — Christian jr. Their services had also been extended from Glacier House and Mount Stephen House to the Lake Louise Chalet, where a rustic cabin built on the lake shore known as the "Swiss Guides' House" was becoming the base camp for the Valley's climbing activities. Passenger Traffic Manager Robert Kerr came up with an idea that year to build a picturesque Swiss village somewhere close to the line where it could be seen by tourists and provide housing to allow the guides stay in Canada year-round. Named Edelweiss, it was to be situated just outside of Golden and to consist of six, six-room cottages designed to emulate Swiss chalets, surrounded by pasture lands intended for the growing of flowers and vegetables and the keeping of the traditional goats and chickens. Part of the CPR's attempt to attract the Swiss to stay for the winter was a promise that the company would keep their mountain hotels open and develop them as winter resorts.

In *Canadian Pacific Empress Mail*, a brochure issued in 1911, the writer quoted Kain's skiing and winter carnival success at Banff and went on to expostulate on the company's new campaign:

As a matter of fact, the mountains in winter are even more beautiful than in the summer, and provide quite as much entertainment. The Canadian Pacific Railway Company, in its determination to hold up this viewpoint, will leave open its chain of beautiful mountain hotels, and will establish a Swiss village at Golden, B. C. where the guides, who have hitherto gone home to Switzerland for the winter months, will have a place to stay and a headquarters from which to begin the work of making the Rocky Mountains a more desirable winter stamping ground than Switzerland itself.

Skeeing, tobogganing, skating, ice-boating, mountain-climbing, and hunting are just a few of the sports the guides will supervise, while Providence and the railway company will provide an unexcelled climate, mountains, lakes, the best hotels, and plenty of mechanical contrivances to add to your enjoyment.[11]

Perhaps the CPR found the cost of renovating and heating their hotels for winter use too expensive or other exigencies intervened, but in any case while Edelweiss was completed in 1912 the hotels did not stay open as proposed (nor would they for another sixty years). Undoubtedly, this was greeted with disappointment in Banff where some hotels, such as Norman Luxton's King Edward and Dr. Brett's Sanitarium, were already staying open all winter and many other businesses were expecting to benefit. In the circumstances, it was not surprising that with the winter advertising already done by the CPR, with the growth of the annual Banff Curling Club Bonspeil, and with such successes as Rossland's Winter Carnival, begun in 1898 and featuring "the Ski Running and Ski Jumping championships for the Dominion of Canada," the idea for a winter carnival in Banff would soon surface.

In fact, the carnival organized by George Paris and Jack Standly described by Kain in 1911 was already a successful local event. All that was needed was some impetus to make it a major attraction. Popular lore has it that the idea to do this came from the fertile brains of Norman Luxton and Barney Collison, Banff's police magistrate. The two "temporary bachelors" were sitting in Luxton's home one evening in 1916 whiling away the hours "with music, refreshments, and social chat, while thick clouds of tobacco smoke filled the air." The conversation drifted to a much discussed topic of the day, "what could be accomplished along the line of bringing people to Banff during the winter months, when all Nature is greatly enhanced by the work of the supreme artist — Winter." Many methods were discussed until finally "the idea of holding a week's series of winter sports events was decided upon as the most feasible." Both realized that to move to such a concept funds would be needed, and a hasty telegram was sent off to Harkin requesting the Dominion Government pitch in. To their amazement, a reply came back stating that the Parks Department would contribute a few hundred dollars, and the pair immediately decided to hold a public meeting to gain local support. Few came. Undaunted, Luxton undertook to canvass Banff residents individually and "armed with the strength of his convictions, he argued so convincingly that business men and citizens in general promised substantial contributions to the Banff Winter Carnival, as its originators named it."[12]

A meeting held in the firehall at the end of December, 1916 began the formal organization of the event. At that time it was reported that the government had agreed to make the labour of the alien internees available for the construction of an ice palace on Banff Avenue. This was to be a sixty foot by ninety foot structure with "towers, battlements and bastions" as well as a maze "of intricate passages calculated to puzzle those who attempt to thread its windings," and was to provide the focal point for the Carnival's activities. Events were planned to build around the already proven success of the Banff Bonspeil and the operation of the Cariboo Street toboggan slide, a long, manicured run from the top of the street on Tunnel Mountain to Banff Avenue and a winter entertainment that had made money from both Banffites and visitors since 1914. The cooperation of different groups in the town was announced in early January in the *Crag and Canyon*:

> *. . . the Banff Winter Sports club, the Banff Curling club and Banff citizens have joined hands and united their interests and for two weeks, commencing Tuesday, February 6, they will enact the role of hosts to the people of Manitoba, Saskatchewan, Alberta and British Columbia. . . . Ski-ing, tobogganing, ice-boating, hockey, snowshoeing, speed and fancy skating, trap-shooting, swimming contests in the hot sulphur pools, etc., will each and all be staged.*[13]

Although it was admitted that mistakes were made, the events went off well, with ladies' hockey matches and speed-skating, pony ski races and ski-jumping being particularly well enjoyed. The pony ski races were described as "a new sport in Banff" with the object being "to fasten a pair of skis to one's feet, grasp a rope hitched around the saddle horn of a horse, with a rider, and endeavor to keep one's feet upon the snow or ice while the horse is sent over the course at a mad gallop." Ski-jumping attracted the largest crowds, it being estimated that "fully a thousand people were perched on bare spots, bumps on the mountain side and limbs of trees" to watch the three competitors — Maland, Elvinson and Ofrim — who had stopped off on their way back from the Revelstoke sports meet the week before. The carnival was brought to a close with a masquerade ball in Brewster's Hall at which Miss Mary McHugh of Calgary was chosen as Carnival Queen, the first of many young western Canadian ladies who would proudly bear the title.

The initial Banff Winter Carnival lost money, which had to be made up by dances and whist drives, but its value to the future of winter tourism was immediately recognized. Within a month Banff's leading businessmen had met and created the Banff Winter Sports Association to carry on its future activities, with Jim Brewster serving as president, Sam Armstrong, Dave White's business partner, as secretary-treasurer, and Superintendent S. J. Clarke, King Edward manager L. C. Orr, and Lou Crosby as an executive committee. Thereafter each carnival improved, although it was not until after the war that any money was made and the books balanced. By 1920 the Banff Winter Sports Association was publishing a major promotional brochure explaining the various sports, lavishly illustrating them with photographs, and appealing to the growing number of those holidaying on the coast in the winter to "include a stop-over at Banff. . . and continue your journey with renewed vigor, prepared to take the full value out of your trip." New and unique activities were added as time went on, including children's events such as tug-of-wars and obstacle snowshoe races, as well as automobile ski-joring, whippet races, and dog sleigh races. The latter took on a primary role for a period beginning in 1923 when the Trimble-Murfin Picture Company sponsored a "dog derby" on Lake Minnewanka to be filmed for use in one of their movies starring "Strongheart," the dog hero of the day. The Strongheart Trophy and a $1,000 prize was put up, attracting professional mushers from as far away as The Pas, Manitoba, and after the first year the derby was run from Calgary to Banff so that audiences could see it finish in town.

The greater inclusion of Calgary in Carnival events as time went on became a conscious effort to draw on the city's increasing population to support Banff's winter activities. Mayor Costello officially opened the first carnival and Calgary curling rinks, hockey teams, and individual competitors were a part of the Carnival's participants from the beginning. By the late-twenties a special train was being laid on for the first day of the Carnival, which was dubbed "Calgary Day," with a parade to the ice palace and a greeting by the local school children and the carnival queen following the arrival. Addresses at the 1929 event included those by M. L. A. George Webster, Mayor Fred Osborne, Calgary Rotary Club President Frank Freeze, Calgary *Herald* Manager Charles Hayden and Calgary Exhibition Association President Nat Christie. Writing on the background of the Carnival in 1929, W. E. Round made mention of the importance of Calgary to Banff's welfare and vice-versa:

In time the possibilities of the Banff Winter Carnival and Banff as an all-winter playground appealed to many prominent Calgarians. The Banff Winter Sports Association was affiliated with the Banff-Lake Louise-Calgary Tourist Association and Calgary thus put her shoulder to the Carnival wheel. As a tourist magnet, be those tourists of the summer or winter variety, Banff's destiny — her place in the sun is inseparably joined with Calgary's welfare. What benefits Banff must ultimately benefit Calgary and this fact the progressive business leaders of the Foothills City realised.[14]

Appreciation of the importance of Calgary to Banff's tourism success, first publicly voiced in connection with the Winter Carnival but also made manifest by the growth in automobile traffic to the park, would thereafter become one of the primary tenets of the Valley's economic life. As Round's comments predicted, the future of the two were inextricably linked, and much of that linkage would be based on winter sports, particularly skiing.

One of the important influences of the Banff Winter Carnival was the impetus that it gave to the growth of skiing at the local Banff level. The ski-jumping event was mainly a spectator sport with only professionals jumping, a practice that became even more pronounced when a new and larger jump was built on the side of Tunnel Mountain overlooking the Buffalo Paddock in 1919. However, that year Gus Johnson, one of the competitors from Camrose, decided to stay in Banff after the carnival and through his efforts with some of the youth, who had first learned to ski from Kain, organized the Banff Ski Club. The club had a nucleus of about fifteen members and through Johnson's construction of

Ski-jumping at the Buffalo Paddock jump was a popular Banff Winter Carnival event

smaller jumps, such as the one on Learn's Hill on Buffalo Street, they gradually improved their skills. Never-the-less, the increasing professionalism of jumping, with Banff being awarded a date on the American Professional Ski Jumping Circuit in 1921, meant that the local jumpers were relegated to the B and C events. In these circumstances, skiing attention began to turn to "sliding," or what we would now call downhill, on some of the area's better slopes. It also appears that several of the Swiss guides, in particular Edward Feuz jr., Walter Feuz, and Rudolph Aemmer, would sometimes come to town to instruct the Banff lads in the proper form of ski-running, climbing with a side step, diagonal traverse and herringbone and coming down with a telemark turn to the right and a christiana to the left. They also told the boys stories about some of the remoter areas of the mountains they had explored on skis, being particularly enthusiastic about the terrain of the Ptarmigan Valley and the Mount Assiniboine area.

About 1920 Peter White, Fulton Dunsmore and Cyril Paris had begun skiing from Banff through the Edith Pass area and had found some slopes where forest fires and logging activities had provided several good downhill runs. In 1923 the lads met Owen

Bryant, an entomologist from the eastern United States working in the Banff area, and told him of their discoveries. Bryant, an avid skier, was particularly attracted to the slopes of nearby Mount Norquay and suggested a ski cabin should be built there for the following winter. Hiring Johnson to do the work of clearing a good ski run and piling the logs for seasoning, Bryant was disappointed when the logs were stolen. This set the project back and it was not until after Johnson's death in 1927 that the Mount Norquay Ski Company Ltd. was formed by Cliff and Jack White and Cyril Paris and construction began on the first Norquay cabin. The work was reported on by a correspondent of the *Crag and Canyon* just prior to the cabin's completion in January, 1929:

> *Truly, the site chosen is ideal for the purpose for which it is intended. The level meadow in the gap — the gradual slopes leading into it in several places — the steep slopes in others — farther around Norquay the innumerable slides of varying grades and lengths —all are conducive to enjoyable skiing with plenty of variety. . . .*
>
> *At the present time there are several slides cleared and with the passage of two or three more seasons a slide will be completed practically from the top of Norquay upon which the ski jump with a three hundred foot landing will be built. . . .*
>
> *Club members are to be seen on the slides, and last Sunday five or six of the younger members enjoyed themselves alternately between working (?) on the cabin and skiing on several of the slides.*[15]

Although the partners in the Mount Norquay Ski Camp did not intend that it become a business venture, the populace of Banff were soon flocking to the slopes. The era of commercial skiing, an activity that would fundamentally re-shape the Valley's future, was at hand.

Chapter Fourteen
An Identity of Our Own

The initiation of the Banff Winter Carnival in 1917 during the difficult days of World War I and the response it received from the populace was an important progression for Banff. For the first time the businessmen and community leaders of the town had taken the ball in their own hands and had not relied on direction from either the CPR or the Parks Branch in launching a community initiative. As such, it was a key step in breaking the almost total dependency of Banff-Bow Valley communities on either corporate or government entities. But it was not the only one, as in their local institutions and their social, cultural and political lives these communities had begun to take on well-defined identities. Although there had been close affinities between Valley communities in the years prior to the formation of the Parks Branch, Banff now saw itself as increasingly distinct from the surrounding resource towns and began to pursue its own unique vision of the future. In the process, differences would appear between local wishes and points-of-view and those of the federal government, which had quite a different perspective. One of the defining tensions in the subsequent unfolding of Valley life would therein be revealed.

There is little doubt that in their early histories the Valley's settlements found themselves firmly under the paternalistic thumbs of both corporate and government interests. As mentioned, the fact that most of them owed their existence to resource extraction meant that they were company towns. In Anthracite and Canmore, first the H. W. McNeil interests and later the Canadian Anthracite Coal Company and the Canmore Coal Company were responsible for community infrastructure and employment, with the United Mine Workers local being the only somewhat inde-

Company sponsored bands, such as the H. W. McNeil Company brass band pictured here in Canmore about 1900, played an important role in providing mining community identity

pendent community voice. However, apart from projects that contributed towards community betterment, such as the hospital and Union Hall in Canmore's early years, the union was not in a position to overcome the dominance of company interests. This was particularly so in Bankhead where it was the huge CPR itself, as represented by the Pacific Coal Company, that had carefully planned and developed its "model community," and mine superintendent D. G. Wilson and his staff were by far the foremost community citizens and spokesmen.

In Banff, where the CPR was also the dominant interest, there was a somewhat similar, if less pronounced, situation. The Banff Springs Hotel was the largest employer in town and the centre of its economic well-being, but it was not a place where the townsfolk felt particularly welcome. An obvious social gulf emerged in the community's early years which Bart Robinson, in his book *Banff*

Springs: The Story of a Hotel, succinctly describes :

Despite the town's pride in the hotel, as well as its dependence upon the hotel for a portion of its meal ticket, few of the townspeople ever saw the inside of the hotel, and most were only vaguely aware of the elegant activities that transpired behind the great carved doors. It was very much "a place unto itself" and very few of the local populace would consider directly transgressing its glittering domain. The concept of social class was a very vigorous doctrine at the turn of the century and it operated most effectively to keep the "downtown people" downtown.

Yet there were some annual events which tended to bring the hotel and the town into direct contact with each other on a social plane. The annual hotel summer ball carried the established families of Banff and Calgary briefly into the sequestered realm of New York and Boston social registers, and lucky guests of the occasions could later speak in casual tones of mingling with European and Eastern royalty.[1]

Another event that helped to bring the hotel and the townspeople into contact was their shared promotion of Banff Indian Days. As described, this had been initiated due to expediency — the need to entertain stranded CPR guests when the rails washed out in June, 1894. The Stoney had continued to come to Banff during the summer thereafter, usually to participate in the annual Dominion Day celebration, but it wasn't until 1907 that the CPR and local businessmen grasped the potential of a full week's Indian celebration for the tourist trade. Despite the fact that Calgary and other western Canadian communities were rapidly beginning to modernize, local entrepreneurs understood that part of Banff's appeal was its "frontier" and "wild west" personality, and nothing was more popular or interesting to international tourists at the time than native peoples. Banff boosters such as Norman Luxton, Jim Brewster and Dave White for years formed the local Banff Indian Days Committee (and thereby provided the model for the later Banff Winter Carnival) working with the Banff Springs Hotel manager. Each day there was a parade of natives down Banff Avenue and across the bridge to the hotel and for many years some dancing events were held in its environs (today's Banff Springs playing field). Originally, many of the races and other competitive events of the Dominion Day celebrations had been staged right on Banff Avenue, but when it was decided to hold a more formal Indian Days the government was approached about providing a special location, resulting in the designation of the Banff Indian Grounds just north of town. While the CPR made a financial contribution to the event, which was strictly a break-even proposition with all monies used for payment to the natives to attend and the purchase of food and prizes, most of the funds were raised from local business subscription.

Perhaps the best example of the influence exhibited by the CPR on community activity was in a field spanning the relationship between sport and social life — golf. When the CPR began building its golf course in 1911, the intention was, according to Howard Douglas, to "elect members" who could pay a membership fee and thereby have the right "to use the course at any time." The company expected these members be drawn from the more prominent representatives of the community, and, indeed, many of the town's growing middle class had come from urban centres where they had experienced the game. Several were invited to an organizational meeting at the Banff Springs on July 13, 1911, those in attendance representing an eclectic mix of CPR management personnel, summer visitors and prominent residents. They included F. W. Peters, general superintendent of the CPR's British Columbia Division, G. A. Walker, CPR solicitor for Alberta, G. H. Rawlins, manager of the Banff Springs Hotel, Mr. MacMahon, a summer resident from Calgary, A. B. Macdonald, superintendent of Rocky Mountains Park, A. E. Foster, manager of the Imperial Bank, Lou Crosby and Dr. Harry Brett. The organizing group created the first executive, which decided to limit membership to twenty "inside" or resident members and thirty "outside" or non-resident members. This limitation set a trend that would be continued within the Banff Springs Golf Club thereafter, with CPR management determining the number of local members allowed into the club and securing two positions on the club's executive that would, to

Stoney Indians at the Banff Springs Golf Course in a Banff Indian Days publicity photograph

a great extent, determine exactly who those members were.

Despite the corporate dominance exhibited in the early life of the Valley's communities, they did manifest aspects of activity that could be found in any other western Canadian settlement of the time. During this period the over-riding Anglo-Saxon flavour of the west meant that the institutions that flourished were, with a few exceptions, those reflecting this background. Churches were a mainstay of community life, with the traditional Presbyterian, Anglican, Methodist and, particularly in the mining communities, the Roman Catholic congregations being early in evidence. Methodist and Roman Catholic missionaries had, of course, been at work in the Valley from the 1840s, but with the McDougalls' concentration on the Stoney at Morley it appears that it was the latter sect that was most prominent in the area. The Oblate missionaries (O.M.I.) were well-established with diocesan headquarters at St. Albert under Bishop Vital Grandin and an active mission at Calgary from its earliest days. From there Reverend Father

Edmund Claude was regularly travelling through the mountains ministering at construction camps as the railhead pushed westward. On October 13, 1883, within days of the rails having reached Siding 29, he preached the first Catholic service in the Banff area and eight days later offered the first mass at Silver City. Father Claude performed this missionary work until the fall of 1884, one his last services being the first offered at Canmore. He was followed by Father Leon Doucet, who began holding monthly masses in Canmore in 1887 and by Father Cocola who came all the way from Kamloops to preach to the growing number of Italian miners. It took until 1893 for the first permanent Catholic church, Sacred Heart, to be built on land donated by the mine company at Canmore by Reverend Father Comire and two Oblate brothers. Father Comire then took charge of the Canmore parish as well as Banff, where a Catholic church, St. Mary's of the Assumption, had been built on Lynx Street in 1888, and undoubtedly Anthracite as well. In 1896 a diocesan census showed there to be ninety Catholics at Canmore, fifty at Banff and twenty at Anthracite, and by 1906 the Catholic (and only) church had been built in Bankhead, followed by a small Catholic church, St. Bernard's, at Exshaw in 1907.

Given the presence of large numbers of Valley residents of Scots origin, the Presbyterians were quick to follow. Reverend Charles Gordon (who later became famous writing under the pen name of Ralph Connor) was the minister in charge of Canmore from 1890 to 1893. He oversaw the completion of the first log Presbyterian Church in 1891 (this became the United Church after the union of the Methodists and Presbyterians in 1925), and Ralph Connor Memorial Church remains today one of Canmore's most significant heritage resources. Presbyterian services were preached in Banff at a resident's home as early as 1886 by Reverend I. Dyke of Calgary, and in 1888 when the Reverend J. J. Macleod was stationed there, the first Presbyterian church was built near the Catholic St. Mary's recently constructed on Lynx Street. That year, 1888, witnessed a real building boom in churches, at it also marked the only appearance of a Methodist church, constructed at the corner of Banff Avenue and Buffalo Street by Reverend Clement Williams, who formed the Banff Mission in June, 1887. However, in a gesture of local church cooperation between the Methodists and Presbyterians that preceded official union by more than a decade, the Methodists shared the Lynx Street building with the Presbyterians in the early years of the new century. With respect to the Anglicans, their first services in Banff were held, again in 1888, in a log building where the King Edward Hotel would eventually stand, while in Canmore they were preached in the Presbyterian church in rented space beginning in 1893. As with the Catholics, the Canadian Anthracite Coal Co. eventually donated land in Canmore on which the Anglicans could erect a church, this occurring in 1895 with the building of St. Michael's under the supervision of Reverend R. W. Barnes. The next year Lord Stanley, Governor-General of Canada, laid the cornerstone for what would become St. George's-in-the-Pines on Beaver Street in Banff. By the turn-of-the-century then, all the major denominations had gained a strong presence, and an equally strong influence, in the Valley's life.

A second mainstay of district affairs was provided by the influential fraternal organizations that appeared in the pre-war era. These organizations were based on the premise that the creation of fraternal feelings and the extension of benevolent activities to their members and other needy elements of society justified their social usefulness. Their importance to community life in the west has been well described by Donald Wetherall in his social history *Useful Pleasures: The Shaping of Leisure in Alberta 1896-1945*:

In general, even without an analysis of membership of these organizations, it is apparent that, among the fraternal clubs, the Masons were generally seen as the elite organization, whereas the Knights of Pythias and Oddfellows were of somewhat lower rank. Business interests, personal needs, and tradition undoubtedly played a part in attracting members to these organizations. Most were linked to national and international organizations that provided a social framework transcending the local chapters. Nonetheless, it is clear the local chapters played an impor-

tant social role in the everyday lives of their members. The regular meetings, with their ritual, regalia, emphasis upon secrecy, and claims to origins in antiquity created a socially secure environment in which one could meet friends and acquaintances. Most of these groups had their own meeting halls or buildings and many of them mounted several annual events.[2]

Most of these clubs traced their lineage to ancient times and had certain secret initiation and meeting rites, something that was expressed in a unique way in the Mason's case. Cascade Lodge, No. 5, A..F. and A. M., exhibited a rather peripatetic nature during the early years of its existence. Begun at the instigation of H. Ransford, New York lawyer and Secretary of the Canadian Anthracite Coal Co., the first meeting, or "communication," was held on May 25, 1888 in a Masonic Hall located on the second storey of the Carlin and Lake store in Anthracite. Among the Masons in attendance, in addition to Ransford, were Dr. R. G. Brett, Archibald McNeil of the H. W. McNeil Co., and David Keefe, CPR section foreman, and by the end of the year there were nineteen members, including Billy MCardell and Frank McCabe. The Lodge was relocated to Banff in 1892 to a building provided by Dr. Brett after problems developed with the Anthracite hall, but it did not stay, returning to Anthracite early in 1898 after O. E. S. Whiteside, the new mine manager, found better quarters for it in the McNeil building. The dedication ceremony for this new location was performed by Hamilton Lang, assisted by T. McNaught of Golden and Dr. Brett, Dave White and Tom Wilson of Banff. There it remained until the closing of the mines in 1904 when it returned to Banff to be housed in the new Brewster Opera House. On December 2, 1901, the lodge members had staged their first mountain communication on the summit of Tunnel Mountain, and this unique Masonic event was repeated on the summit of Cascade Mountain on August 26, 1907, the summit of Mount Aylmer on August 14, 1910 and at several other high altitude locations thereafter. The influence, prosperity and social standing of the Masons was well-exhibited in 1924 when they decided to build a grand

Cascade Lodge, No. 5, A.F. & A. M. "communication" on the summit of Mount Aylmer, August 14, 1910

new hall on a triangular lot at the intersections of Cariboo, Bear and Lynx Streets. Contracted by Arthur Unwin for the large sum of $15,000, the press called it "a pretentious affair of stucco design, one-story high with semi-basement," housing a kitchen and dining room as well as "a community hall forty by forty feet."

Other fraternal organizations followed, several of them being the usual women's auxiliaries of male-dominated orders. The Cascade Chapter of the Order of the Eastern Star, the distaff side of the Masonic Order, was installed at Banff in December, 1914, complementing the Bow Valley chapter already in existence west of Calgary. The Banff Rebekahs, Lodge No. 34 had appeared a year earlier to mirror the activities of the Independent Order of Odd Fellows, Lodge No. 48 which had been formed a few years previously, duplicating the situation in Canmore where the Oddfellows established in 1908 and the Rebekahs in 1914. At Banff, both groups initially held their meetings in the rooms above Dave White's store and later in the Standish Hardware building. After church union in 1925 the original Methodist Church was to be replaced by the new Rundle United Church on the corner of Banff Avenue and Buffalo Street, and these organizations were able to acquire the use of the old church and move it back to Beaver Street to be a home, not only for the Oddfellows and Rebekahs but also for a number of other community organizations.

The Mount Rundle Chapter of the Imperial Order Daughters of the Empire was one of these, they too having been formed in 1913, and having used the Methodist Church in its original location for most of their history. This organization was, as its name implied, a patriotic order, the motto of which was "Fear God and honor the King," and embraced in its membership many of those who were also part of Eastern Star, including Mrs. Eva Atkin, Mrs. Pearl Moore, Mrs. James Brewster and Miss Dell Sibbald. Its first efforts included purchasing patriotic pictures to decorate the schools and sponsoring a patriotic essay contest, while entertainment at the meetings included papers read by members on such subjects as "The Union Jack," "Life of Nelson," "Wellington," and "Laura Secord." However, as time went on this organization became what was to be Banff's first real "service club," a concept that began to become popular during the inter-war period. Its male manifestation did not appear until 1924 when the Chicago-based International Rotary organization chartered a club in Banff which included in its membership leading business and professional men who met weekly for lunch at the Mount Royal Hotel to determine ways of fulfilling Rotary's mandate of "service above self."

The usefulness of the large number of fraternal organizations that were created just prior to 1914 was to be tested by the impacts of the First World War on community life in the Valley. It has been said that the bloody battles of the war, such as Vimy Ridge and the Somme, were the crucible in which Canadian nationhood was formed. In a similar way, its effects on the home front helped many young communities to foster their identities and community spirit, and Banff, Canmore, Bankhead and Exshaw were to be no exception. Given their relatively small populations at the time, the number of casualties experienced in the trench warfare of France and Belgium were keenly felt by all the Valley's residents and, likewise, all at home pitched in to support the war effort in any way possible.

By early 1915, the *Crag and Canyon* was stating that more than ten percent of Banff's estimated winter population of 1,000 had signed up and boasted that "this town has contributed more men for king and country than any other town or city, in proportion to population, in the Dominion." A recruiting drive held by Major Parry of the 50th Battalion in Calgary in early February was typical, he in one day examining and accepting applications for enlistment from thirty-four volunteers — twenty from Banff, twelve from Bankhead, and two from Exshaw. As these men gradually made their way overseas, and the local "Honor Roll" of casualties mounted, all the Valley's communities threw themselves headlong into war activities. Succouring the wounded through the agency of the Red Cross was a major goal of all existing fraternal organizations and the new Overseas Clubs and Patriotic Leagues created as a result of the conflict. In Bankhead, the Ladies Patriotic League held a 1915 New Year's Eve dance reported as "one of the most successful affairs ever held in the briquet town," with the proceeds going to the Red Cross Fund. Similarly, at Banff during the same period it was being reported that: the I.O.D.E. ladies had distributed $276 to the "Hospital Ship Fund," $25 to "Belgian Relief," and $5 to "Local Relief;" the Overseas Club had held a whist drive, the proceeds of which were to "be devoted to the purchase of tobacco for the boys from Banff who are at the front;" the Red Cross Bonspeil had just been completed; the Banff Winter Carnival Club was planning a "Patriotic Fund Carnival on the Toboggan Slide;" and the young married men had issued a hockey challenge to the young unmarried men, with the proceeds to be donated to the Red Cross Fund.

The ability of the Valley's communities to sustain both their level of recruitment and support of those overseas as the war dragged on was remarkable. By February, 1917, 266 men from Banff, seventy-seven from Canmore, thirty-four from Bankhead, and four from Exshaw had enlisted, and the tally of "Banff heroes who have sacrificed their lives that you and I may enjoy freedom from the curse of militarism" stood at thirteen. The clubs and organizations were, at the same time, squeezing every last dollar out of their strained communities to support the growing number of causes, now including several prisoners-of-war funds, holding such unique events as raffling a cord of wood at the Lux Theatre for the Belgian Relief Fund. In April, 1917 the monthly returns to the Canadian Patriotic Fund, Southern Alberta Branch from the area stood at $430 for Canmore, $400 for Banff and $200 from Bankhead, with $150 per month coming from the donations of government employees alone. By war's end over 300 men from Banff and almost 100 from Canmore had answered the call to arms, and seventy-four had paid the ultimate price, fourteen from Canmore, fifty-two from Banff and eight from Bankhead.

A new and important organization that emerged as a result of the war was the Great War Veteran's Association, which in 1926 became the Royal Canadian Legion. Re-integration of returned veterans into community commerce and life was a major post-war issue — while the country went all out to support the boys overseas it was almost totally unprepared to look after veterans' problems when they returned. Groups to deal with these issues sprang up all over the country, and as early as May, 1917 the Calgary Returned Veteran's Association was running a railway excursion to Banff to provide an outing for veterans. The largest such organization was the G. W. V. A., which eventually had over 700 branches across Canada, one of being the "Rocky Mountains Branch" formed on March 30, 1918, originally incorporating Banff, Bankhead and Canmore. The first eighteen members quickly grew to thirty as returned men trickled back home, including such local worthies as Bill Peyto, Art Beattie, Joe Woodworth, Charlie Fullbrook and the community's most senior military man Colonel Phil Moore, who had been promoted to Brigade Major early in the war and after returning from overseas was appointed commander of the Alberta depot battalion responsible for conscription in the province. Acting under the direction of its orginal executive, which included Bill Noble, Tom Davidson and William Birney of Banff and W. Letcher of Canmore, the branch's main activity was attempting to find employment for its members, lobbying government to hire returned men and the setting up of a "Veteran's Taxi

Stand" in Banff being two of its more successful efforts.

Within a few years the original Rocky Mountains Branch was split in three when Bankhead formed its own branch in April, 1919 as did Canmore in 1921 after the Canmore Coal Company constructed a Memorial Hall. The Rocky Mountains G.W.V.A. originally met in an unfinished room above Dave White's store, but a movement was soon afoot to build a Banff Memorial Hall, and fund-raising whist drives and dances for this purpose replaced those which had been previously held to support the soldiers overseas. This led to the beginning of construction of the hall on a property adjacent to the Imperial Bank in August, 1921, and upon its partial completion in 1923 the G. W. V. A. took its place among other groups in participating actively in fraternal and community work. The annual children's "Christmas Tree" became a long-time project, but it also took on the important task of organizing Remembrance Day services and banquets and maintaining the Banff cenotaph, built on the same site by the I. O. D. E. in 1923, as well as the Bankhead cenotaph after the closing of the mine.

Another feature of community identity in the Valley that began to emerge in the years around World War I was related to cultural activities and a growing sense of the area's history. The first movies had been shown in the Lux Theatre in Banff when Luxton opened it in 1913 and at the Opera House in Canmore at about the same time. Halls and opera houses in the towns had also provided a home for some form of musical and theatrical entertainments, usually staged by local children or by touring performers. The Opera House in Canmore performed this function, while in Banff, the National Park Theatre held concerts and recitals given by visiting artists attracted by the tourist trade, an example being the August, 1917 report on the "singing of Madame Perry and the piano solos by Miss Ethel MacDonald with Indian tableaux scenes well staged and very effective." At the same time, Banff had just hosted its first "Chautauqua," an opportunity for Valley residents to experience some of the best performers and lecturers in America. The Ellison-White Chautauqua was an American troupe that toured through western Canada and appeared in towns where guarantors would put up $1,000 to secure a week's diversion, featuring such performers as the Chautauqua symphony orchestra, soloist Olive McCormick, Canadian baritone Ruthven Macdonald, lecturer-astronomer Dr. A. D. Carpenter, the Conus Players presenting "Carson of the North Woods," and a special program of "Junior Chautauqua" for the children. The Chautauqua thereafter became a mainstay of the Banff summer season's entertainment for several years.

But these events had little to do with promoting local culture, a role that tended to be fulfilled by a small number of community leaders. Tom Wilson began assembling Banff's most significant historical library in 1897 when Collie sent him an invaluable copy of the Palliser Blue Book. It and the publications of his clients Wilcox, Collie, Outram and others, which typically included an introduction recounting the Rockies' historic background, formed a core of material that was freely lent to other residents to enable them to understand the region's heritage. Mary Schäffer, who settled permanently in Banff in 1913, also became a local oracle for those interested in travelling the backcountry, assembling an excellent library and collecting native and other historic materials. One of her most treasured acquisitions was a copy of Reverend Robert Rundle's journal which she obtained from his daughter in England for the I. O. D. E. chapter named in his honour. In February, 1915 she shared this remarkable artifact of Valley history with her compatriots at a chapter meeting:

Mrs. Schaffer read extracts from the diary of Rev. Dr. Rundle, a missionary, who lived and toiled among the Indians of this country some 75 years ago. . . . The hearers were taken back, in imagination, to the days when civilization was in its infancy in western Canada. What made the knowledge of Dr. Rundle's daily life more interesting from a local standpoint was the fact that one of the giant peaks overlooking Banff is named after him, as is the local chapter of the the Imperial Daughters of the Empire.[3]

Mrs. Warren, as she became in 1915, also believed that her

friend Tom Wilson was worthy of recognition as the area's most famous pioneer and the "trailblazer of the Canadian Rockies." Along with Mary Vaux Walcott, in whose company she had first visited Glacier House in 1891, she suggested to John Murray Gibbon, the CPR's general publicity agent and a strong promoter of Canadian culture, that Tom be honoured in 1924 at the launch of the first camp of the Trail Riders of the Canadian Rockies in the Yoho Valley. Gibbon had himself first ridden the trails under Wilson's guidance, and agreed to acknowledge him, both to recognize his contributions to Rocky Mountain history as well as to also be able to utilize him as "local colour" in CPR publicity. He commissioned leading French-Canadian sculptor Henri Hebert to design and cast a bronze plaque memorializing his discoveries of Lake Louise and Emerald Lake in 1882, and at the camp it was unveiled after a speech by Mrs. Walcott and a song rendered by Banff Springs Hotel soloist Frances James. Wilson, for his part, seemed to be at a loss for words with all the attention, stating that "I am not accustomed to speaking extemporaneously unless a cayuse has stepped upon my foot." Any shying from notoriety was was soon overcome, however, as from 1927 until his death in 1933 he was employed by the company entertaining their guests at the Chateau Lake Louise and Banff Springs Hotel with stories of the "good old days on the trail."[4] For his part, Gibbon quickly recognized the value of linking heritage with tourism, already evident with the success of Banff Indian Days, and in 1927 began holding an annual fall festival at the Banff Springs Hotel, known as the Highland Gathering and Scottish Music Festival, that played upon Banff's and the CPR's Scots traditions to spur shoulder season visitation.

Norman Luxton was another community builder who understood the importance of the Valley's heritage and used his resources to foster it where he could. As a lad of sixteen, Luxton had spent a period employed as an apprentice clerk working for the Indian Agency at Rat Portage (Kenora) and thereafter began a lifelong interest in natives and native culture. Shortly after arriving in Banff, he began operating Dave McDougall's old trading

Norman Luxton and his tame bear at the Sign of the Goat Curio Store and "Free Museum"

post near Morley securing good quality native furs and crafts, and it was there that he met his future wife Georgina, McDougall's daughter and the first recorded white child born in the lands that would become Alberta. This Stoney and Cree material became the basis for both the stock-in-trade at the Sign of the Goat Trading Store at Banff and his personal collection of the best examples of native work. Luxton understood the value of what he was doing went beyond mere commerce, writing to his future wife in 1903 on the eve of opening his Banff store that "I shall call it the Sign of the Goat and I shall make it look like a museum so people will be interested, even if they do not always buy."[5] When the store was moved to a new location on a lot south of the river owned by his mother-in-law Annie McDougall, a large sign was erected advertising it as a "free museum" in conjunction with the trading post itself. As his interests grew, he found other ways to promote Banff, being largely responsible for the writing of its first homegrown advertising, a pamphlet entitled *Fifty Switzerlands in One — Banff the Beautiful*, and "boosting" the town in the columns of the *Crag and Canyon*. By the 1920s the newspaper was beginning to publish articles and series that recognized Banff's history, including a serial constructed from his own journals, entitled *The Voyage of the Tilikum,* and articles that included reflections on the Valley's history and culture written by William E. Round, a local music teacher and newspaper correspondent who may be regarded as Banff's first real historian. Round worked with Tom Wilson in 1929 to record his reminiscences of the days working on the CPR survey, later published as *Trail Blazer of the Canadian Rockies,* and in the mid-thirties the *Crag* took an extremely important step in documenting Banff's history when it published William McCardell's *Reminiscences of a Western Pioneer*.

On the museum front, Luxton's informal efforts were given a more substantive life in the activities of Norman Sanson as the curator of the Banff Natural History Museum. The first Banff Museum, which was in fact the first museum in western Canada, was opened in 1895 and, as previously mentioned, was in part of Superintendent Stewart's former residence moved to a location at the corner of Spray and Mountain Avenues. Originally under the direction of the Natural History Branch of the Geological Survey of Canada, the museum's first exhibits had been collected in 1891 by none other than Professor John Macoun, the man perhaps most responsible for Banff existing in the first place. Macoun, who at the time worked for the Natural History Branch, was ordered by Dr. A. R. C. Selwyn, Director of the Geological Survey, "to make a collection of specimens of the fauna and flora of the Rocky Mountain Park and vicinity for the museum proposed to be established at Banff." The exhibits, which included eight specimens of mammals, 259 birds, a turtle, fifty-seven specimens of wood, 814 plants and 201 minerals, were in place and open to the public by July, 1895. The first curator was George MacLeod, who also performed the duties of meteorological observer, but due to his death in March, 1896 he was replaced by Sanson, who had been assisting him during his lingering illness. Although not formally trained in natural history, he was a quick study and soon began making regular field trips throughout the park to augment the collections.

The sheer volume of these and the facility's popularity among visitors eventually led to a call for a new museum, the ultimate result of which was the building of the museum and superintendent's office in today's Central Park. The new building, described by the *Crag and Canyon* as "that magnificent structure located on the north bank of the Bow river close to the bridge" was completed in 1903 in a distinctive, rustic "railway pagoda" style designed by former CPR construction superintendent John Stocks.

While the focus of the museum's collections was natural history, Sanson worked under no clear mandate, and after the "new" museum opened donations began to come in from a variety of private citizens and government agencies. For his part, Sanson actively sought material to illustrate the human history of the park, given that no-one else was formally carrying out this role. In 1920 purchases included a bison leg-bone imbedded in a piece of Douglas fir along with a picture of the Reverend Rundle, and the same year he attempted to acquire old logging material from the Eau Claire Lumber Company. However, his chief interest was Indian artifacts and he put together an impressive collection, partly belonging to himself and partly on loan from Canon H. W. Gibbon-Stocken, an early Anglican pastor on the Blackfoot and Sarcee reserves, which was exhibited on the Museum's second floor. When faced with the very real possibility that the Gibbon-Stocken collection would be sold to a private buyer and removed in 1923, Sanson was able to convince the Department of the Interior to purchase it. By the time of his retirement in 1932 (after which his position remained unfilled), and largely because of the persistence of his collecting activities, the museum held broad and interesting exhibits on natural and human life in the Valley.[6]

Another node of culture in Banff resided in the home of Jimmy and Billie Simpson near the corner of Bear and Buffalo Streets. While next-store on Bear Street Dave White's young son Peter was just beginning to study cartooning by correspondence, Simpson was busy putting together the town's best art collection, featuring wildlife artists that would eventually influence his neighbour's son. Jimmy's "packhorses for paintings" deal with Carl Rungius meant it was his paintings and etchings that formed the core of the collection, but there were numerous other painters who Simpson escorted, such as Belmore Browne and Philip Goodwin, whose works found their way onto his walls as well. These and other accoutrements reflecting his artistic tastes adorned every nook and cranny of the house, a fact noted by one of his foremost hunting clients, New York diamond dealer and Tiffany appraiser Joseph McAleenan, when he first visited it in 1915:

An upright piano stood against the east wall. Pelts of bear, cat and wolf covered the floor and hung over comfortable chairs. There was the latest Victrola, with records of Caruso, Kubelik and other great artists. On the walls hung paintings of landscapes and animals, typical of the owner's taste. Here, appearing at their best, were the works of Carl Rungius, a friend of Simpson's, a splendid library of books, the titles of which paid eloquent tribute to their owner. . . .

Here was a man whose days and years had been spent in the mountain wilderness, who knew from close association the life habits of its animals. Who had rubbed elbows with the roughest side of life. Yet here we found him, knowing and loving and living with the best of music, art and literature.[7]

Jimmy's wife Billie (Williamina), who had come out from Scotland in 1912 and had been trained as a nurse, was equally imbued with a love of art and literature, but her real passions were figure skating and drama. Beginning in 1924, she cooperated with a few other ladies in the community in the formation of a club, known as the Banff-Literary Dramatic Society, to study the works of Irish dramatists and produce informal plays. Heading the group was another energetic community member, Margaret Greenham, a former headmistress of Havergal College in Toronto who along with her husband Henry began The Mountain School for girls in Banff in 1919. Together with the wives of Dr. Dean Robinson and Dr. Ernest Kennedy and one or two others, Mrs. Greenham and Mrs. Simpson produced three one-act plays held in the Simpson's living room, and within a year of its creation the

Society could boast of a library containing over 100 volumes of classical writers such as George Bernard Shaw and Oscar Wilde. In time, the group's influence would grow to the extent that they publicly produced plays at the Bretton Hall Theatre, and the Society would remain the major manifestation of the community's dramatic life for a quarter-century.

Billie Simpson, one of Banff's sport and culture sparkplugs

As important as cultural, social and religious activities were in establishing the Valley's identity in the years prior to 1930, they paled in comparison with the influence of its political life. The dependency that all Valley communities exhibited towards the CPR and resource development interests were equally apparent in their relationship with the federal government, who almost completely controlled their destinies. However, as time went on and the populace gained confidence and local leadership, acceptance of the government's total direction of their affairs began to be challenged, particularly in Banff.

The early political history of the Valley was dominated by Robert G. Brett, the CPR doctor who had begun by performing operations in a boxcar during railway construction days but had cleverly used his influence to gain a strong economic foothold in Banff in the guise of numerous commercial interests and residential properties. His business acumen was equally well-reflected in politics, leading him in 1888 to contest a seat in the district west of Calgary for the Legislative Assembly of North West Territories, which advised the federal government in administering the area. His success in obtaining the seat and his growing notoriety as the president of the Royal College of Physicians and Surgeons in the Territories thereafter made him a virtually unstoppable political force. Running nominally under the Conservative banner, he won the subsequent elections of 1891 and 1894, and in the session of 1896 during debate on territorial finances had the distinction of being the first member to suggest the formation of the Province of Alberta. Although initially defeated in 1898 by Liberal opponent Arthur Sifton, he regained the seat on the strength of a judicial recount. Thereafter, until his retirement from active politics in 1901, he remained a powerful voice in the Legislative Assembly as the official Leader-of-the-Opposition.

Brett, who became Alberta's second Lieutenant-Governor in 1915, was an effective spokesman for the Valley's interests, but after the creation of the Province of Alberta in 1905 a new and more partisan dimension was added to the political scene. Until this time, Valley residents unquestioningly accepted federal government authority and depended on it for all their infrastructure and operational needs, just as they depended on the CPR for their livelihoods. Yet as the growth of Valley communities accelerated, the government, while starting to withdraw as the primary development force, felt the need to retain control through a growing list of regulations affecting all manner of daily life and commerce, dictated by Ottawa but administered by the local park superintendent and his staff. This state of affairs meant that administrators had less time to devote to park management, as municipal issues constantly pressed themselves to the top of the agenda, a trend that would affect park management for generations.

Despite the tight grip of the federal government on Banff's affairs, it was actually the CPR that sparked the birth of local political activity. It was not in the nature of Banff's citizenry to stand up to the CPR, but a proposal to relocate the CPR main line through the Bow Valley being studied by the federal Board of Railway Commissioners in the fall of 1912 was serious enough to stir them to action. The proposal would see the line located close to Major Rogers's intended route, passing through Tunnel Mountain and then crossing the Bow River near Bow Falls and running in proximity to the Banff Springs Hotel. Local entrepreneurs realized that this would signal the death knell for their downtown businesses, and on November 18, 1912 a public meeting of Banff citizens was held to protest the new route which, as the minutes stated, "threatens the destruction of a great portion of the town of Banff." The meeting decided the best form of protest was to organize a Banff Board of Trade to unite their voices, and thirty citizens signed the roll and agreed to pay a $5 membership fee. A committee was set up to begin the task of drafting a constitution and by-laws and it created the first temporary executive, led by D. C. Bayne as president, and Bill Mather, Norman Luxton, Herbert Robarts, George Paris and George Hunter as officers. The threat of the rail re-alignment soon disappeared, perhaps at least partly due to the arguments the Board of Trade mustered against it, but it was determined that the Board had been a useful body to put forward a consistent position on matters affecting the town and the park and it was soon active on a number of other fronts.[8]

Representations were made to the government concerning community needs, including the requests of inhabitants at the north end of town to have electric lights, the wishes of citizens to have the telephone exchange kept open in the evening, and the desire for a local board of health. As well, requests were made of the CPR to have the special Saturday summer rate to Banff apply in winter and to have the company accept responsibility for livestock killed by trains in the park. However, it was the rising debate over the allowing of automobiles into the park that really caught the Board's attention, particularly after Jim Brewster, who was initially opposed to their appearance, became the organization's vice-president in December, 1913. Unfortunately, representations on this issue, as well as demands that proposed new park regulations be submitted to them for scrutiny before coming into force, were largely ignored by Harkin. He took an undue length of time to respond to communications on what were regarded locally as important issues, and when he did respond he made clear the primacy of national interests. His position was apparent in a meeting with the Board during his May, 1915 visit to Banff. In reply to a question about the setting up of a health board he stated that "the whole aim in framing any regulations bearing on the subject of the kind was to see that there was no unfair burden on the dominion as the governing authority of the park." Similarly, on the matter of increasing the hours of the telephone exchange his response was that "the park belonged to the whole dominion, that the total revenue of the park was trifling in comparison to the total expenditure, and that they had to consider very seriously any expenditure calculated to increase that expenditure."[9] Harkin's attitude, and the Board's lack of success on such key issues as gaining control over the local volunteer fire department, led to a weakening of its effectiveness. Combined with the growing exigencies of the war, these problems resulted in the May, 1915 meeting with Harkin being the Board's last.

This did not mean that local political life was dead. During the war years petitions were circulated calling on the government to assist in creating a more democratic voice for Banff citizens, and Norman Luxton, through his control of the opinions expressed in the *Crag and Canyon*, strongly supported them. His philosophy, shared by many in Banff, was perhaps best exhibited in an emotional editorial in the December 23, 1916 issue of the *Crag*, aimed squarely at Harkin, under the by-line "This Article is For YOU:"

It was only the other day, seemingly, that Howard Douglas was the commissioner of the Rocky Mountain Park. When the people of Banff had a grievance they went to the government office and invariably found Howard on the job, always ready to listen to their complaint and discuss with them the best method of righting any wrongs caused by the miscarriage of Parks regulations. In those days it was not necessary to write long-winded letters to Ottawa, with weeks of delay before an ambiguous reply was received. It was owing, in a great measure, to the proper latitude allowed the local government office to settle all petty disputes that many of the business houses have expanded to the magnitude they are today. . . .

What a vast difference exists today. Regulations governing the business that gives the people of Banff their livelihood, business that has taken years of hard work, self-denial and persistent effort to build up, are made in Ottawa. By men who live in Ottawa, by fly-by-night men who visit Banff in summer only, by men who have no knowledge of local conditions the year around. . . .

Immediately there will be presented to the people of Banff a petition which, as British subjects, as business men, as property owners, as thinking men and women, each will be asked to sign. This petition will set forth to Dr. Roche, minister of the Interior; to R. B. Bennett K. C., member of the house of commons representing this part of Alberta; and to Sir James Lougheed, western senator; the rights of the Banff people to representation in the civic government. It will request that a body of citizens, composed of men and women, be appointed to confer with one or more appointees from government on all subjects beneficial or inimical to the prosperity and well-being of the people of Banff.[10]

It took until the completion of the war, and the appointment of Sir James Lougheed as Minister of the Interior, a man personally familiar with the situation in the park dating as far back as representing the McCabes and McCardell at Pearce's hot springs inquiry, for these pleas to be answered. In August, 1920 a delegation of Banff citizens met Lougheed and wrung from him agreement to sanction the formation of an organization to act in an advisory capacity relative to the management of affairs in the park. On February 28, 1921 an organizational meeting attracting some eighty interested Banffites was held under the chairmanship of Lou Crosby to discuss Lougheed's permission to form "an elected body to confer with the Superintendent of Rocky Mountains Park and present any grievances or suggestions they may have." It was agreed to call the new organization the "Banff Citizens' Association" and a further meeting the next month decided to seek nominations for nine councillors, a number agreed upon by the Department. On March 21, 1921 Banff held its historic first election of advisory councillors and the two hundred plus electors chose Sam Armstrong, Byron Harmon, Sam Howard, Bill Mather, Hugh

Gordon, Tom Dunsmore, Colonel Philip Moore, Dan McCowan and Ted Balderson to represent them. At the first regular meeting, held in Byron Harmon's photography shop, Gordon was elected chairman and Balderson secretary. The council got right to work, making a number of recommendations to the superintendent and beginning to explore ways to collect funds from property owners to aid volunteer firemen injured while performing their duties. This would be the beginning of a long process of finding a means to levy taxes on local residents to support community goals that the federal government was unwilling or unable to accomplish.[11]

As the Citizens' Association had been officially sanctioned by the Minister, government officials had to pay it more attention than its Board of Trade predecessor. None was more attentive than Harkin himself, who took pains to respond to its numerous letters (although not always in the affirmative) and made a point of meeting with them on his annual visits to the park. The first such meeting took place on September 21, 1921 in Superintendent R. S. Stronach's office and dealt with such matters as proper business licensing, the need for additional campgrounds, the desire to have tungsten lights replace the arc light streetlighting system, and a request to have the Bankhead road kept open in the winter. An important area of agreement concerned the opening of a government tourist information bureau in Banff provided the council came up with a suitable publication on Banff and its beauties. This was the beginning of long-term, mutually beneficial relationship between the town and the government in promoting Banff tourism, evident in the production of *Fifty Switzerlands in One* and its distribution from a small log tourism information building adjacent to the Park Museum beginning in 1924.

The Banff Citizens' Association, or Banff Advisory Council as it took to calling itself, was an effective organization that was well-supported by the community's residents throughout the twenties. Its affairs were dominated by a fairly tight-knit group of influential businessmen who let their name stand for office after it went to a format of having three seats elected each year for a three year term. In 1922 Sam Armstrong was elected president and he held the position until 1925 when Jim Brewster, who was quickly becoming Banff's most powerful and influential citizen, took over the reins. As a body whose mandate extended to the park as well as the town, its business was largely dominated by transportation and tourist interests during the twenties as a result of the major growth in roads and tourism infrastructure that were the hallmark of the decade. A sampling of issues brought to the table illustrates this tendency, as they included pushing for the completion of the Banff-Windermere Highway prior to 1923, promotion of its use by American auto-tourists after is opening, improvements to park roads and better government maintenance over winter months so they could be re-opened earlier in the season, and the obtaining of reciprocal rights for transportation companies in Canadian and U. S. parks. This did not mean that Banff townsite issues were not given their due, as the council was also successful in having the Minister of the Interior lower domestic power rates in 1924 and 1925 and having proposed new business licenses presented to them for comment before being issued.

Other issues produced no common ground, the council and officials locking horns on the matter of the government's desire to issue commercial business licenses on the south side of the river and a major dust-up when the government decided to move the Rundle campground to a new and larger location on Tunnel Mountain in order to allow the CPR to expand the golf course in 1927. Disagreements such as these resulted in several calls by council for the superintendent to be given more power to decide local matters with the advice of the Advisory Council or have the Commissioner of Dominion Parks reside in the west, where most of his responsibilities lay. In September, 1923 a meeting was held with the M. P. for Calgary West, Captain J. T. Shaw, to discuss this matter and Shaw ended his presentation by stating that "Banff was just as competent to govern itself as any community." The idea of more powers for council began to grow thereafter and in November, 1924 was brought even further to the fore when Canmore, which had formed its own council, wrote and asked what new powers had been gained in a recent meeting between the Advisory Council and the new Minister of the Interior, Charles Stewart. The secretary advised that no new powers had been granted, but invited Canmore's council to meet with Banff's to discuss how the situation might be addressed. The joint meeting took place on November 25, 1925 and the minutes recorded that there was "full discussion of the requirements of the Councils as regards finances and wider powers in civic affairs." Joint resolutions to the Minister emerged from the meeting, calling on the government to fund the activities of the councils, as they had no power to tax, and to grant the broader powers being sought in municipal matters. Copies of the resolutions were sent to Stewart and R. B. Bennett, but the Minister quickly responded that no such powers could be granted, attempting to nip in the bud any idea of true representative government. But the genie of self-government had been let out of the bottle as a result of these discussions, and it would never be fully put back in. This issue would thereafter dominate the subsequent relationship between the town and federal authorities responsible for park administration, ultimately providing a battleground for the struggle between development and preservation that would become the hallmark of its subsequent history.

Despite some setbacks, the Banff Advisory Council could take pride in providing an authentic voice for the strong and tight-knit community that Banff had become by 1930. Growth in community identity had been nurtured by a variety of social and political influences that were also present to a degree in other park towns. By that time, though, their number had shrunk, with both Anthracite and Bankhead being nothing more than ghost towns, causing federal authorities headaches with land management issues for decades to come. Canmore and Exshaw remained static, as the resources they depended on waxed and waned on national and international markets, and they were about to undergo a further baptism by fire in the coming Depression. To the west of Banff, with the beginning of a long and sustained growth in skiing, a new community forming around the old station at Lake Louise would soon be making its presence felt. The Banff-Bow Valley was about to enter its modern age.

Watershed

By 1930 the Banff-Bow Valley had undergone a complete transformation from the days some 150 years earlier when European fur traders had first laid eyes on it. The pristine wilderness had given way to man's hand with its rails, trails, mines, roads and townsites, while still maintaining many elements, such as its geographic wonders and fascinating natural life, which provided its unique character. It had become known to the world, and now the world was increasingly coming to see it, creating new pressures and demands. All the signs of its future character and heritage were now discernible.

It was a place where the early history of native peoples was recognized — even celebrated — but where these same peoples were to be welcomed only as guests, not to stay. It was a place where the Canadian Pacific Railway dominated much of the business and social life, and where that same company exercised its political power on the government at every opportunity to achieve its corporate ends. It was a place of wonder and delight for those wishing to hike or ride the trails used by intrepid tourist-explorers and early guides and packers for generations. It was an alpine world where the growing challenge of mountaineering and the understanding of the meaning of mountains and appreciation of their natural and aesthetic beauties was becoming strongly engrained. It was a place where people were beginning to celebrate winter and its myriad of outdoor activities, rather than dread it. It was a home to people, some of whom understood the power and the fragile nature of the land and worked to sustain it, or took advantage of the incomparable recreational opportunities it provided, while attempting to make everyday life in unusual circumstances reflect a normal community.

In the final analysis, the Valley was a paradox — a society built on the fundamentals of tourism where access to and activities in the park were to be promoted through development of amenities and services and heavily dependent on resource extraction, yet existing in a place which belonged to all Canadians and which was increasingly seen as of high aesthetic and natural value and in need of further protection.

At the same time, it was changing. By the end of the twenties the Banff Advisory Council was in the thick of a Royal Commission on lease renewals in the townsite and in discussions about the proposed new National Parks Act that was to accompany the constitutional amendment transferring natural resources to the western provinces. This same Act would give the park its new name, Banff National Park, and would provide important powers for conservation and preservation. However, it would also redraw park boundaries, a decision which would fundamentally alter the Valley's subsequent development and character. In 1927, when an examination of possible new park boundaries was being made by the Department of Mines and the Water Powers Branch with a view towards identifying areas that could be excised for mining and water power development, the Canmore Advisory Council had written Charles Stewart requesting that the town be allowed to remain in the park. Stewart's reply signalled the new set of circumstances providing the framework for the Valley's evolution:

> *I may say that the Park boundaries are being revised with the sole object of leaving outside the Park areas which are considered to be more valuable from the standpoint of the commercial utilization of the natural resources than from the standpoint of national playgrounds, the original natural scenic features of which are to be preserved inviolate for all time for the enjoyment of ourselves and the generation to follow. The Provinces have decided that these areas should be opened to commercial development and it is, therefore, manifestly impossible to retain them in these Parks.*[1]

The boundary revision accompanying the National Parks Act of 1930 only reduced the area of the park from 2,751 square miles, which it had become in 1917, to 2,580 square miles, but critical changes were afoot in the lands of the lower Bow Valley. While major additions were made to the park on its northern boundary,

Canmore, Exshaw and surrounding lands, including the Spray Lakes and Kananaskis Valley, were excised from federal authority and allowed to develop under a far different provincial mandate. From 1930 onward the lands in the Valley inside national park boundaries would increasingly undergo pressures for preservation while those outside would have a purpose that was seen to be just the opposite.

The Act of 1930 was therefore a watershed in the Valley's history and heritage. It affected the area's direction in ways that were for a time masked by the exigencies of the Depression and the Second World War but which would eventually come to light in the debates and varying viewpoints that would gain momentum in the period of rapid post-war growth. The National Parks Act changed the Valley forever.

Notes

Chapter One -- People of the Shining Mountains

[1]Gwyn Langemann, "A Description and Evaluation of Eight Housepit Sites in Banff National Park, Alberta," Canadian Archaeological Society, May, 1998, p. 2.

[2]For a good summary of the early native occupation of the Rockies, see Jon Whyte, *Indians in the Rockies*, (Altitude Publishing, 1985).

[3]V. G. Hopwood, *David Thompson, Travels in Western North America, 1784-1812*, (Macmillan, 1971), p. 199.

[4]J. G. MacGregor, *Peter Fidler, Canada's Forgotten Surveyo*r, (McClelland and Stewart, c. 1966), pp. 78-79.

[5]Hopwood, p. 220.

[6]Barbara Belyea, ed., *Columbia Journals David Thompson*, (McGill-Queen's University Press, 1994), p. 15.

[7]For a discussion of the various theories of Stoney migration see John Larner, *The Kootenay Plains (Alberta) Land Question And Canadian Indian Policy, 1799-1947*, (Doctoral Thesis, West Virginia University, 1972).

[8]John Maclean, *McDougall of Alberta*, (The Ryerson Press, 1927), p. 78. While the Stoney name for the Banff-Bow Valley was *Mun-uh-cha-ban*, the name for the river itself was *Minnihsno*, meaning "cold water." See Marius Barbeau, *Indian Days on the Western Prairies*, (Bulletin No. 163 Anthropological Series No. 46 National Museums of Canada, 1960), p. 211.

[9]Barbeau, p. 211.

[10]Peter Erasmus, *Buffalo Days and Nights*, (Glenbow Alberta Institute, 1976), p. 74.

[11]Hugh Dempsey, *The Rundle Journals, 1840-48*, (Historical Society of Alberta and Glenbow Alberta Institute, 1977), p. 61.

[12]John Snow, *These Mountains Are Our Sacred Places*, (Samuel Stevens, 1977), p. 11.

[13]Ella E. Clark, *Indian Legends of Canada*, (McClelland and Stewart, 1960), p. 96.

[14]Barbeau, p. 209.

[15]Clark, p. 97.

[16]Barbeau, pp. 99-100.

[17]Snow, p. 4.

Chapter Two -- The Great River of the West

[1]Belyea, p. 13.

[2]Ibid., pp. 18-19.

[3]Hopwood, p. 239.

[4]Writer Jack Nisbet maintains that Thompson was not in a race to the mouth of the Columbia with the Astorians. He states that in a meeting of the North West Company partners at Fort William in the spring of 1811, they had voted to accept

a 1/3 interest in the Astorian Company and that Thompson would have known this. See Jack Nisbet, *Sources of the River; tracking David Thompson Across Western North America*, (Sasquatch Books, 1994), p. 166.

[5]E. H. Oliver, ed., *The Canadian North-west*, (Ottawa, 1914), I, p.678.

[6]Sir George Simpson, *An overland journey round the world during the years 1841 and 184*, (Lea and Blanchard, 1847), p. 75.

[7]Ibid., p. 76.

[8]Dempsey, p. 67.

[9]Ibid., p. 164.

[10]Ibid., p. 261.

[11]Pierre J. De Smet, *Oregon missions and travels over the Rocky Mountains in 1845-4*, (Arthur Clark, 1906), p. 215.

Chapter Three -- The Amazing Doctor Hector

[1]Irene M. Spry, "Routes Through The Rockies," *The Beaver*, Autumn, 1963, p. 33.

[2]Spry, p.34.

[3]Captain H. J. Warre, *Sketches In North America And The Oregon Territory*, (Imprint Society, 1970), p. 16. Warre's comparison of the Rockies with the "Alps of Switzerland" appears to be the first time this analogy appeared in print.

[4]Spry, p. 34-35.

[5]D. Geneva Lent, *West of the Mountains, James Sinclair and the Hudson's Bay Company*, (University of Washington Press, 1963), p. 253

[6]Barbeau, pp. 221-22.

[7]Lent, p. 258.

[8]Irene M. Spry, ed., *The Papers of the Palliser Expedition, 1857-60*, (The Champlain Society, 1968), p. 4.

[9]Ibid., p. 259. The phrase "deeply regretted" was used by Palliser in reference to Sinclair's death at the hands of the Klickitats Indians on the Columbia in 1856.

[10]Ibid., p. 295.

[11]Ibid., p. 318.

[12]Ibid., p. 325.

[13]Ibid., p. cxxi.

[14]Ibid.

[15]The Earl of Southesk, *Saskatchewan And The Rocky Mountains*, (Edmonston and Douglas, 1875), p. 1.

[16]Spry, ed., p. 326.

Chapter Four -- Steel Through the Wilderness

[1]George M. Grant, "The C.P.R. By The Kicking Horse Pass And The Selkirks," *The Week*, January 10, 1884, p. 85.

[2]Whyte Museum of the Canadian Rockies Archives, "Reminiscences of a Western Pioneer" by William McCardell, p. 87.

[3]Ibid., pp. 223-24.

[4]John Macoun, *Autobiography of John Macoun, M. A., Canadian Explorer and Naturalist, 1831-1920*, (The Ottawa Field Naturalist's Club, 1922), p. 185.

[5]Thomas E. Wilson, *Trail Blazer of the Canadian Rockies*. (Glenbow Alberta Institute, 1972), p. 14.

[6]Whyte Museum of the Canadian Rockies Archives, Copy of Wilson scrapbook, Tom Wilson to J. B. Harkin, 1924.

[7]Ibid., Ina Burns, "Mountain Miracles," Calgary *Herald*, n.d.

[8]David Cruise and Alison Griffiths, *Lords of the Line, The Men Who Built The CPR*, (Penguin Books, 1996), p. 108.

[9]Charles A. Shaw, *Tales of a Pioneer Surveyor*, (Longman Canada, 1970), p. 146.

[10]Grant, February 7, 1884.

[11]Shaw, pp. 147-48..

[12]Morley Roberts, *The Western Avernus*, (J. M. Dent, 1924), pp. 48-49.

[13]Peter Turner Bone, *When The Steel Went Through, Reminiscences of a Railroad Pioneer*, (Macmillan of Canada Ltd., 1947), p. 78.

[14]A. Thomas, "How Banff Got Its Name," *Crag and Canyon*, October 27, 1939 (reprinted from Vancouver *Province*). According to this account, the name "Banff" was originally suggested by Harry Sandison, a prominent Winnipeger, who had been born at Banff, Scotland, the well-known seaport and watering place at the mouth of the Deveron River. Sandison was an acquaintance of John McTavish, CPR Land Commissioner, and when informed in 1883 that McTavish was about to attend a meeting in Montreal to discuss the establishment of the resort in the vicinity of the hot springs, Sandison suggested that he bring up the name "Banff" and watch the reaction of George Stephen and Donald Smith. McTavish agreed, and later recounted to the reporter, A. V. Thomas, what had happened: "Mr. McTavish did as I suggested. He told the C.P.R. directors that Banff was an ancient watering place in Scotland and went on to describe its beauties. As soon as the word "Banff" was mentioned, Donald Smith looked at Mr. Stephen and went over to him and whispered. They both seemed quite excited, and Mr. Van Horne wondered what it was all about. Donald Smith then explained that he knew Banff very well, as he had been born close to there. Then Mr. Stephen said he had been born within twelve miles of Banff, and had known ever since he was a boy that it was a famous watering place. It was now Mr. Van Horne's turn to say something. 'I like that name "Banff",' he said, 'It's a short, snappy name. Suppose we call it Banff.' And Banff it was."

Chapter Five -- The National Policy Comes to the Rockies

[1]McCardell, p. 151.

[2]Rev. R. J. McGuiness, "The Story of Silver City," *The Western Catholic Almanac*, 1938, p. 3.

[3]McCardell, p. 351.

[4]McGuinness, p. 5.

[5]A. R. Byrne, *Man and Landscape Change in Banff National Park,* (U. of C., 1968), p. 95.

[6]The best source on the development of Canmore and the Kananaskis-Exshaw area is Edna Hill Appleby, *Canmore, The Story of An Era,* (The Author, 1975).

[7]National Archives of Canada, R. G. 15, Item 137193.

[8]Ibid.

[9]McCardell, p. 250.

[10]Ibid., p. 254-55.

[11]Fergus Lothian, *A History of Canada's National Parks, Vol. 1,* (Parks Canada, 1976), p. 22.

[12]Robert Craig Brown, "The Doctrine of Usefulness: Natural Resources and National Park Policy in Canada, 1187-1914 in J. G. Nelson, ed., *The Canadian National Parks Today and Tomorrow,* (U. of C., 1968.)

Chapter Six -- A Public Park and Pleasure Ground

[1]Sandford Fleming, *England and Canada, A summer tour between Old and New Westminster,* (Sampson, Low, Marston, Searle and Livingstone, 1888), p. 414.

[2]Brown, p. 52.

[3]House of Commons Debates, May 3, 1887.

[4]E. J. Hart, *The Selling of Canada, the CPR and the Beginnings of Canadian Tourism,* (Altitude Publishing, 1983), p. 41.

[5]Debates, May 3, 1887.

[6]Earnscliffe Cottage now forms part of the Manager's residence at the Banff Springs Hotel, immediately east of the hotel's parkade.

[7]*Crag and Canyon,* November 10, 1933.

[8]For a good description on the development of "the Banff style' see Edward Mills, *Rustic Building Programs in Canada's national parks, 1887-1950,* (Parks Canada, 1994). The best remaining example of this design treatment is the Banff Park Museum, designed by former CPR construction supervisor John Stocks and built in 1903. In 1994 architect Jeremy Sturgess was given the commission to design the new Banff Town Hall on Bear Street and revived elements of "the Banff style," in particular the crossed-log motif, in the Town of Banff's first public building.

[9]Bart Robinson, *Banff Springs, The Story of a Hotel,* (Summerthought, 1973), p. 14.

[10]*The Canadian Pacific, The New Highway to the East Across the Mountains, Prairies and Rivers of Canada,* (Montreal, 1887), p. 11.

[11]W. H. H. Murray, *Daylight Land,* (Cuples and Hurd, 1888), p. 186.

Chapter Seven -- This Way to the Stars

[1]A. O. Wheeler, *The Selkirk Range*, (Ottawa: Dept. of the Interior, 1905), p. 4.

[2]Canada. Department of the Interior Report, 1886, Part II, *Report of J. J. McArthur, DLS,* p. 40.

[3]Walter D. Wilcox, "Early Days in the Canadian Rockies," *American Alpine Journal,* IV (1941), p. 177.

[4]Walter D. Wilcox, *Camping in the Canadian Rockies,* (The Knickerbocker Press, 1896), pp. 111-12.

[5]Although it was believed for many years that Moraine Lake had been formed by a moraine blocking the outlet creek, geologists later determined that the blockage was actually formed by a rockslide from the slopes of Mount Babel.

[6]Glenbow Archives, Wilson Papers, Barrett to Wilson, November 1, 1924.

[7]A. P. Coleman, *The Canadian Rockies, New and Old Trails,* (Henry Frowde, 1911), pp. 202-03.

[8]Charles E. Fay, "The Casualty on Mount Lefroy," *Appalachia,* VIII, (November, 1896), p. 150.

[9]Quoted in E. J. Hart, *The Selling of Canada,* p. 64.

[10]Charles E. Fay, "The First Ascent of Mount Dawson," *Appalachia,* IX, (1901), pp. 260-61.

[11]R. W. Sandford, The Canadian Alps: *A History of Mountaineering in Canada Vol. I,* (Altitude Publishing, 1990), p. 164.

[12]Wheeler, p. 4.

[13]A. O. Wheeler, "Origin and Founding of the Alpine Club of Canada, 1906" *Canadian Alpine Journal,* Vol. XXVI, (1938), p. 89.

Chapter Eight -- Trail Language

[1]Coleman, pp. 121-46, 170.

[2]For a description of Tom Wilson's role as the first outfitter in Banff and the development of the guiding and outfitting profession see E. J. Hart, *Diamond Hitch, The early outfitters and guides of Banff and Jasper,* (Summerthought, 1979).

[3]Walter Wilcox, *The Rockies of Canada,* (The Knickerbocker Press, 1916), p. 115-16.

[4]E. J. Hart, *Jimmy Simpson, Legend of the Rockies,* (Altitude, 1991), p. 21.

[5]Stanley Washburn, *Trails, Trappers and Tenderfeet In The New Empire of Western Canada,* (Henry Holt and Company, 1912), p. 175.

[6]Pat Brewster, *Weathered Wood,* (F. O. Brewster, 1977), pp. 35-36.

[7]H. E. M. Stutfield and J. N. Collie, *Climbs and Explorations in the Canadian Rockies,* (Longmans, Green and Co., 1903), pp. 41-42.

[8]*Jimmy Simpson, Legend of the Rockies.*

[9]For a complete account of the history of the Brewster family and companies see E. J. Hart, *The Brewster Story, from pack train to tour bus,* (Brewster Transport, 1981).

[10]Whyte Museum of the Canadian Rockies Archives, Thompson Little Collection, Charles E. Fay to Charles S. Thompson, August 17, 1898.

[11]The account of Mary Schäffer's explorations was originally published as Mary

T. S. Schäffer, *Old Indian Trails of the Canadian Rockies*, (The Knickerbocker Press, 1911). This work was later reprinted, along with a biographical sketch and her previously unpublished memoir of the 1911 trip to Maligne Lake as E. J. Hart, ed., *A Hunter of Peace*, (The Whyte Foundation, 1980).

[12]*Crag and Canyon*, May 6, 1922.

Chapter Nine -- The Eye of the Beholder

[1]For a complete treatment of the influence of the early railway photographers , see Margery Tanner Hadley, *Photography and the Landscape of Travel: Western Canada 184-1914,* (M.A. thesis, University of Calgary, 1984).

[2]Canadian Pacific Corporate Archives, Van Horne letterbook 14, p. 857, Van Horne to Fraser, Jan. 6, 1886.

[3]The importance of Van Horne's influence on Canadian art is well documented in E. J. Hart's *The Selling of Canada.*

[4]Van Horne letterbook, Van Horne to Rev. Thomas Sommerville, June, 1885.

[5]F. M. Bell-Smith, "An Artist's Reminiscences," *Canadian Alpine Journal*, 1918.

[6]"Mountain Sketches, Beautiful Scenery Transferred to Canvas by Mr. Bell-Smith, R. C. A.," Winnipeg *Free Press*, October 18, 1887.

[7]The best source for Bierstadt's activities in Canada is Allan Pringle, "Albert Bierstadt in Canada," *The American Art Journal*, Vol. XVII, No. 1, Winter, 1985.

[8]Jon Whyte & E. J. Hart, *Carl Rungius, Painter of the Western Wilderness,* (Douglas & McIntyre, 1985), p. 88.

[9]Belmore Browne, "Paintbrush on the Heights," *The American Alpine Journal,* Vol. IV, No. 2, 1941.

[10]Lisa Christensen, *A Hiker's Guide to the Art Of The Canadian Rockies* (Glenbow-Alberta Institute, 1996), p. 71.

[11]Elizabeth Brown, *A Wilderness For All: Landscapes of Canada's Mountain Parks*, 1885-1960, (Whyte Museum of the Canadian Rockies, 1985), p. 11.

[12]Jon Whyte, *Mountain Glory, The Art Of Peter and Catharine Whyte,* (Whyte Museum of the Canadian Rockies, 1988), p.23.

Chapter Ten -- Sanctuaries of the Original and the Wild

[1]J. B. Harkin, "Canada's National Parks," *Handbook of Canada*, (University of Toronto Press, 1924), p. 98.

[2]Canada. Department of the Interior Report,, 1886, Part I, *Report by W. F. Whitcher,* p. 86.

[3]National Archives of Canada, RG84, Vol. 80, U3, Part 1, John Connor to William Pearce, Supt. of Mines, July 8, 1899.

[4]For a discussion of this and other game preservation initiatives at the time see Janet Foster *Working for Wildlife,* (U. of T. Press, 1978)

[5]The Stoney, in particular, were the main target for most critics of the day, the accusation being that they hunted in the park and in the neighbouring foothills

and killed all game without regard for the future. Typical was an interview with a Montreal newspaper in 1909 wherein Bill Brewster complained that "we allow our Indians to slaughter indiscriminately in our vast park" and that he "had seen as many as sixteen heads of wild animals in one Indian tepee." There was little recognition that the park encompassed traditional hunting grounds and those few who recognized Stoney dependence on Rocky Mountain wildlife stated that they should be given more rations on the reserve to solve hunting problems.

[6]National Archives of Canada, RG84, Vol. 80, U3, Part 2 Memo to R. H Campbell, Forestry Branch, Department of Interior, Feb 6, 1909.

[7]National Archives of Canada, RG84, Vol. 93, U3-15 , Minister of Interior to Governor General, May 1, 1915. Although official documents called the positions "game guardians," they were soon being referred to in departmental correspondence mainly as "fire guardians" in their forest protection role and as "game wardens" in their wildlife activities. The term "warden" began to be used more frequently as time went on and in 1915 it was declared the official terminology.

[8]Robert J. Burns, *Guardians Of The Wild: A History Of The Wardens Of Canada's National Parks,* (n.p., 1994), p. 17.

[9]RMP No. 3 "Windy Cabin" on the Panther River was moved from its original location to a site on the grounds of the Whyte Museum of the Canadian Rockies in 1977 and was restored by the Banff Warden Service in 1985 as Banff National Park Centennial project.

[10]Canada. Department of the Interior Report, 1915, Part V, *Report of Superintendent of Rocky Mountains Park,* p. 19.

[11]Canada. Department of Interior Report, 1912, Part V, *Report of the Commissioner of Dominion Parks,* p. 2.

[12]Foster, p. 73.

[13]Department of the Interior Report, 1916, Part V, *Report of the Superintendent of Rocky Mountains Park,* pp. 15-35.

[14]Burns, p. 93.

[15]Canada. Department of the Interior Report, 1915, Part V, *Report of the Commissioner of Dominion Parks,* p. 6.

[16]*Just A Sprig of Mountain Heather,* (King's Printer, 1914), p. 7.

[17]Harkin, pp. 97-98.

[18]Burns, p. 76.

[19]Leslie Bella, *Parks for Profit,* (Harvest House, 1987), pp. 45-46.

[20]*Canadian Alpine Journal,* Vol. XIV, 1924, p. 147.

Chapter Eleven -- Islands of Industry and Commerce

[1]J. D. R. Holmes, *The Canmore Corridor: The Historical Geography of a Pass Site, 1880 to the Present,* (M. A. thesis, University of Calgary, 1978), pp. 40-41.

[2]This building, the only known log "Opera House" in Canada, now is on exhibit at Heritage Park in Calgary.

[3]The name Bankhead was provided by Lord Strathcona, Donald Smith, after a

Scottish town near Banff, Scotland whose name meant "coal mine entrance."

[4]Canada. Department of the Interior Report, 1905-06, Part V, *Report of the Superintendent of Rocky Mountains Park*, p. 11.

[5]Ben Gadd, *Bankhead, The Twenty Year Town,* (The Friends of Banff National Park, 1989), p. 32.

[6]The name Exshaw was provided by Sandford Fleming, one of the founders of the company, after Lord William Exshaw, his son-in-law and the managing director of the company.

[7]Canada. Department of the Interior Report, 1907, Part V, *Report of the Superintendent of Rocky Mountains Park*, pp. 14-15.

[8]William S. Green, *Among the Selkirk Glacier,* (MacMillan & Co., 1890), p. 236.

[9]"Coming of the Surveyors -- Growth of Banff Begins," *Crag and Canyon*, May 6, 1935.

[10]Statistics taken from hotel registrations show that the number of tourists coming to Banff grew from 4,924 in 1888-89 to 60,825 in 1913-14.

[11]E. W. Elkington, *Canada, The Land of Hope,* (Adam & Charles Black, 1910), p. 139.

[12]Canada. Department of the Interior Report, 1915, Part V, *Report of the Proposed Artistic Lay-out Of Banff by Thos. H. Mawson*, pp. 72-84.

Chapter Twelve -- The California-Banff Bee Line

[1]Whyte Museum Archives, Wilson Papers, Contract between T. E. Wilson, Field, B. C., Liveryman and the CPR, 1902.

[2]*Brewster Story*, pp. 23-24.

[3]W. R. Marshall, "On the Trail to Banff, 1912," *Alberta Historical Review*, Autumn, 1966.

[4]Canada. Department of the Interior Report, 1913, Part V, *Report of the Commissioner of Dominion Parks*, p. 8.

[5]Ibid., p. 5.

[6]Quoted in W. F. Lothian, *p. 59.*

[7]*The Banff-Windermere Highway* (Department of the Interior, nd.), p. 5.

[8] For a complete account of the internment situation in Rocky Mountains and other national parks see W. A. Waiser, *Park Prisoners, the Untold Story of Western Canada's National Parks, 1915-46,* (Fifth House, 1995).

[9]See E. J. Hart, *Golf on the Roof of the World,* (Banff Springs Golf Club, 1999), for a full description of these events.

[10]*Bungalow Camps in the Canadian Pacific Rockies,* (np., nd.), 1927, p. 1.

Chapter Thirteen -- Making Fun of Winter

[1]Stutfield and Collie, pp. 248-49.

[2]*Diamond Hitch*, p. 73.

[3]*Jimmy Simpson*, p. 52.

[4]R. E. Campbell, *I Would Do It Again,* (Ryerson Press, 1959), p. 115.

[5]Calgary *Weekly Herald*, Jan. 6, 1898.

[6]Calgary *Weekly Herald*, Mar. 23, 1899.

[7]Appleby, p. 112

[8]*Crag and Canyon*, January 22, 1916.

[9]Whyte Museum of the Canadian Rockies (Archives), Fulmer Collection, unidentified newsclipping, 1939.

[10] Conrad Kain, *Where The Clouds Can Go,* (American Alpine Club, 1979), p. 275.

[11]"Winter Sports In The Rockies," *Canadian Pacific Empress Mail*, 1911.

[12]"The Banff Winter Carnival,"*Crag and Canyon*, February 1, 1929.

[13]*Crag and Canyon*, January ?, 1917.

[14]Ibid., February 1, 1929.

[15]"Mount Norquay Ski Camp," *Crag and Canyon*. Jan. 11, 1929.

Chapter Fourteen -- An Identity of Our Own

[1]Robinson, p. 34.

[2] Donald G. Wetherell, *Useful Pleasures: The Shaping of Leisure in Alberta 1896-1945,* (Canadian Plains Research Center, 1990), pp. 105-06.

[3]*Crag and Canyon*, Feb. 13, 1915.

[4]*The Selling of Canada*, p. 105-06. The Wilson plaque was moved to Wilson's grave in the Old Banff Cemetery after his death in 1933 and remains today one of the most storied gravemarkers in that historic place. See the Whyte Museum of the Canadian Rockies' cemetery walking guide, *At Rest In The Peaks.*

[5]Eleanor G. Luxton, ed., *Tilikum/Luxton's Pacific Crossing*, (Gray's Publishing Ltd., 1971), p. 16.

[6]David Smyth and W. B. Yeo, "The Banff Museum," undated Parks Canada staff report.

[7]Joseph McAleenan, *Hunting with Rifle and Camera in the Canadian Rockies,* (privately printed diary of twenty copies, 1916), p. 2.

[8]Whyte Museum of the Canadian Rockies (Archives), Minutes of the Banff Board of Trade, 1912-13.

[9]*Crag and Canyon*, May 29, 1915.

[10]Ibid. , December 23, 1916.

[11]Whyte Museum of the Canadian Rockies (Archives), Minutes of the Banff Citizens' Association, 1921.

Watershed

[1]Great Plains Research, p. 181.

Index

Credits/Acknowledgements

Glenbow Museum 47, 59, 101, 112, 121, 259, 288
Montreal Museum of Fine Arts 185
National Archives of Canada 38, 53, 225
Notman Archives 189
Whyte Museum of the Canadian Rockies 6, 22, 43, 69, 77, 81, 84, 87, 91, 97, 103, 117, 163, 166, 170, 175, 195, 202, 208, 213, 215, 220, 231, 233, 247, 273, 281, 301, 308, 315, 319; (Alpine Club of Canada) 144, 157, 158; (Elliott Barnes) 240, 287; (Byron Harmon) 17, 27, 125, 139, 198, 265, 298, 304; (George Noble) 128, 255; (George Paris) 20; (Mary Schäffer) 178; (Vaux family) 149, 152
University of Alberta Archives 33

The author would like to extend his sincere thanks to Bob Sandford, Jim Swanson, Craig Richards, Lena Goon and the Whyte Museum of the Canadian Rockies for their assistance.